*Dedicated to*
*my teachers who inspire me*
*my students who challenge me*

D1568069

# PRAISE FOR
# *MODERN JUDAISM*

*MODERN JUDAISM* expertly captures the essence of Reform Judaism, demonstrating both its roots in tradition and its embrace of modernity. Rabbi Sonsino has written scholarly works on Jewish history and theology while serving with distinction as a congregational rabbi. In this volume, he combines scholarly wisdom with a deep knowledge of Jewish life to provide readers of all faiths with a superb introduction to a complicated but vitally important subject.

> **Rabbi Eric H. Yoffie**
> Immediate part-president of the
> Union for Reform Judaism

*MODERN JUDAISM* provides even more than its title suggests, for it is more than an introduction to Progressive Judaism—it is a comprehensive overview and analysis of Judaism itself. Rifat Sonsino offers an overarching view of the history of the Jewish people in his first chapter of the book, and then proceeds to explore and explain the theology, beliefs, holiday, and lifecycle practices and observances of the Jewish people both within the synagogue and the home. In addition, he describes the relationship of Judaism to other religions, and focuses on the differences and similarities that mark diverse religious movements within Judaism. The book concludes with a description of Progressive Judaism—its accomplishments and challenges. Rabbi Sonsino succeeds in displaying his scholarly erudition and mastery of Jewish tradition in an accessible and articulate manner throughout this work, and provides a first rate introduction to Judaism that will delight and inform both those beginning their studies in Judaism as well as those with more advanced knowledge. I am honored to give this book my highest recommendation.

> **Rabbi David Ellenson**, President
> Hebrew Union College–Jewish
> Institute of Religion

# Modern Judaism

## An Introduction to the Beliefs and Practices of Contemporary Judaism

### Rabbi Rifat Sonsino, Ph.D.

*Boston College*

cognella

San Diego, CA

Bassim Hamadeh, CEO and Publisher
Michael Simpson, Vice President of Acquisitions
Jamie Giganti, Managing Editor
Jess Busch, Senior Graphic Designer
John Remington, Acquisitions Editor
Brian Fahey, Licensing Associate

First published in the United States of America in 2014 by Cognella, Inc.

Printed in the United States of America

ISBN: 978-1-62131-437-0 (pbk)/ 978-1-62131-438-7 (br)

www.cognella.com  800.200.3908

# CONTENTS

NOTES AND ACKNOWLEDGMENTS     IX

ABBREVIATIONS     XI

PREFACE     XIII

CHAPTER ONE: A BRIEF HISTORY OF THE JEWISH PEOPLE     1

CHAPTER TWO: BASIC AFFIRMATIONS     29
    Part I: God
    Part II: Torah
    Part III: Israel, People, and Land

CHAPTER THREE: MODERN JEWISH RELIGIOUS MOMENTS     85

CHAPTER FOUR: THE JEWISH FESTIVALS     95

CHAPTER FIVE: JEWISH LIFE-CYCLE CEREMONIES     127

CHAPTER SIX: JEWISH VIEWS ON LIFE AFTER DEATH     147

CHAPTER SEVEN: JEWISH COMMUNITY ORGANIZATIONS     157

CHAPTER EIGHT: THE JEWISH HOME AND JEWISH SYMBOLS     169

CHAPTER NINE: JUDAISM AND OTHER RELIGIONS     179

CHAPTER TEN: PRESENT AND FUTURE CHALLENGES     195

EXCURSUS: FAITH STATEMENTS     203

INDEX     231

# NOTES AND ACKNOWLEDGMENTS

This book is the result of many years of study and teaching, both at a congregational and a college level. My aim is to provide an extended introduction to Judaism for those who are interested in its development from ancient times until now, and to discuss current issues facing Jews and Judaism. The book contains not only a survey of the Jewish history, but also the basic Jewish beliefs, the various religious denominations today, all the religious festivals and life-cycle events, as well as Judaism's position vis-à-vis other religions of the West. The excursus at the end of the book includes an analysis and text of all the major faith pronouncements made by various Jewish religious groups today.

Unless it is otherwise indicated, all biblical texts have been taken from the Tanakh, published by the Jewish Publication Society, 1985. Transliteration of Hebrew into a non-Semitic language is always problematic, as many diverse systems appear to indicate. In this book, for easier reading, I chose to render the Hebrew letters *heh* and *het* as *h*, the letter *kaf* as *kh*, and *a'yin* as the consonant itself, plus a single quotation mark (such as *a'gunah* or *o'lam*). The vowels *tzere* and *segol* have been kept as *e*.

Like every other culture, Judaism has its own technical vocabulary in Hebrew and other languages, which expresses its singular ideas. For convenience sake, I have compiled an index of the major Hebrew words where the first mention contains its primary meaning. This will also function as a subject index for the book.

I want to thank Jamie Giganti, my Project Editor; John Remington, Senior Field Acquisitions Editor (Northeast Region); and the professional staff at Cognella Academic Publishing for providing valuable advice on all aspects of the production process of this book. I am grateful to each of them.

Even though "the making of many books is without limit" (Eccl. 12:2), I hope this *Modern Judaism* text is a solid beginning for those who wish to pursue the subject matter further. I encourage such individuals to read the books indicated at the end of each chapter.

**Rifat Sonsino**

# ABBREVIATIONS

| | |
|---|---|
| Av | *Avot* |
| BB | *Baba Batra* |
| BCE | Before Common Era |
| BT | Babylonian Talmud |
| CCAR | Central Conference of American Rabbis |
| CE | Common Era |
| Cent | Century |
| Dan | Daniel |
| Deut | Deuteronomy |
| Eccl | Ecclesiastes |
| Est | Esther |
| Ex | Exodus |
| Ez | Ezekiel |
| Feb | February |
| Gen | Genesis |
| HUC-JIR | Hebrew Union College-Jewish Institute of Religion |
| Isa | Isaiah |
| Jer | Jeremiah |
| JPS | Jewish Publication Society |
| Jon | Jonah |
| Judg | Judges |
| K | Kings |
| Ket | *Ketubot* |
| Lev | Leviticus |

| | |
|---|---|
| M | *Mishnah* |
| Mac | Maccabees |
| Mal | Malachi |
| NAB | New American Bible |
| Neh | Nehemiah |
| NJPS | New Jewish Publication Society (Bible) |
| Num | Numbers |
| Pes | *Pesahim* |
| Prov | Proverbs |
| Ps | Psalms |
| R | *Rabbi, Rabbah* |
| Rom | Romans |
| RSV | Revised Standard Version (Bible) |
| S of S | Song of Songs |
| Sam | Samuel |
| Sanh | *Sanhedrin* |
| Shab | *Shabbat* |
| Tos | *Tosefta* |
| UAHC | Union of American Hebrew Congregations |
| URJ | Union for Reform Judaism |
| WUPJ | World Union for Progressive Judaism |
| Yev | *Yebamot* |

# PREFACE

Judaism, both as religion and culture, has a long and rich tradition. Some Jews are more religiously observant than others, and many hold different beliefs about God and Torah. But almost all Jews have a sense of kinship with one another. Furthermore, unlike some religions, Judaism places little emphasis on creed or dogma, and tolerates a great deal of diversity in matters of faith and practice.

In covering the many facets of Judaism, it is necessary to start with a survey of the Jewish history in order to provide a context for the thoughts and practices of Judaism. This will be followed by a discussion of the basic principles of Judaism, the festivals, the life-cycle events, the Jewish views of the afterlife, the organization of the Jewish community today, the Jewish home, and the relationship between Judaism and other religions. Some selected texts as well as a few of the basic Hebrew prayers have been added to help the reader with some of the most important religious rituals at home and in the synagogue.

Every religion and culture uses certain technical vocabulary that characterizes its approach to the vicissitudes of life. It is not always easy to translate these into another language. Therefore, when studying Judaism, it is important to review first some of these terms, ever so briefly, in order to provide a better understanding of some of the concepts that stand at the center of this rich tradition.

## JUDAISM

The definition of Judaism has always created controversy among scholars. Some stress the element of religion as its dominant feature, as for example, "Judaism is the religion of the

Jewish people." The problem with this definition is that it attempts to define Judaism with another word requiring its own definition, namely, "Jewish people." Who is part of the Jewish people is still a matter of internal dispute.

Others claim that the most characteristic feature of Judaism is its culture, and, therefore, characterize it by saying that "Judaism is the culture or mores of Jews."

Yet others combine religion and culture in their definition of Judaism, based upon the observation that in Judaism it is almost impossible to differentiate between religion and peoplehood. Though some prefer to say that Judaism is the "religious culture" of the Jewish people, others opt for "the religion and culture of the Jews."

For the purposes of this study, I will define Judaism as "the religion and/or culture of the Jewish people."

In reality there are many Judaisms: the Judaism of the Rabbis is very different from the Judaism of the biblical period, and modern Judaism deals with many issues that medieval Jews did not have to face. Therefore, to do justice to the subject matter, one must place it in its historical context.

One of the positive aspects of the Jewish tradition has been its ability to adapt to new conditions through creative interpretation of ancient texts and often by bold moves carried out at important historic intersections. Throughout history, the religion and culture of the Jews have allowed, and, at times, even fostered, diversity. Even though certain themes remained constant and dominant, many of the details have shifted depending on the location and times. So, it is rather misleading to say in general terms, "Judaism teaches ..." One needs to identify the period and even the individual who dealt with this issue.

## GOD

For most of their history, Jews have affirmed the existence of one, indivisible, and incorporeal God as the main source of all there is, and encouraged their adherents to proclaim, "Hear, O Israel, The Eternal is our God, the Eternal is One/alone" (Deut. 6:4). However, in time, Jews developed different views of God, some of which are even incompatible with others. Jewish theologians have differed, and will continue to differ, regarding the definition of God for the Jewish community. (For more details, see Chapter Two.)

## JEW

The term "Jew" is traced back to the term *Yehudi*, one who was a member of the tribe of Judah (one of the twelve sons of the patriarch Jacob), and the eponymous head of the tribe that was named after him in ancient Israel. After the split of the kingdom in the tenth century BCE (see details below in the section about Jewish history), the Northern Kingdom was called Israel, whereas the Southern Kingdom carried the name of Judah, even though it also included the tribe of Benjamin. So the term *Yehudi* was applied to anyone who lived in the Southern Kingdom of Judah. Later on, even Mordecai, the cousin of Queen Esther, who was originally a Benjaminite but lived in Persia, is referred to as *Yehudi* (Esther 2:5; 5:13). The term eventually entered into Greek as *Ioudaois* and into Latin as *Judeaos*. After the first century CE, the early Christians identified Judas Iscariot, the one who "betrayed" Jesus, as the Jew-devil, and the term began to carry a derogative connotation for many centuries. A major change took place in our days; the term "Jew" shed most of its negative references in the Western World and became, once again, a term of respect.

The modern term "Jew" has various nuances. For some, a Jew is simply a person who belongs to the Jewish people. Others say that a Jew is someone who considers him/herself a Jew. This is too broad a definition, because there are some people, like the Jews-for-Jesus, who consider themselves Jewish but are not accepted as such by the organized Jewish communities around the world. For others, a Jew is one whom others view as a Jew, whether or not they themselves would consider themselves Jewish. For the Nazis, if you had one Jewish grandparent, you were a Jew. This definition is highly problematic, because it imposes on some people an identification that they do not accept or claim. In 1970 the Israeli Knesset (parliament) had to tackle this issue because a number of people, who were immigrating to Israel from around the world, claimed to be Jewish and demanded privileges given to Jews by virtue of the Law of Return. So, for this purpose, the Israeli law defined a Jew as, "A person who was born of a Jewish mother or has become converted to Judaism and is who is not a member of another religion." This definition was later on changed by Reform Judaism in 1983, by adding that Jews can derive their identity not only through the mother but also through the father, provided they are willing to make certain commitments for Jewish living. (For details, see Chapter Two).

## HEBREW

The term "Hebrew" may refer to the Hebrew language and/or to the Hebrew people. The origin of the word "Hebrew" is obscure. The connection between the term "Hebrew" and the marauders who, as early as the eighteenth century BCE, swept through ancient Canaan called *hap/biru* is highly contested among scholars. Most likely, the Israelites were related to some pastoralists coming from the steppes east of the Jordan River, called *shasu* (c. 15th century BCE).[1]

In the Bible, the term "Hebrew" is often used by the Israelites whenever they identified themselves to foreigners. Thus, for instance, Abram/Abraham—the first patriarch—is called *ha-i'vri*, "the Hebrew" (Gen. 14:13). Similarly, Jonah identified himself as a "Hebrew" to the sailors who wanted to heave him overboard (Jon. 1:9).

In the last century, most Jews in America called themselves Hebrews—as in the Bible—in response to the prevalent anti-Semitism that viewed "Jews" negatively. Thus, for instance, the first union of all the Reform congregations in the United States, established by Rabbi Isaac Meyer Wise in 1873, was called "The Union of American Hebrew Congregations" (changed to "Union for Reform Judaism" in 2003). Similarly, the name of the Reform Rabbinic seminary in Cincinnati, OH—established in 1875—was and remains today "Hebrew Union College" (now, "Hebrew Union College–Jewish Institute of Religion"). Today, however, hardly any Jew calls himself a Hebrew. The proper term today is "Jew."

The Hebrew language, belonging to the West-Semitic family of languages, is closely related to Moabite and other Transjordan dialects. It has evolved ever since biblical times. Early Israelites adopted the Phoenician alphabet for their own use. Around the fifth century BCE, Israelite scribes began to use the Aramaic "square letters," thus abandoning forever the old Phoenician characters. The classical books of Judaism are written primarily in Hebrew, whether biblical or rabbinic.

Hebrew has 22 consonants, and is written from right to left. It does not have capital letters and, for a long time, vowels were not represented by any signs. Consonants also have numerical values. Thus, the first letter, *alef*, is 1, and the second letter, *bet*, is 2. Hebrew does not recognize the neutral gender. All nouns are either masculine or feminine. Before the introduction of the vowel-signs, some consonants (i.e, *heh*, *vav*, and *yud*) were used to represent long vowels. The complete vowel system, in the form of diacritical marks, was created later on, perhaps around the tenth century CE, by some scribes in Tiberias to make reading easier. However, in Israel, newspapers and many books are still printed without any vowels, and Israelis write Hebrew cursively without adding any vowels. Often, the context determines the meaning of the words. Thus, for example, the root *KTB* can be read as *koteb* ("writing" or "writer"), *katub* ("written"), *kitteb* ("to inscribe"), *ketab* ("document"), or *kattab* ("correspondent").[2]

Transliterating Hebrew into English is no easy task, because English does not have many of the phonemes found in Hebrew. Various transliteration systems have been created, from the most scholarly to the popular, with neither being totally satisfactory.

## ISRAEL

The word "Israel" refers both to the people and the land, and the context determines its proper meaning. The name is attributed to the patriarch Jacob, when his name was changed from Jacob to Israel (Gen. 32 and 35). This term remained as the basic term by which Jews were called during biblical times. For example, "The Philistines drew up in a battle formation against Israel" (I Sam. 4:2), or, "Hear, O Israel, the Eternal is our God, the Eternal is one/ alone" (Deut. 6:4). In English texts, Jews of the biblical period are usually referred to as "Israelites" as a direct translation of *bene Yisrael* ("the children of"—or, better, "belonging to [the people of] Israel"). The land upon which the Israelites lived was also called "Israel" or, fully, "the Land of Israel." (For more details, see Chapter Two.)

## ISRAELI

This is a modern term referring to the citizens of the State of Israel, whether Jews or not.

## TORAH—"INSTRUCTION"

The word Torah comes from a Hebrew root, *Y-R-H*, meaning, "to throw," "to point out," and, therefore, "to direct" and "to instruct." The ancient priests used to give authoritative direction to the people, namely Torah (e.g., Lev. 10:11; Deut. 33:10), by using the *Urim* and *Thummim*. These were sacred lots, perhaps in the shape of dice, which were "thrown" in order to determine the will of God. Later on, the word Torah assumed a wider meaning and often referred to specific priestly injunctions, such as the "Torah of the meal offering" (Lev. 6:7) or the "Torah of the Nazirite" (Num. 6:21). It was the responsibility of the priests to teach and to impart Torah (Lev. 10:11; Deut. 24:8; Jer. 18:18). Their role continued into the postexilic period (sixth century BCE), when the returnees gathered around Ezra, the priest, to study the teachings of the Torah with priests and Levites (Neh. 8:13).

Today, in its strictest meaning, the word Torah refers to the Five Books of Moses or to the scroll in the synagogue's Ark that contains these books. However, it also has a wider meaning referring to the totality of Jewish sacred texts, both past and present. (For more details, see Chapter Two.)

## MITZVAH—"COMMANDMENT"

In popular language, the Hebrew word *mitzvah* (*mitzvot* in the pl.) is usually translated as "good deed." However, in reality the word conveys a sense of obligation, and is better rendered as "commandment" or as "sacred obligation." *Mitzvah* refers to the biblical and rabbinic obligations, both religious and moral, such as, lighting the Sabbath candles or observing the rules and regulations of the Passover holiday, as well as giving charity or visiting the sick.

The ancient sages have identified 613 such *mitzvot* that are incumbent upon every Jew. They are usually divided into two categories: 248 of them are positive ("You shall ...') and 365 are negative ("You shall not..."). Then there are some commandments that stem from the Bible (*deorayta*) and others that were prescribed by the Rabbis (*derabbanan*). Some people also divide the *mitzvot* into "ritual" (e.g., Sabbath and festivals, Kosher food) and "ethical" (e.g., honoring parents, not taking bribes). However, it is difficult to separate the two, because the line of demarcation is not so clear. Thus, in the celebration of Passover, there are both ritualistic (e.g., the ritualized meal) and ethical concerns (e.g., slaves becoming free).

In modern times, many of these 613 *mitzvot* cannot be fulfilled, because some of them refer to the rituals that took place in the ancient Temple of Jerusalem or to priestly obligations that were carried out by the clergy of the time. Today, only about 200 *mitzvot* can be carried out by observant Jews around the world.[3]

## HALAKHAH—"JEWISH LAW"

This word, coming from the Hebrew root *H-L-K* (meaning, "walking"), refers to the practice of the Jewish law, and derives from the assertion that Judaism is a way of life and a style of living. In popular language, for example, one would ask, "What is the *halakhah* on this subject?" meaning, what does Jewish law require in this case?

## KADOSH—"HOLY"

The Hebrew term *kadosh*, based on the three Hebrew consonant-roots, *K-D-Sh*, is usually translated as "holy," and basically means, "to be set aside for a special purpose." Holiness can be applied to an object, a human being, or even God. Thus, for example, the Israelites are called *goy kadosh* in the Bible (Ex. 19:6), because they were "set apart" by God from other peoples to be God's own (Lev. 20:26). The same three Hebrew consonants, in their different configurations, yield a similar meaning. Thus, the wedding ceremony in Jewish life is called *kiddushin*, and refers to the fact that the bride and the groom have "sanctified" themselves by turning their love and attention to each other for a sacred union. The Bible commands the Israelites to "sanctify" (*lekaddesho*) the Sabbath day (Ex. 20:8), by setting it apart from all other days of the week. The books of the Torah are usually called *kitve kodesh* ("holy Scriptures") and deserve special consideration, because they are different from all other types of books and therefore, sacred. In Jewish liturgy, the *kedusha*, "Sanctification" (what the Christian liturgy calls, "Sanctus") is pronounced as a special prayer mostly in the mornings, leading to the proclamation, "Holy (*kadosh*), Holy, Holy, the Lord of Hosts! His presence fills all the earth" (Isa 6:3). In Rabbinic literature, God is often called *ha-kadosh barukh hu*, "The Holy One, Blessed is He," because God is viewed as being unique, indescribable, and totally different from any other existents we know, and therefore, "Holy."[4]

## SHALOM

In modern Hebrew, the word *shalom* means "hello" as well as "peace." However, in the lexical usage of this term it has a much wider significance. Coming from the Hebrew root, *Sh-L-M*, the word basically means "being complete and sound." Thus, the word *shalom* implies wholeness, completeness, tranquility, security, safety, and well-being. When one greets another by saying "*mah shelomkha*" (in the feminine, *mah shelomekh*)—literally, "How is your *shalom?*"—we are not simply asking "How are you?" but we are inquiring about the other's general well-being. When on the Sabbath we wish another person *Shabbat Shalom* ("Sabbath of Peace"), we are hoping that this person will be restored to wholeness on this special day. When God promises Abraham that "You shall go to your fathers in peace (*beshalom*)" (Gen. 15:15), the text means that he would die naturally and without pain at the end of his long life. When the prophet Jeremiah sent his famous letter to the Judeans living in exile, he urged them to settle in the country, and "seek the welfare of the city (*shelom i'r*) to which I have exiled you and pray to the Eternal in its behalf" (Jer. 29:7).

In Jewish teachings, peace is not a negative notion, implying the absence of war. It is a positive term and a situation that must be achieved. Thus, Jews are required to establish *shelom bayit* ("peace in the house") by making sure there is domestic tranquility reached through kindness and consideration among the family members. In Jewish life, one is not to be satisfied with living "in peace" but must *bakesh shalom*, pursue wholeness and reach it (Ps. 34:15).

These special terms and other cultural and religious expressions that will be discussed in the following pages reflect the worldview of Jews in different times of their history.

## ENDNOTES

1. For the problem about the *habiru/hapiru*, see the article, "Hebrew" in the *Anchor Bible Dictionary*, 1992, Vol. 3, 95.
2. For more details about the "Hebrew Language," see the *Encyclopaedia Judaica (EJ)*, 2007, Vol. 8. 620–683.
3. On *mitzvah*, see op.cit., Vol. 14, 372.
4. On Holiness, see, the *Anchor Bible Dict. Vol. 3*, 237–248.

# CHAPTER ONE

# A BRIEF HISTORY OF THE JEWISH PEOPLE

## INTRODUCTION

Jews tend to be very conscious of their history. Collective memory often shapes their character and identity. In Jewish classical texts, God is conceived as one who is personally involved in the affairs of human beings. God is a redeemer, who took the Israelites out of Egypt and brought them to the Land of Israel. The Exodus is the model for all future redemptions.

Judaism has a long history, and Jews have lived in many countries throughout the centuries: in Canaan, Egypt, Babylonia, Persia, the Mediterranean basin, and eventually all over the globe. Thus a survey of the history of the Jewish people not only has to account for the individual Jewish communities spread around the world but also must consider the periodization of these histories that may be at variance with other Jewish Diasporas. Often, the status of Jewish communities depended on the degree of modernization of the host country. So while one community may have entered the modern period, another could still be living in medieval times. In this book, using broad categories, the history of the Jews will be divided into these historical periods:

a.  The Biblical Period: It goes from Creation of the world to the destruction of the Second Temple in 70 CE, even though the last three hundred years or so are also known as the Hellenistic period.
b.  The Early Rabbinic Period: It formally begins about the year 70 CE and goes through the 7th century CE, with the completion of the Jerusalem and then the Babylonian Talmud.

c.   The Medieval Period: This is much longer than its Western division of historical times, and goes from the 7th to the 18th/19th century.

d.   The Modern Period: This refers to the 19th/20th century to the present time.[1]

# THE BIBLICAL PERIOD

## Origins

In the Bible, the Book of Genesis first covers some universal themes in the first eleven chapters, such as the story of creation, the garden of Eden, and Noah and the deluge, most of which are found in (and possibly taken over from) the literature of the ancient Near East, and then turns its attention to the beginnings of the Jewish people with the patriarch Abraham (then called Abram). It provides a genealogy from Adam to Abram, and then has God saying to the patriarch: "Go forth from your native land and from your father's house to the land that I will show you" (Gen. 12:1. NJPS).[2]

Jewish history covers a span of time of about 4,000 years. In reality, we don't really know how and when the Jewish people made their appearance in ancient Canaan. According to Genesis, at the beginning of the patriarchal period (Abraham, Isaac, and Jacob), traditionally placed between the 20th and 18th centuries BCE, the Hebrews, as they were called then, sprang from the south of Mesopotamia, went to Haran, in southeast Turkey,[3] and moved south to Canaan. During the days of Jacob, because of a famine in the land, the group, now about 70 people, sojourned in Egypt in order to find food and join one of their own, Joseph the son of Jacob, who had acquired an important position in the Egyptian administration. But after a while, a new king emerged in Egypt who "did not know Joseph" (Ex. 1:8); in other words, he did not recognize the good that Joseph had done for the wellbeing of Egypt during its own famine. This new king, perhaps Ramses II (1279–1212 BCE), imposed a heavy burden on the Israelites and had them work as slaves. Thus, they lived for many years (the Bible says, about 400) in miserable conditions.

## Moses and the Exodus

During this time, a young man by the name of Moses, who was born to Jewish parents belonging to the tribe of Levi but raised in the palace by a princess, took note of the plight of his own people and decided, along with his brother Aaron and sister Miriam, to free his fellow Israelites (Ex. 1-2).

The rise of Moses is shrouded in legends and falls within the literary pattern of many leaders of the ancient world who come from lower classes but reach greatness because of their skill, determination, and wisdom. The Bible portrays Moses as a baby, three months old, who was left by his mother in a basket in the river because of the king's order to murder all the Israelite males. The baby is luckily discovered by an Egyptian princess bathing in the same river, who adopts him but ironically leaves his grooming to Moses' own mother, without knowing who she was. The closest literary parallel to this legend is that of Sargon I, an Akkadian king who ruled in Mesopotamia in the third millennium BCE. There, too, Sargon is left in the water within a basket and discovered and reared by a water-drawer. (See sidebar below.)

Under the leadership of Moses, the Israelites, or a number of them, following the legendary ten plagues that fell upon the Egyptians, escaped from Egypt sometime between the 15th and 13th centuries—this transformative historic event is traditionally called "The Exodus"—and then spent a few decades in the Sinai wilderness. Modern scholars continue to debate whether all the 12 tribes left Egypt en masse and settled in Canaan as the Bible claims, or, in a more likely scenario, if the few departing tribes joined up with others already living in Canaan, thus creating a loose confederation of tribes called "Israel" under the divine guidance of *YHVH*. There are even some biblical historians who claim that the Exodus never took place, and that Israel emerged primarily within Canaan in due time.[4]

During their stay in the wilderness of Sinai, the Israelites covenanted themselves to God, whom they called *YHVH*, and received the Torah (lit. "Instruction") on a mountain called either Mt. Sinai or Mt. Horeb. Its exact location is still unknown.

The Israelites remained in the wilderness forty years, according to the biblical tradition. Moses died before entering the land of Israel, and the mantle of leadership fell

---

### The Legend of Sargon

Sargon, the mighty king, king of Agade, am I.
My mother was a high priestess, my father I knew not.
The brother(s) of my father loved the hills.
My city is Azupiranu, which is situated on the banks of the Euphrates.
My mother, the high priestess, conceived me, in secret she bore me.
She set me in a basket of rushes, with bitumen she sealed my lid.
She cast me into the river which rose not (over) me,
The river bore me up and carried me to Akki, the drawer of water.
Akki, the drawer of water lifted me out as he dipped his e[w]er.
Akki, the drawer of water, [took me] as his son (and) reared me.

(ANET, 119)

upon Joshua, his disciple, who, according to the Bible, led the twelve Israelite tribes into Canaan and settled them in the mountain regions around the early part of the thirteenth century BCE.

The earliest reference to an entity known as "Israel" is found in the victory stele of the Egyptian Pharaoh Merneptah (1213–1203 BCE). This indicates that by the thirteenth century BCE there was already an entity in Canaan called "Israel" that suffered defeat. (See sidebar below.) The inscription, discovered in 1896 by Sir William Petrie, in the modern city of Luxor, Egypt, reads: "Israel is laid waste, his seed is not" (ANET, 378).

## Judges and Kings

Joshua was the first of the twelve *shoftim* "judges" (really "military rulers") who ruled the Israelites for about two centuries, one after the other, from the twelfth to the tenth century BCE in their new land. The early Israelite tribes lived in an area surrounded by small kingdoms. In the east were the Edomites, the Moabites, and the Ammonites; in the north were the Phoenicians; and in the southwest, the powerful Philistines. Every so

### Victory Hymn of Merneptah

The princes are prostrate, saying: "Mercy!"
Not one raises his head among the Nine Bows.
Desolation is for Tehenu;
Hatti is pacified;
Plundered is the Canaan with every evil;
Carried off is Ashkelon;
seized upon is Gezer;
Yeno`am is made as that which does not exist;
Israel is laid waste, his seed is not;
Hurru is become a widow for Egypt!
All lands together, they are pacified;
everyone who was restless has been bound
by the king of Upper and Lower Egypt;
Be-en Re Meri-Amon; the Son of Re;
mer-ne-Ptah Hotep-hir-Maat, given life
like Re every day.

(see ANET, pp. 376-378)

often, one of these kingdoms attacked their neighboring Israelite tribes. When these foes grew stronger and the assaults more devastating, the Israelites felt the need to establish a united front against their enemies, and particularly against the Philistines in the southwest. First, King Saul brought a few of the tribes together to fight the Philistines and ended their monopoly over the iron smelting in the region. Subsequently, his successor, David (c. 1000–960 BCE), not only united all the tribes—both in the South and in the North—but also conquered Jerusalem, making it the capital of the united monarchy. His son, Solomon (c. 960–922), maintained the peace among the tribes and was able to build a temple in the new capital of Jerusalem. This temple functioned as the royal sanctuary. After the destruction of the other local temples around the country (the so-called Deuteronomic Reformation in the seventh century BCE), the Jerusalem Temple became the religious center of all the Israelites.

After Solomon's death, internal dissent led to the split of the kingdom. The northern tribes, led by the rebellious Jeroboam I, formed the "Kingdom of Israel," and the southern tribes, under the leadership of Solomon's son, Rehoboam, set up the "Kingdom of Judah." Though both kingdoms were populated by Israelites, there were some differences between the north and south. Whereas the small southern kingdom, centered in Jerusalem, maintained the Davidic dynasty, the northern kingdom, much larger and more powerful, with its capital in Samaria, had various dynasties following one another. The main sanctuary of the southern kingdom was in Jerusalem. The northern kingdom had two major temples, one in Beth-El in the south and the other in Dan, in the north (I K. 12:29). At times, the two kingdoms cooperated (e.g., I K. 22:2), but sometimes they fought each other (e.g., II K. 14:1-14).

In 722/1 BCE the Assyrians, led by Sargon II,[5] conquered the Northern Kingdom, and dispersed part of its population to many parts of the ancient Near East, thus giving rise to the myth of the lost ten tribes. Over a hundred years later, Judah lost its freedom to the Babylonians in 586 BCE, who destroyed the Temple in Jerusalem and exiled many of its citizens to Babylon. (This period is called the Exilic Period.) Those who were exiled to Babylonia, including the prophet Ezekiel, established themselves as a productive community. After a 70-year hiatus, in 538 BCE, the Persian king Cyrus II (550–530) allowed the Israelites to return to their own land and to build a new temple. Some Jews remained in Babylonia, but others took advantage of this offer, returned to Israel and—under the leadership of Nehemiah—began to rebuild the walls of Jerusalem, and finally dedicated the Second Temple in 515 BCE.

## The Hellenistic Period and the Destruction of the Second Temple

With the arrival of Alexander the Great into the region (c. 333 BCE), the small Judean community felt the impact of the dominant Greek culture. After Alexander's death in 323

BCE, his generals divided his huge Greek Empire into various parts: Ptolemy I Soter took Egypt and Seleucus I Nicanor obtained Syria and the eastern provinces. In 301 BCE, Judea and Phoenicia were finally transferred to Seleucus. In those days, Jews were ruled internally by the High Priest who often depended on the Greek rulers for their authority.

In 175 BCE, when Antiochus Epiphanes IV became king in Damascus, the capital of Greek-Syrians, he displayed great ambitions for his empire by attempting to conquer Egypt and other surrounding countries. He even gave himself the surname Epiphanes (meaning "the visible god") and started to interfere in the politics of Judah. This did not sit well with many Jewish leaders, many of whom facetiously called the king *Epimanes* (meaning "the madman"). The king appointed Jason (for Joshua) (175–171 BCE) as High Priest instead of his brother Onias III. However, under the influence of the Tobias family, Antiochus replaced Jason with Menelaus (for Onias) (171–167 BCE), in exchange for a large sum of money (II Mac. 4:24), even though Menelaus was not a member of the High Priestly family.

In 169–168 BCE, Antiochus IV set out to conquer Egypt. While he was fighting there, Jason, the deposed High Priest, left the Ammonites with whom he had taken refuge, and attacked Menelaus in order to regain the High Priesthood. A civil war broke out between Jason and Menelaus, and Jason successfully entered the city of Jerusalem. King Antiochus was furious. On his way back from Egypt, Antiochus attacked Jerusalem, imposed restrictions on Judea, and eventually desecrated the Temple. The First Book of Maccabees describes these tragic events as follows:

> He [Antiochus IV] directed them to follow customs strange to the land, to forbid burn offerings and sacrifices and drink offerings in the Sanctuary, to profane Sabbaths and feasts, to defile the Sanctuary and the priests, to build altars and sacred precincts and shrines for idols, to sacrifice swine and unclean animals, and to leave their sons uncircumcised (I Mac. 1:44–48, RSV).

On the fifteenth day of the month of Kislev, in 167 BCE, the Syrian-Greeks erected "a desolating sacrilege upon the altar of burnt offering" (I Mac. 1:54). Though the meaning of this expression is not altogether clear, it probably meant a pagan altar or statue. That was too much for many pious Jews. A priest by the name of Mattathias of the Hasmonean family from the town of Modein, not far from Jerusalem, along with his five sons decided to rebel. Some of their followers refused to fight on the Sabbath, and as a result many were massacred on this holy day. Mattathias and his sons believed otherwise: They believed that the Sabbath was given to Israel to live and not die. So they urged their compatriots to carry weapons even on the Sabbath. Eventually, many of the Jews joined the Hasmoneans in their fight for freedom.

The Hasmonean revolt continued after the death of Mattathias, with considerable success. Under the leadership of Judah (called the Maccabee), Mattathias's son, Jewish armies defeated the Syrians in 166 BCE. As a result of these military victories, parts of Judea were liberated and the Temple was cleaned. After two years of defilement, the Temple was purified and rededicated to the worship of the one invisible God. This dedication (literally *Hanukah* in Hebrew) took place on the twenty-fifth day of Kislev, 165 BCE. The festival of *Hanukah* celebrates this major achievement. (For details about this holiday, see the chapter on the Religious Festivals.)

Greek-Syrian domination of Judah soon gave way to the Romans who came in with great military might on account of an internal conflict between two of the Hasmonean pretenders to power in Judea, Hyrcanus II and his brother Aristobulus. Each wanted Rome to supply military aid. Pompey (106–48 BCE), the Roman general, marched into Jerusalem in 63 BCE. By 37 BCE, Jewish self-rule came to an end. When military oppression became overbearing, the Jews revolted against their Roman masters However, this attempt failed miserably. Titus, the future Roman emperor, attacked and destroyed the city as well as the Second Temple of Jerusalem in 70 CE. Thus ended the Second Commonwealth of Jewish life in ancient Israel. Jews were expelled from Jerusalem to many places in Galilee. Many joined other Jews living in communities around the Mediterranean basin.

During the first centuries before and after the Common Era, the Jewish community was divided into various sects, each one with its own political agenda and theological approach. The Jerusalem Talmud speaks of 24 sects (JT Sanh. 10.6.29c). According to the Jewish historian, Josephus (first century CE), the major sects were Sadducees, Essenes, and Pharisees (Ant. 18:1, 2-6; Wars 2:8.2). The Jewish philosopher, Philo of Alexandria (first century CE), also mentions a Jewish ascetic group, the Therapeutae, which flourished around the city of Alexandria (De Vita Contemplativa, Ascetics, III). In addition there were Samaritans and early Christians who lived in many parts of Galilee.

The Sadducees represented the ruling elite, and often worked along with the Roman authorities. The Essenes, in total disagreement with the Jerusalem priesthood, soon withdrew to the Dead Sea area. The Pharisees, representing the majority of the population, maintained Jewish life by creating new ideologies, and accommodated different schools of thought, such as the followers of Hillel and Shammai, which became entangled in the deliberation of Jewish law and Torah teachings. Furthermore, whereas some Jews preferred to deal harshly with the Romans (namely, the Zealots), others proclaimed the arrival of a new age and the coming of the end of times. Josephus loosely calls them "The Fourth Philosophy," perhaps an umbrella group for all the revolutionaries acting against Rome. Proclaiming the end of times implied the end of the Roman Empire, and that was a sign of rebellion. Anyone who argued this line was crucified by the Romans. Early Christians were among these groups of visionaries who proclaimed the coming of the kingdom of God. Jesus and his followers were born Jewish and died as Jews. (For more on this subject, see Chapter Nine.) The separation between Judaism and Christianity took place in progressive stages during the late first century, and more clearly in the second century after the Bar Kohba (132–135 CE) rebellion against Rome.

## THE RABBINIC PERIOD

With the destruction of the second temple in Jerusalem, the sacrificial system and the priesthood came to an end. Instead, religious sages, who were part of the early Pharisaic group, emerged as the new leaders. They were the rabbis who adapted the biblical teachings to a new world. Away from Jerusalem—and now with some internal autonomy restored by the Romans—they met as an organized group in other cities, first at Yavne (about 30 miles southwest of Jerusalem) and afterwards in a few places in the Galilee (including Tiberias) and began to re-establish Jewish life by collecting and editing the teachings of the religious teachers of the past generations. Even after a short rebellion by Bar Kohba against the Romans, a revolt that failed miserably, spiritual creativity continued in earnest among Jews of the Holy Land. In the early part of the third century, under the leadership of Judah Hanasi (c. 138–217 CE), the leader of the community, early rabbinic teachings were collected and edited. This collection of law and lore, written in Hebrew, was named *Mishnah* (for details, see below), and the teachers of the time were referred to as *Tannaim*.

Fundamental to the rabbis' ideology was the belief that Moses received on Mt. Sinai not only a written Torah but also its interpretation in the form of an "Oral Torah." Thus, the rabbis maintained,

> Moses received the (oral) Torah from Sinai, and he delivered it to Joshua, and Joshua to the elders, and the elders to the prophets, and the prophets delivered it to the men of the Great Synagogue. They said three things: Be deliberate in judgment; raise up many disciples; and make a fence to the Torah. (M Avot 1:1)

This assumption allowed the rabbis to adapt the written divine word to the conditions of their time, reasoning that the real meaning of the text was transmitted orally from one teacher to another. Furthermore, the rabbis introduced the belief of the resurrection of the body after death, thus giving hope to the people that good behavior will ultimately be rewarded in the distant future, around the time when the Messiah, a descendent of David, will redeem the oppressed. They also established the Jewish calendar, canonized the Hebrew Bible, created the prayerbook, and changed the derivation of the Jewish identity from the father to the mother. From then on, one was considered a Jew if his/ her mother was Jewish.

The *Mishnah* was subject to interpretation by other sages who came after its completion. These rabbis—called *Amoraim*—debated different aspects of the *Mishnaic* texts, and these discussions—called *Gemara* ("conclusion")—were conducted in the vernacular Aramaic and were eventually compiled by combining the *Mishnah* and the *Gemara*, thus creating the Talmud (for details, see below). There were two versions of this compilation. The Jerusalem Talmud was probably completed in Tiberias around 450 CE, and the Babylonian Talmud around 500 CE at the Sura academy in Babylonia, located in the southern part of the country and west of the Euphrates River, where a large Jewish community lived after the destruction of the Second Temple. There are some differences between the two in terms of methodology as well as content. Whereas the Jerusalem Talmud places more emphasis on agricultural matters, the Babylonian Talmud reflects a more commercial world. In case of conflict between the two, the Babylonian Talmud is usually given priority.

# Medieval Times

## The Gaonic Period (8th to 11th centuries)

The Talmudic period gave way to the post-Talmudic times when the heads of the renowned rabbinical academies in Babylon held sway. They were called *geonim* (pl. of *gaon*, meaning "learned"), and set up court in the cities of Sura or Pumpedita from the third century CE on. One of the most famous rabbinical leaders of this Gaonic period was Saadia Gaon of Sura (882–942). He was a philosopher who authored one of the first systematic theological treatises, *Emunot vedeo't* (*The Book of Beliefs and Opinions*), originally written in Arabic, wherein he attempted to reconcile Judaism with the ideas of Plato and Aristotle. During the days of Saadia, the major threat to the Jewish community came from a Jewish sect called *Karaim* (Karaites, in English) who believed that only the written Bible was valid and that the Talmudic laws were not binding on Jews. Saadia fiercely defended rabbinic authority against them and declared Karaites heretics.

## Jews in Europe

The center of Jewish life quickly moved to Europe, both east and west. How the Jews came to Europe is still a matter of dispute. It is known that during the first century, there were Jewish communities in the eastern Mediterranean basin. According to the dominant theory, Jews moved through North Africa and crossed into Spain, while others moved through Italy, went north into France and Germany, and then went east into Poland

and Russia. The first group became known as Sephardic Jews (from the word *Sefarad*, meaning Spain) and the second as Ashkenazic Jews (from the word *Ashkenaz*, meaning Germany). These two Jewish groups developed social institutions and religious patterns, at times even in conflict with each other. This division is still prevalent today. Historically, they have disagreed on many issues of theology as well as religious practice.

## The Golden Age of Spain

It is estimated that large number of Jews came to Spain in 711 following Tarik ibn Ziyad, a Berber Muslim, who crossed the straits of Gibraltar with a huge army and conquered Southern Spain. The small Visigothic Jewish communities welcomed these Jews but were soon overwhelmed by their number. The Jewish community quickly prospered. Arab leaders trusted Jews more than they trusted the Christians. Because of their knowledge of various languages, Jews played an important intermediary position, translating books from Arabic into Hebrew, Latin and Greek, thus making them available throughout Europe.

During the Muslim domination of Spain, which spanned from the eight to the thirteenth centuries, Jews reached the highest status possible under Muslim law, a period

usually described as "The Golden Age of Spain."[6] Various Jewish personalities excelled beyond expectation: Thus, for example, Hasdai ibn Shaprut (925–975) of Cordoba became the personal physician to Khalif Abd-al-Rahman III and worked as a diplomat; Samuel ibn Nagdela (993–1065), a poet and Talmudic scholar, became the secretary of the Vizier in Malaga as well as the adviser to the king in Granada; his son, Joseph, was also the vizier of Granada and the Nagid ("leader") of the Jewish community; Solomon ibn Gabirol (1021–1057) of Malaga and Judah Halevi of Toledo (1086–1145) became the poet laureates of the Spanish communities; Abraham ibn Ezra of Tudela ( 1092–1167) was a renowned grammarian and a commentator;

*Statue of Maimonides in Cordoba, Spain*

Moshe ben Nachman (Nahmanides) of Girona (1194–1270), was famed as a great mystic and commentator.

## Maimonides's Daily Schedule

"I live in Fostat, and the Sultan lives Cairo. The distance between them is 4000 cubits [a mile and a half]. My duties to the Sultan are very heavy. I must see him every morning to check on his health. If one day he doesn't feel well, or one of the princes or the women of his harem doesn't feel well, I cannot leave Cairo that day.

It often happens that there is an officer or two who needs me, and I have to attend to healing them all day. Therefore, as a rule, I am in Cairo early each day, and even if nothing unusual happens, by the time I come back to Fostat, half the day is gone. Under no circumstances do I come earlier. And I am ravenously hungry by then. When I come home, my foyer is always full of people—Jews and non-Jews, important people and not, judges and policemen, people who love me and people who hate me, a mixture of people, all of whom have been waiting for me to come home.

I get off of my donkey, wash my hands, and go out into the hall to see them. I apologize and ask that they should be kind enough to give me a few minutes to eat. That is the only meal I take in twenty-four hours. Then I go out to heal them, write them prescriptions and instructions for treating their problems.

Patients go in and out until nightfall, and sometimes—I swear to you by the Torah – it is two hours into the night before they are all gone. I talk to them and prescribe for them even while lying down on my back from exhaustion. And when night begins, I am so weak, I cannot even talk anymore.

Because of all this, no Jew can come and speak with me in wisdom or have a private audience with me because I have no time, except on *Shabbat*. On *Shabbat*, the whole congregation, or at least the majority of it, comes to my house after morning services, and I instruct the members of the community as to what they should do during the entire week. We learn together in a weak fashion until the afternoon. Then they all go home. Some of them come back and I teach more deeply between the afternoon and evening prayers."

*From his letter dated September 30, 1199, to his disciple, friend, supporter, and translator, Rabbi Samuel ibn Tibbon of Provence.*

One of the most famous Spanish Jews was Moses Maimonides of Cordoba (1135–1204), the philosopher and leader of the Jewish community in Spain and—later on—in Fustat, Egypt. He left an indelible mark in the Jewish community for centuries. Maimonides wrote extensively, including *The Book of the Lamp*, a commentary on the *Mishnah* (*Kitab al-Siraj* in Arabic); the *Mishneh Torah* (a code of Jewish law in Hebrew); and the *Guide to the Perplexed* (in Arabic), a major philosophical work that he addressed to one of his pupils, Rabbi Joseph ben Judah. In it he attempted to reconcile the Jewish teachings with the philosophy of Aristotle. Maimonides died in Egypt at the age of 69 but was buried in Tiberias.

Things began to change within a short time after the Arab conquest. Christians in the North began the Reconquista as early as 718, as they tried to push the Arabs down and away from the Spanish peninsula. The good fortune of the Jewish community also began to suffer. In 1263 during a disputation that was held in Barcelona in the presence of King James I of Aragon, Nahmanides had to defend rabbinic teachings against Pablo Christiani, a converted Jew, who claimed that he could prove the truth of Christianity by using the Talmud. Though he fared well during the debate, Nahmanides had to go into exile afterwards.

By the 14th century, most of the Arabs were pushed down to the southern part of Spain. Aragon and Castille were already in the hands of the Christians. Jews looked to kings for their protection. The kings, in turn, used them as administrators and tax collectors, a position that created deep hatred against them by the local population. In June of 1391, there were riots in Seville, and many Jews were killed. In 1413, another disputation took place in Tortosa between Joshua Lorki, also called Geronimo de Santa Fe, an ex-Jew, and Vidal Benveniste, which lasted almost a year. During these debates the Talmud was condemned, and Jews were forbidden to study it.

In the last few decades of the 15th century, a number of Jews, trying to escape oppression or by sincere conviction, became Christians. Some adhered to their new faith, whereas others led a double life, Jew at home but Christian in the streets. In order to monitor these new Christians, known as "Conversos," (also called derogatorily "Marranos" ("pigs")), the Spanish kings, Ferdinand of Aragon, and Isabella, queen of Castille, approved the establishment of the Spanish Inquisition in Castille. It is to be noted that the Inquisition did not monitor the Jews directly, only newly converted Christians.

By Jan. 1492, Granada, lost to the Arabs, surrendered to the armies of Ferdinand and Isabella. On March 31, 1492, claiming that Jews were corrupting the new Christians, Ferdinand and Isabella, influenced by Tomas de Torquemada, the queen's confessor, issued a decree of expulsion at the palace Alhambra in Granada, thus putting an end to Jewish life in Castille and Aragon. Jews had until Aug. 1 to leave. This day corresponded to the 9 of Av, a day of fasting when Jews commemorate the destruction of the First and the Second Temple. A delegation of Jewish dignitaries, Abraham Senior and Isaac Abravanel, tried to meet with the authorities in order to have the edict revoked, but to no avail. The number of Jews who actually left Spain is not known, but it is assumed that it was around 200,000. Spanish Jews found refuge in Southern France, North Africa, and later on, in Italy, the Balkans, as well as in different parts of the Ottoman Empire, bringing with them their Spanish culture and their Judeo-Spanish, called Ladino, a language still spoken today among many Sephardic Jews. The impact of this expulsion has been tremendous, and many Jews today still recall it among the greatest tragedies that has befallen them.

## The Edict of Expulsion from Spain:

*The Alhambra decree, an edict of expulsion was issued against the Jews of Spain by Ferdinand and Isabella. It ordered all Jews of whatever age to leave the kingdom by the last day of July, 1492.*

(1) King Ferdinand and Queen Isabella, by the grace of God, King and Queen of Castile, Leon, Aragon, (etc) ... to the prince Lord Juan, our very dear and muched love son, and to the other royal children, ... and to councils, magistrates..., and all good men of the noble and loyal city of Burgos and other cities, towns, ... and to all Jews and to all individual Jews of those places, and to barons and women of whatever age they may be, and to all other persons ... and to all to whom the matter contained in this charter pertains or may pertain. Salutations and grace.

(2) You know well or ought to know, that whereas we have been informed that in these our kingdoms there were some wicked Christians who Judaized and apostatized from our holy Catholic faith, the great cause of which was interaction between the Jews and these Christians, in the cortes which we held in the city of Toledo in the past year of one thousand, four hundred and eighty, we ordered the separation of the said Jews in all the cities, towns and villages of our kingdoms and lordships and [commanded] that they be given Jewish quarters and separated places where they should live, hoping that by their separation the situation would remedy itself. Furthermore, we procured and gave orders that inquisition should be made in our aforementioned kingships and lordships, which as you know has for twelve years been made and is being made, and by many guilty persons have been discovered, as is very well known, and accordingly we are informed by the inquisitors and by other devout persons, ecclesiastical and secular, that great injury has resulted and still results, since the Christians have engaged in and continue to engage in social interaction and communication they have had means and ways they can to subvert and to steal faithful Christians from our holy Catholic faith and to separate them from it, and to draw them to themselves and subvert them to their own wicked belief and conviction, instructing them in the ceremonies and observances of their law, holding meetings

at which they read and teach that which people must hold and believe according to their law, achieving that the Christians and their children be circumcised, and giving them books from which they may read their prayers and declaring to them the fasts that they must keep, and joining with them to read and teach them the history of their law, indicating to them the festivals before they occur, advising them of what in them they are to hold and observe, carrying to them and giving to them from their houses unleavened bread and meats ritually slaughtered, instructing them about the things from which they must refrain, as much in eating as in other things in order to observe their law, and persuading them as much as they can to hold and observe the law of Moses, convincing them that there is no other law or truth except for that one. This proved by many statements and confessions, both from these same Jews and from those who have been perverted and enticed by them, which has redounded to the great injury, detriment, and opprobrium of our holy Catholic faith.

(3) Notwithstanding that we were informed of the great part of this before now and we knew that the true remedy for all these injuries and inconveniences was to prohibit all interaction between the said Jews and Christians and banish them from all our kingdoms, we desired to content ourselves by commanding them to leave all cities, towns, and villages of Andalusia where it appears that they have done the greatest injury, believing that that would be sufficient so that those of other cities, towns, and villages of our kingdoms and lordships would cease to do and commit the aforesaid acts. And since we are informed that neither that step nor the passing of sentence [of condemnation] against the said Jews who have been most guilty of the said crimes and delicts against our holy Catholic faith have been sufficient as a complete remedy to obviate and correct so great an opprobrium and offense to the faith and the Christian religion, because every day it is found and appears that the said Jews increase in continuing their evil and wicked purpose wherever they live and congregate, and so that there will not be any place where they further offend our holy faith, and corrupt those whom God has until now most desired to preserve, as well as those who had fallen but amended and returned to Holy Mother Church, the which according to the weakness of our humanity and by diabolical astuteness and suggestion that continually wages war against us may easily occur unless the principal cause of it be removed, which is to banish the said Jews from our kingdoms. Because whenever any grave and detestable crime is committed by members of any organization or corporation, it is reasonable that such an organization or corporation should be dissolved and annihilated and that the lesser members as well as tile greater and everyone for the others be punished, and that those who perturb the good and honest life of cities and towns and by contagion can injure others should be expelled from those places and even if for lighter causes, that may be injurious to the Republic, how Much more for those greater and most dangerous and most contagious crimes such as this.

(4) Therefore, we, with the counsel and advice of prelates, great noblemen of our kingdoms, and other persons of learning and wisdom of our Council, having taken deliberation about this matter, resolve to order the said Jews and Jewesses of our kingdoms to depart and never to return or come back to them or to any of them. And concerning this we command this our charter to be given, by which we order all Jews and Jewesses of whatever age they may be, who live, reside, and exist in our said kingdoms and lordships, as much those who are natives as those who are not, who by whatever manner or whatever cause have come to live and reside therein, that by the end of the month of July next of the present year, they depart from all of these our said realms and lordships, along with their sons and daughters, menservants and maidservants, Jewish familiars, those who are great as well as the lesser folk, of whatever age they may be, and they shall not dare to return to those places, nor to reside in them, nor to live in any part of them, neither temporarily on the way to somewhere else nor in any other manner, under pain that if they do not perform and comply with this command and should be found in our said kingdom and lordships and should in any manner live in them, they incur the penalty of death and the confiscation of all their possessions by our Chamber of Finance, incurring these penalties by the act itself, without further trial, sentence, or declaration. And we command and forbid that any person or persons of the said kingdoms, of whatever estate, condition, or dignity that they may be, shall dare to receive, protect, defend, nor hold publicly or secretly any Jew or Jewess beyond the date of the end of July and from henceforth forever, in their lands, houses, or in other parts of any of our said kingdoms and lordships, under pain of losing all their possessions, vassals, fortified places, and other inheritances, and beyond this of losing whatever financial grants they hold from us by our Chamber of Finance.

(5) And so that the said Jews and Jewesses during the stated period of time until the end of the said month of July may be better able to dispose of themselves, and their possession, and their estates, for the present we take and receive them under our Security, protection, and royal safeguard, and we secure to them and to their possessions that for the duration of the said time until the said last day of the said month of July they may travel and be safe, they may enter, sell, trade, and alienate all their movable and rooted possessions and dispose of them freely and at their will, and that during the said time, no one shall harm them, nor injure them, no wrong shall be done to them against justice, in their persons or in their possessions, under the penalty which falls on and is incurred by those who violate the royal safeguard. And we likewise give license and faculty to those said Jews and Jewesses that they be able to export their goods and estates out of these our said kingdoms and lordships by sea or land as long as they do not export gold or silver or coined money or other things prohibited by the laws of our kingdoms, excepting merchandise and things that are not prohibited.

(6) And we command all councils, justices, magistrates, knights, squires, officials, and all good men of the said city of Burgos and of the other cities, towns, and villages of our said kingdoms and lordships and all our new vassals, subjects, and natives that they preserve and comply with and cause to be preserved and complied with this our charter and all that is contained in it, and to give and to cause to be given all assistance and favor in its application under penalty of [being at] our mercy and the confiscation of all their possessions and offices by our Chamber of Finance. And because this must be brought to the notice of all, so that no one may pretend ignorance, we command that this our charter be posted in the customary plazas and places of the said city and of the principal cities, towns, and villages of its bishopric as an announcement and as a public document. And no one shall do any damage to it in any manner under penalty of being at our mercy and the deprivation of their offices and the confiscation of their possessions, which will happen to each one who might do this. Moreover, we command the [man] who shows them this our charter that he summon [those who act against the charter] to appear before us at our court wherever we may be, on the day that they are summoned during the fifteen days following the crime under the said penalty, under which we command whichever public scribe who would be called for the purpose of reading this our charter that the signed charter with its seal should be shown to you all so that we may know that our command is carried out.

(7) Given in our city of Granada, the XXXI day of the month of March, the year of the birth of our lord Jesus Christ one thousand four hundred and ninety-two years.

I, the King, I the Queen,

I, Juan de Coloma, secretary of the king and queen our lords, have caused this to be written at their command.

Registered by Cabrera, Almacan chancellor.

King Ferdinand and Queen Isabella, "The Edict of Expulsion from Spain," *Jewish History*, vol. 9, no. 1, trans. Edward Peters, pp. 23-28. Copyright © 1995 by Springer Science+Business Media. Reprinted with permission.

On Aug. 2, Columbus sailed from Spain toward the New World. Some claim that he was of Jewish descent, although this has never been proven. It is true, however, that he had a few Conversos among his crew.

Even though the Jewish community as such disappeared in Spain at the end of the 15th century, Jews started to enter the country periodically and in small numbers, coming from parts of Europe and North Africa. In 1877 about 400 Jews were listed as living in Spain. In 1916, the first synagogue in modern times opened in Madrid, the capital. The Spanish authorities formally revoked the edict of expulsion in 1968. During the special celebration, the king and queen of Spain as well as the president of the State of Israel, Chaim Herzog, attended the synagogue in Madrid to mark this special occasion. It is estimated that there are 15,000 Jews living now in Spain, half of them in Catalonia.


## Central Europe

Jews have lived in Europe for a very long time. During most of their history and especially in medieval times, they were under royal protection, which made them crown property. Many kings supported them, while others exploited them. Very often Jews were restricted to one profession: money lending. This did not endear them to the population at large.

In 1095, in order to unify all Christians in the Western World, Pope Urban II called upon all Christians to conquer the Holy Land. This was the beginning of the many Crusades (the last one, the Eighth Crusade, took place in 1270) that devastated Europe and the Middle East. Many responded to the pope's appeal, but began the massacre in Europe by destroying numerous Jewish communities on their way to Palestine. Thus, many Jews along the Rhineland were killed. This tragedy is reflected in many liturgical poems written during the First Crusade.

The situation of the Jews in central Europe was very precarious. In 1215, the Fourth Lateran Council, convoked by the Pope Innocent III (1198–1216) at the Lateran Palace in Rome, ruled that all Jews had to wear a yellow badge on their clothes and a funny hat on their heads. The false accusation of the "desecration of the host" (i.e., the profane use of the communion wafer) by Jews as well as the libel of ritual murders that was directed against the Jews made their life miserable. In 1240 Nicholas Donin, an apostate Jew, denounced the Talmud in Paris. Consequently, many copies of the Talmud were burned. There were also massive expulsions of Jews throughout Europe: in 1290 from England and in 1306 from France. During the Black Death of the 1350's, Jews were blamed for the bubonic plague that killed one third of Europe's population. In order to escape death, many Jews moved into Poland, which welcomed them, and where later on Jews created an important cultural center.

In opposition to Spanish Jews who interacted openly with their Muslim and Christian neighbors, most European Jews, under heavy oppression by the authorities, secular as well as religious, preferred to turn inward, withdrawing from the larger society and concentrating on the internal needs of the community. This effort, however, yielded some positive results, and great rabbinic luminaries emerged to help the community cope with its problems and issues. Rabbi Gershom ben Judah (c. 960–1040) of Mainz became famous for the decrees he issued about communal life, such as the abrogation of polygamy among Ashkenazic Jews, the ruling that divorce requires consent from both parties, and that one should not be allowed to read someone else's letter. A French Jew, Rabbi Shelomo ben

Yitzhak, known also as Rashi (b. 1040 in Troyes), studied with some of Rabbi Gershom's students, and upon his return to his native land wrote some of the most enduring commentaries on the Bible and Talmud. After his death, his grandchildren, called Tosafists, wrote *Tosafot* ("additions") to his commentaries. Also, in the thirteenth century, a group of German Rabbis, known as *Haside Ashkenaz* ("The Pious Men of Ashkenaz") dedicated themselves to mysticism and created the *Sefer Hasidim* ("The Book of the Pious"), outlining the proper behavior and correct ethical action. It was also around this time that Spanish as well as German rabbinic masters began to edit a collection of teachings in the form of Codes of Behavior. Rabbi Joseph Karo (1488–1575), a Sephardic scholar at Safed created the Shulhan Arukh ("The Set Table"), the Code of Jewish law, to which Rabbi Moshe Isserless (1520–1572) of Poland added his own notes called The Mappah ("The Table Cloth"), reflecting the customs of Ashkenazic Jews.

## RISE OF KABBALAH

The Hebrew word *Kabbalah* (lit. "reception") often refers to the esoteric and mystical teachings of the rabbinic sages. There has always been a mystical trend in Judaism, but it took off with brilliance in Spain with the rise of modern mysticism. The classical period of this movement began with the publication of the *Zohar*, which became the most important text of Jewish mysticism, by Moses ben Shem Tov in the 1280s. In this major work, the author identified God as *En Sof* ("Endless"), spoke of the ten *sefirot* ("emanations") that emerged from God, stressed *devekut*, cleaving to God by means of prayer and meditation, and promoted the belief in the transmigration of the souls after death. Soon, however, the center of Kabbalah moved to the city of Safed in the Holy Land. Among the mystics there, Rabbi Isaac Luria (1534–1572) became the most celebrated master. He came up with a new paradigm of creation and a mystical way of explaining the condition of the Jews in Exile. He argued that at the beginning, God contracted (*tzimtzum*), giving way to a vacuum into which God sent rays of light, which were supported by vessels. However, these containers eventually broke up (*shevirat ha-kelim*) spreading the divine lights everywhere—an explanation of why Jews live in Exile. The ultimate goal, said Luria, is *tikkun o'lam*, the repairing of the universe, thus bringing wholeness to all existence by observing the Mitzvot indicated in sacred texts.

Kabbalistic teachings expanded throughout the Jewish world, and today they continue to influence, in matters of belief and practice, many Jews, and even some non-Jews, who subscribe to them.

## Jews in Eastern Europe

Until the 18th century, Russia did not allow Jews to move into its territory, so many of them started to establish communities in Poland, Ukraine, and Lithuania. Protected by kings, these Jews established community organizations and rabbinic seminaries (called Yeshivot), and engaged in business or farming. In Poland, they also developed a central Jewish organization in Lublin called "The Council of the Four Lands" (namely, Greater and Little Poland, Ruthenia, and Volhynia) (1580–1764), whose delegates met twice yearly to discuss and resolve community matters. They lived in special restricted enclaves, named *Stiebels*, and had a common language, Yiddish (a combination of German and Hebrew), that enabled them to set up a wide net of ties among Jews living in faraway places.

But life was not easy for these Jews. In 1648, when the Cossacks, under the leadership of Bogdan Chmielnicki, revolted against the ruling authorities, they also inflicted great pain upon Jews. In the late eighteenth century, when Russia, Prussia, and Austria divided Poland, Russia found itself with a huge population of Jews. Most of the czars, however, were hostile to Jews. There were constant "pogroms" (the Russian word for "devastation" or "riot") in various parts of the Russian Empire. During the reign of Nicholas II (1894–1918), the Czar provided the funds for the publication of the notorious pamphlet, *The Protocols of the Elders of Zion*, which wrongly claimed that Jews secretly controlled the financial resources of the world. In 1911, when a Christian boy was murdered in Kiev, Ukraine, Mendel Beilis, a Jew, was accused of using his blood for ritualistic purposes. Eventually the jury cleared Beilis of this "blood libel." In 1917, the Russian Revolution, which was supported by many Jews, brought down the Russian monarchy, but it did not end the vicious anti-Semitism of the country.

## Sabbetai Zevi—The False Messiah of the Ottoman Empire

Judaism has known many "false messiahs." However, the case of Sabbetai Zevi is one of the most dramatic in Jewish history, not only because his was one of the most encompassing messianic movements in Jewish life, but because his conversion to Islam created the deepest disappointment for a very large number of Jews who lived in the 17th century.

*Sabbetai Zevi, the false messiah of the Ottoman Empire*

Rabbi Sabbetai Zevi was born in Izmir in 1626, a major city on the eastern shores of the Aegean Sea, at a time when Jews were dealing with the aftereffects of the Chmielnicki massacres of 1648 in Eastern Europe and the Russian-Swedish war of 1655. Many Jews took refuge in Kabbalah awaiting the arrival of the Messiah. Even Christians expected the Messiah to come in 1666. Zevi was engaged in mystical studies, and because of his charisma, good looks, and beautiful voice, he started to attract many followers. After meeting with Rabbi Nathan of Gaza, a fellow Kabbalist, Zevi declared himself Messiah in 1665 and said he was going to seize the crown from the Ottoman ruler. Soon after, Turkish authorities arrested him and brought him to Constantinople. In 1666, he was summoned to an imperial court in Adrianopolis for trial. There, Zevi, in order to escape the death penalty, agreed to become a Muslim and took the name of Aziz Mehmet Efendi.

His conversion fell like a bomb among the thousands of his followers. Some decided to abandon the cause, while others followed him into Islam, by living a double life, Jew

## Napoleon's Sanhedrin—1806

Jewish high court convened by Napoleon I. to give legal sanction to the principles expressed by the Assembly of Notables in answer to the twelve questions submitted to it by the government (see *Jew. Encyc.* v. 468, *s.v.* France). These questions were:

1. Is it lawful for Jews to have more than one wife?
2. Is divorce allowed by the Jewish religion? Is divorce valid, although pronounced not by courts of justice but by virtue of laws in contradiction to the French code?
3. May a Jewess marry a Christian, or a Jew a Christian woman? or does Jewish law order that the Jews should only intermarry among themselves?
4. In the eyes of Jews are Frenchmen not of the Jewish religion considered as brethren or as strangers?
5. What conduct does Jewish law prescribe toward Frenchmen not of the Jewish religion?
6. Do the Jews born in France, and treated by the law as French citizens, acknowledge France as their country? Are they bound to defend it? Are they bound to obey the laws and follow the directions of the civil code?
7. Who elects the rabbis?
8. What kind of police jurisdiction do the rabbis exercise over the Jews? What judicial power do they exercise over them?
9. Are the police jurisdiction of the rabbis and the forms of the election regulated by Jewish law, or are they only sanctioned by custom?
10. Are there professions from which the Jews are excluded by their law?
11. Does Jewish law forbid the Jews to take usury from their brethren?
12. Does it forbid, or does it allow, usury in dealings with strangers?

at home and Muslim in the street. They were called "Dönme: (a Turkish word, meaning "convert"). The movement, though much smaller now, still exists around the world.[7]

# THE MODERN PERIOD

The beginnings of the Modern Period in Jewish history can be traced back to the Age of Enlightenment of the 18th century Europe, which promoted reason as the primary source of knowledge and the basis of authority. Developed by thinkers in Germany, France, and Britain, the movement quickly spread all over Europe, including Russia, though much later. All traditional institutions were questioned, and customs and morals went through a fresh review. There was also an attempt to supplant the authority of the old aristocracies and established religious institutions in favor of individual rights. In 1791, during the Emancipation, France granted full political rights to Jews. In 1806, Napoleon called the Jewish leaders to a major meeting (the modern "Sanhedrin") in order to inquire about their political loyalties, and was pleased to hear that French Jews considered themselves French first.

The reaction to the Age of Enlightenment within the Jewish communities in Europe was mixed. Some heartily approved it, while others were more cautious if not suspicious of it. Here below are some of the major responses to modernity:

## *The Rise of Reform Judaism*

In the 18th century, some traditional Jews argued that in order to preserve Judaism in the modern period, one has to separate the Jewish culture from the non-Jewish culture, and keep Judaism at home while acting as engaged citizens in the outside world. Others disagreed, and said that one can be Jewish both at home and abroad, without making any sharp distinction. The first group became known as Orthodox, whereas the second, Reform.

The origins of modern Reform Judaism are usually traced to Germany. The movement began not with major theological debates but with simple liturgical changes. In the early 1800's, when Israel Jacobson (1768–1828), a wealthy banker of Halberstadt, established a sectarian boarding school in Seesen, he added a chapel for religious services (1810) where prayers were recited both in Hebrew and German; it had an organ, and often included a sermon in the vernacular. These represented major innovations for that time, and created a split within the community, with some approving and others disapproving. Later on, Jacobson received the support of some of the liberal-minded Rabbis of Germany, such as Abraham Geiger (1810–1874) in Hamburg and Samuel Holdheim (1806–1860) in

Berlin, and started to influence public opinion within the Jewish community all over Europe. However, the movement weakened in Germany because of anti-Semitism, Orthodox Jewish opposition, interference of hostile government officials, and the lack of total emancipation of Jews in Europe, and was transplanted to the Unites States, which welcomed freedom of expression.

In the seventeenth and eighteenth centuries, early arrivals into the United States were mostly of Sephardic origin. German Jews started to arrive at the beginning of the nineteeth century. By 1830, there were about 4,000 to 6,000 Jews in America. Within two decades their numbers went up to about 75,000. New York City, which had one of the largest Jewish populations in the country, had about 16,000 in the 1850s, but 80,000 by the 1880s. At the turn of the century close to one million Jews were already living in different parts of the States, most of them coming from Eastern European countries.

Early Jewish communities in America were primarily Orthodox. The first Reform Temple in the United States was established in January 1825, after splitting off of the Beth Elohim congregation in Charleston, South Carolina. Isaac Harby, a playwright and educator, along with a dozen men, petitioned the leaders of Beth Elohim for a more abbreviated service, a weekly English sermon, and a few minor changes in the liturgy but were turned down. In response they set up a new congregation called the Reformed Society of Israelites. This was followed by the appearance of Har Sinai Society in Baltimore, Maryland (1842), Temple Emanuel in New York City (1850), and a few others. These Reform congregations downplayed Jewish nationalism in favor of universalism, viewed Judaism more as a religion than an ethnic culture, and encouraged their members to become good and loyal citizens.

The first influential liberal rabbi in the continent was Max Lilienthal (1815–1882) who was born in Munich, Germany. After studying for the rabbinate, he received a secular education and got his Ph.D. from the University of Munich (1837). He was then invited by the Russian government to lead a private Jewish day school in Riga, where he introduced confirmation for girls in 1840. In 1844 he came to the United States and at the age of thirty, he became a congregational rabbi in New York City. Here, in response to the needs of the times, he began to realize the necessity of making some changes in Jewish life, primarily in the synagogue liturgy. Thus, for example, in 1846 he set up the first Confirmation service in America. However, the conflict with some of the

*Isaac Meyer Wise (1819-1900)*

more traditional members of his synagogue caused him to resign his position, and he started to operate a private boarding school in the city. Through the influence and friendship of Rabbi Isaac M. Wise (see below), he moved to Cincinnati, Ohio, in 1855 and became the rabbi of B'ne Israel congregation, called Rockdale Avenue Temple. There he instituted a number of reforms; among others, he made some changes in the liturgy and abrogated the auctioning off of synagogue privileges. He also fought for the separation of church and state. He died in 1882 at the age of 67.

The first few Reform Jewish congregations in America had limited success, and awaited the arrival of an organizational genius by the name of Rabbi Isaac Meyer Wise. Originally from Bohemia, Rabbi Wise came to the United States in 1846, and in 1850 he became the Rabbi of Beth El, a Reform congregation in Albany, New York. But his reputation grew when he moved to another temple in Cincinnati, Ohio, B'ne Jeshurun, where he served for 46 years. Wise was not a theologian but had an uncanny ability to bring people together and was instrumental in creating the three major institutions that make up Reform Judaism of America today: In 1873, he united all the Reform congregations of his time by creating the Union of American Hebrew Congregations (UAHC) [today called Union for Reform Judaism (URJ)]; in 1875 he established the first Reform Rabbinic seminary, the Hebrew Union College (HUC) [today, Hebrew Union College-Jewish Institute of Religion (HUC-JIR)]; and in 1889, with 30 members, he set up the Central Conference of American Rabbis (CCAR), a professional organization for all future Reform Rabbis of the United States, now also including Canada. Today, the CCAR has close to 2,000 members.

*Israel ben Eliezer*
*(c.1700-1760)*

## The Rise of Hasidism; the Ba'al Shem Tov

Modern Hasidism emerged in mid-eighteenth-century Poland and stressed strict religious observance, but also joy, enthusiasm, and the opportunity to worship God with the whole being, both body and soul. Many of its leaders wanted to escape the legalism of their time in favor of a warm, vibrant, and inward religious expression. The founder, Israel ben Eliezer, called *Ba'al Shem Tov* ("The Master of the Good Name"), revealed himself as a healer and attracted many followers around his charismatic personality. Living in the Carpathian mountains with his second wife, Hannah, he taught compassion, charity, and love and said that one could worship God through joy in his or her daily life. After his death, many of his followers, each leader calling himself a *tzaddik* ("the righteous one"), established their own independent dynasties, many of which still exist today. Jews who opposed these Hasidic Jews ("the pious ones") were called *Mitnagdim* ("Opponents").

Among their leaders was Rabbi Elijah ben Solomon Zalman (1720–1797), often called the Gaon of Vilna, who believed that Hasidism was a dangerous ideology because of the Hasids' subservience to their charismatic leaders, their special liturgical practices, and their own style of slaughtering animals.

Today a number of Hasidic groups have congregations around the world. Among them the Lubavich-Habad, Gerer, Satmar, Belzer, and Brezlov are the most prominent. Hasidic Jews do not greatly differ from other Orthodox Jews in terms of their theology but express great devotion to their dynastic leader, each of whom is called a Rebbe. Often Hasidic Jews wear distinctive dress and hats, which are reminiscent of Polish life in the upper Middle Ages.

*Moses Mendelssohn*
*(1729-1786)*

## The Rise of Neo-Orthodoxy

There are different shades of Orthodoxy in Jewish life. Even though they all subscribe to the belief that the Torah was divinely revealed, and therefore it is deemed authoritative and binding on every Jew, Orthodox Jews interact with the non-Jewish society differently from one another.

One of the early "modern" Orthodox Jews was Moses Mendelssohn, the great philosopher of the German Jewish community, who believed that Judaism was based on reason. He also maintained that one could live a Jewish life at home while being fully engaged in the general society. He campaigned for Jews' civil rights and translated the Pentateuch and the book of Psalms into German.

The modern Neo-Orthodox Judaism traces its origin to Rabbi Samson Raphael Hirsch (1808–1888), a German Jew, who was born in Hamburg. In addition to a rigorous Jewish education, Hirsch underwent a thorough secular education in the German public schools, and later on at the University of Bonn where he studied philosophy. He was active not only in his Jewish community but also in larger German society. He became the Chief Rabbi of his community and member of the Parliament of Bohemia and Moravia.

Hirsch is considered the father of German Orthodoxy. Believing in the divinity of the Torah, he wrote commentaries on the Pentateuch and philosophical analyses of the Mitzvot. He formulated his doctrine of "*Torah i'm Derekh Eretz*," namely, "Torah in combination of secular studies." In his personal life, he adopted a modern attitude in terms of clothing (he wore contemporary attire) and personal grooming (he was clean shaven).

Though uncommon in his time, he delivered sermons in German and encouraged the study of the Bible.

## Political Zionism

Ever since the destruction of Jerusalem in 70 CE, Jews had yearned for the day when they would be able to return to their sovereign country in Israel. Spread all over the world and lacking political clout, this dream remained alive only in the minds of worshipers who regularly prayed for its realization. But it was the unfortunate event of the infamous Alfred Dreyfus affair that galvanized the energies of some of the Jewish leaders and turned it into a political movement. Among the most prominent Jewish leaders of the time was Theodore Herzl, a Viennese journalist working for the Neue Freie Presse, who was sent to Paris to cover Dreyfus' trial.

*Theodore Herzl (1860-1904)*

Alfred Dreyfus, a Jewish officer of the French army, was accused in 1894 of being a spy for the Germans, an accusation that eventually proved to be false. In the meantime, however, the affair unleashed a disastrous anti-Semitic wave in France and the rest of Europe. During the trial Herzl became convinced that Jews needed their own country. He thus wrote a book entitled *The Jewish State*, which received mixed reviews. Some thought that this was impossible; other saw that he may have been on the right track. In 1897, Herzl managed to set up the First Zionist Congress in Basel, Switzerland, with the participation of many delegates who came from all over Europe and from the United States. Buoyed by the wonderful spirit of the Congress, Herzl uttered a prophetic statement, "At Basel, I founded the Jewish State. If not in five years, then certainly in fifty, everyone will realize it." Fifty years later, the State of Israel was established in 1948. (For more details, see Chapter Three.)

## Judaism in the United States

Organized Jewish life began in the United States when in 1654 a group of twenty three Jews arrived in New Amsterdam (today New York) coming from Recife, Brazil, as the result of the Portuguese conquest of Recife. The governor of New Amsterdam, Peter Stuyvesant, did not want to keep these new arrivals but was forced to do so when the Dutch West Company in Amsterdam compelled him to keep them in the new world.

Jews came to North America in three different waves: after the arrival of Sephardic Jews from the various Dutch colonies in the New World, such as Surinam [Dutch Guiana], Cayenne, or Curacao, Jews emigrated (about 200,000) between 1825 and 1860 from Bavaria and other places in Germany. They settled both in the north as well as in the south of the country, even taking opposite sides during the Civil War (1861–1865). However, the largest Jewish immigration (more than one million) came from Eastern Europe (1880–1920). Most of these Jews were very poor, spoke Yiddish, and supported Zionism.

Today, numbering about five and a half million and only second to the Jewish population of Israel, Jews in America have distinguished themselves in almost every aspect of American life. Most Jews in the United States live on the East or West coasts. The following list identifies the states with the largest Jewish populations in 2011:

| | |
|---|---|
| New York | 1,635,020 |
| California | 1,219,740 |
| Florida | 638,635 |
| New Jersey | 504,450 |
| Illinois | 297,935 |
| Pennsylvania | 294,925 |
| Massachusetts | 277,980 |
| Maryland | 238,000 |

The rest are spread throughout the country.[8]

# The Holocaust (1933–1945)

Of the many events that took place in the Jewish world in the twentieth century, there is nothing that can compare with the tragedy of the Holocaust (the *Shoah* in Hebrew) in Europe. In 1933, declining economic conditions in Germany led to the rise of Adolf Hitler, an Austrian-born former painter, who proposed to resolve the crisis by blaming the "Jewish race" for all the ills that had befallen Germany. In 1935, the Nuremberg laws stripped German Jews (around half a million) of their citizenship rights. In Nov. 1938, gangs attacked synagogues and other Jewish institutions (*Kristallnacht*). This led to the "The Final Solution," a plan to target the extinction of all Jews in German-dominated countries.

During World War II, the systematic annihilation of the European Jews took different forms, including deportations to faraway countries, forcing them to live in concentration camps that were really death camps, and actually gassing them in places like Auschwitz. Anti-Semitism was rampant almost everywhere in Europe. In 1940, there were massacres in Odessa, Kiev, Rovno, Riga, and Vilna. The Jewish resistance in the Warsaw Ghetto in 1943 did very little to ameliorate the condition of the Jews. The rest of the civilized world, including the United States, knew about these atrocities but did very little to save the Jews. It was left to a number of righteous Gentiles who took their life into their hands by helping out individual Jews or groups of Jews. By the time the Second World War was over in May 1945, about six million Jews had perished at the hands of the Nazis and their acolytes. It was the greatest human tragedy of the century, from which Jews have not yet fully recovered, and there are still a number of survivors yet alive who can tell the story of what happened to them.[9]

## The Establishment of the State of Israel (1948)

The second most significant event of the twentieth century was the establishment of the State of Israel after a hiatus of almost 2,000 years. (For details, see the end of Chapter Two.)

## Endnotes

1. There are a number of books on Jewish History. See, among them, H.H. Ben-Sasson, Ed. *A History of the Jewish People*. Cambridge, Mass: Harvard University, 1985; Paul, Johnson, *A History of the Jews*. New York: Harper-Collins, 1999; Michael A. Meyer, *Responses to Modernity: A History of the Reform Movement in Judaism*. New York and Oxford: Oxford University, 1995; Howard Morley Sachar, *The Course of Modern Jewish History*. New York: Random House, 1990; Jonathan, D. Sarna, *American Judaism: A History*. Yale University, 2004.

2. Unless otherwise indicated all biblical passages are taken from *Tanakh*, Philadelphia: The Jewish Publication Society, 1999.

3. According to Gen. 11:31, Abraham (here called Abram) came from "Ur of the Chaldees," implying southern Babylonia. This is an anachronism. The Chaldeans became a ruling class only in the seventh/sixth centuries BCE. See, Nahum Sarna, *Exodus*, Philadelphia: Jewish Publications Society (JPS), 1989, 87.

4. The issues surrounding the Exodus are highly complicated. A good summary of these issues is found in Eric H. Cline, *From Eden to Exile*. Washington, DC: National Geographic, 2007, 61-92; See also, Rifat Sonsino, "Did the Israelites Escape Through the Sea?" in *Did Moses Really Have Horns?*, New York: Union for Reform Judaism (URJ), 2009, 70-81.

5. The Bible states that it was Shalmaneser who actually captured Samaria (II K. 17:1-7). Sargon took the credit.

6. Though called "Golden," this does not mean that Jews were considered equal to Muslims. They, along with the Christians, both considered by the Muslims as "People of The Book," still had to pay special taxes.

7. On Sabbetai Zevi, see, Gershom Scholem, *Sabbatai Sevi-The Mystical Messiah.* Princeton University Press, 1989; Rifat Sonsino, "Sabbetay Zevi: The Fall of the False Messiah," Central Conference of American Rabbis (CCAR) Journal, Fall 1996, 71–83.

8. Data taken from www.jewishvirtuallibrary.org, "Jewish Popluation of the United States, by State; Updated Dec. 2011."

9. The literature about the Holocaust is extensive. In addition to various articles in the Encyclopaedia Judaica, see the comprehensive work by Nora Levin, *The Holocaust; The Destruction of European Jewry, 1933–1945.* New York: Schocken, 1984.

# BASIC AFFIRMATIONS—GOD, TORAH, AND ISRAEL

The traditional view of Judaism is that it is based on three basic pillars: God, Torah, and Israel. In fact, according to mystical teachings of Judaism, "God, Torah, and Israel, are One."[1] In order to understand Jewish thought through the centuries, it is necessary to know some of the particulars of each of these basic affirmations.

## THE FIRST PILLAR: GOD

### God Is One but Viewed Differently

Historical Judaism proclaims the Unity of God as the Ultimate Reality and the Supreme Being of all existence, though the concept of the divine has been understood differently by sages throughout history. The unity as well as the uniqueness of God is expressed daily through a liturgical formula called the *Shema'*, based on a biblical text: "Hear, O Israel, the Eternal is our God, the Eternal/alone" (Deut. 6:4).

According to the traditional Jewish view, God is unique, intangible, and demands moral behavior. However, this Ethical Monotheism represents the latest stage in the development of the God concept in Judaism. Having overcome the earliest periods of polytheism, the early Israelites became practicing monolatrists (or, henotheists) who believed that, even though there were many gods ruling the universe, the Israelites were to worship only one of them, namely, *YHVH*. Thus, for example, they proclaimed, "Who is like you, O Eternal, among the gods; Who is like You, majestic in holiness" (Ex. 15:11). The answer is, no one. You are greater than the other divinities. The idea that other gods were not even gods at all but sheer idols emerged most likely during the Exilic times, and became the basic affirmation of Jews for centuries to come. Thus, speaking in the name of one and unique God, the prophet Second Isaiah stated, "I am the Eternal (*YHVH*), and there is none else" (45:18).[2]

In biblical times, no one felt the need to prove that such a God existed, because people lived in a world that took for granted the existence of divine powers. As the Psalmist states, "The fool says in his heart, 'There is no God'" (Ps. 14:1). What worried the Israelites was this: does God care for us? What can we do to get God's attention? The attempt to prove the existence of God using philosophic arguments clearly appears for the first time during the Hellenistic period, and became a prominent issue during medieval times.

Throughout history, Jews have tolerated a great deal of diversity with regard to the understanding of this One God. Both the Hebrew Bible and rabbinic literature contain various conceptions of God (See selected texts.) During the Hellenistic period, the dominant Greek philosophy influenced Jews on how to conceptualize God. Thus, for example, Philo of Alexandria (20 BCE–50 CE) followed the thinking of Plato (fourth century BCE) in his views about God. During medieval times, most Jewish thinkers subscribed to the ideas of Aristotle (fourth century BCE). The great Jewish philosopher Moses Maimonides (1135–1204) was one of these thinkers. In the modern period, contemporary thought has influenced the way in which Jews describe God. Thus today, even for some liberal Jews like Emil Fackenheim (1916–2003), God is a personal God who is all-knowing, all-good, and all-powerful. These are the Classical Theists. Other theists, such as Harold S. Kushner (b. 1935), still maintaining that God is all-good, are compelled to accept that God is not all-powerful in order to account for evil in the universe. These are the Limited Theists. On the other hand, for religious naturalists, like Roland B. Gittelsohn (1910–1995), God is not a personal God, but an impersonal energy of the universe that sustains it from within. For other Jews, God is not a reality but an idea. For instance, religious humanists claim that God is the highest image of oneself. There are some Jews who, following the teachings of Martin Buber (1878–1965), argue that God can be met only in relationship, and others, like Michael Benedikt, maintain that God is simply the good we do.[3] (For selected texts, see below.) Even within this diversity, it is possible to articulate certain common features that could apply to any Jewish God concept. They are:

1. God is One and intangible.
2. God is unique and beyond description.
3. God is moral.
4. God is beyond gender.
5. An individual can transcend his/her humanity, but can never become God.

## God's Names

In Hebrew, God is referred to by various names, such as *El, Elohim, Shaddai,* and *Tzevaot.*[4] However, in the Bible and modern Jewish liturgy, God's proper name is *YHVH.* The correct pronunciation of this name is not known and is now read as *Adonai* (meaning "My Master").[5] In the rabbinic period, the sages came up with other nomenclatures for God, including "Our Father in Heaven," "The Holy One, Blessed is He," "The Merciful One," "The Place," "The Master of the Universe." In Jewish mystical literature we have, *En Sof* ("the Endless One") and *Shekhinah,* referring to the feminine aspect of God's Presence in the world. In modern times, one also finds gender-sensitive as well as non-hierarchical terms, such as, "The Source of Life," "The Eternal," and "the Holy One of Being."

## The Covenant

According to the Hebrew Bible, God, for reasons that are not clear, "chose" the Israelites as a group, and established a special covenant (*berit* in Hebrew) with them. According to Jewish tradition, this covenant was first established with Abraham, the patriarch (Gen. 15:17-24). The Israelites are, as the book of Deuteronomy puts it, God's "treasured possession" (Deut. 7:6). This covenant, signed with the people of Israel on Mt. Sinai (or Mt. Horeb, according to Deuteronomy) during the Exodus period, bound God and Israel, when Israel accepted the Torah as binding on them (Ex. 20; Deut. 5).[6] God promised to care for the Israelites, and the Israelites agreed to live according to God's teachings. However, for many biblical prophets, this covenant between God and the Israelites is conditional, and does not give them only privileges but also duties and responsibilities to live according to God's commandments. The prophet Amos (eighth century BCE) makes this clear: "You alone have I singled out from all the families of the earth; therefore I will call you to account for all your iniquities" (3:2). Israel was told that they would be judged by higher standards. The "covenant of circumcision" (*berit milah*), which is projected back to the days of the patriarch Abraham, is a "sign" of this spiritual bond (Gen. 17). In our times, other Jews, like the Jewish Reconstructionists, argue that, on the contrary, it was the Israelites who actually "chose" God, and covenanted themselves to God.

## The Problem of Evil-Theodicy

The word theodicy comes from *theos* (God, in Greek) and *dike* (justice, in Greek) and refers to the problem of God's justice in view of the presence of evil. How to explain evil as well as the death of the innocent in a world dominated by God's goodness has been debated by thinkers for centuries, with no satisfactory answer yet given. The issue can be summarized as follows: If God is all-powerful, all-knowing, and all-good, where does evil come from?

One of the basic assumptions in the Hebrew Bible is that God punishes the wicked and rewards the righteous. One Psalmist wrote, "I have been young and am now old, but I have never seen a righteous man abandoned, or his children seeking bread" (Ps. 37:25; cf. Prov. 10:28). Yet, along with others in the ancient Near East, the Israelites too, at times, complained that this is not always the case. On many occasions, they said, the innocent do suffer for the sins of others. Thus, another Psalmist stated, "I have seen the wicked at ease" (Ps. 73:3), and the prophet Jeremiah (seventh century BCE) complained, "Why does the way of the wicked prosper?" (Jer. 12:1).

The answer to this terribly disturbing realization is not uniform in biblical texts. Some have maintained that suffering is, in fact, the deserved punishment for sin (see, for example, the argument of the friends of Job in Job 4:8); others argued that suffering is only a test to see if people are still faithful to God (e.g., Deut. 8:2). There were others still who believed that evil is haphazard and morally meaningless (e.g., Eccl. 9:3). Some simply gave up and said that the suffering of the innocent is beyond human comprehension (e.g., Isa. 55:9).

In the early rabbinic period and in medieval times, rabbis probed the question with renewed interest: some spoke of *yisurin shel ha-havah* ("the suffering of love"), and argued that evil is temporary and that those who suffer in this world will ultimately be rewarded in the world-to-come. In medieval times, some said that evil is simply the absence of good.

In modern times, especially after the Holocaust, the question of theodicy has become personal for many survivors and those who thought about the impact of the unspeakable tragedy. Some said that God simply "hid His face" during the Holocaust for reasons that are unknown. Others claimed that God, as we know it, is "dead" but, we still need to create religious rituals that will ensure we do not live in an uncaring world. And others maintained that, not being all-powerful, God had nothing to do with these massacres; they represent the inhumanity of some people against others and evil is a reality that we must accept, because it is part of the structure of the universe. People who choose evil over good misuse their human freedom.[7]

As long as innocent people suffer loss, the question of God's justice will continue to be raised. Satisfactory answers still fail us, because we do not fully know how the universe operates, and cannot fathom the mind of God.

## Offenses Against God; Sin and Atonement

An offense against God is called a sin. In the Bible, the word "sin" (*het*, in Hebrew) means "to miss the mark." Thus, when we read in King Solomon's Prayer, "There lives no person on earth who is so righteous that he does not sin" (I K 8:46), it implies that we often miss the mark and deviate from the rightful course by acting against the divine will as recorded in our sacred texts. This sin can be committed not only against God but also against other human beings.

Many Jewish teachers taught that people are born with a clean slate and are able to choose between right and wrong, but they also recognized that this human freedom is in tension with the idea of pre-determination (M Avot, 3:15). According to the teachings of the Rabbis, human beings enter the world with two inclinations: the inclination to do good (*yetzer ha-tov*) and the inclination to do bad (*yetzer ha-ra'*). Every person struggles with these opposing forces. The study and practice of Torah are supposed to function as an antidote by turning the inclination to do bad into the inclination to do good (BT BB. 16a).

In mainstream Christianity, however, the view is different. One is born with the imprint of "original sin." The death of Jesus is, therefore, considered a sacrificial atonement for the Fall of Humanity, resulting from the sin of the first human beings on earth who disobeyed God's commandment in Paradise by eating from the fruit of the Tree of Knowledge (Gen. 3). Those who believe in Jesus share in the atonement of his death. (See, for example, Rom. 5:12, 18-19; 6:3-4, 6.) Most rabbis, however, do not consider the episode in Paradise as a "Fall." On the contrary, the event actually represents the discovery of Adam and Eve's humanity and their potential for progress.

According to the ancient Rabbis, of the two types of sins (i.e., those committed against God and those against human beings), the contrition expressed during the Day of Atonement (Yom Kippur)—in the past, through an appropriate sacrifice at the Temple, and today with sincere prayers—clears the sins against God. But, in the second case (i.e., sins against other humans), sins can be atoned for only by winning the forgiveness of the wronged person. (M Yoma, 8:9). Confession of sin is simply not enough. One needs to follow the rule of the three C's: a) Confession: after honest searching of one's soul one must verbalize his/her mistake; b) Contrition: the individual must feel sorry for his/her shortcomings; and, finally, c) Change: the offender must seek pardon of the wronged individual, make appropriate restitution, and promise never to do it again.

Mainstream Judaism does not accept the idea of vicarious atonement by another human being. Everyone is responsible for his/her own actions[8], for which proper atonement and restitution are required. It is different in Christianity, which affirms that Jesus died for human sins. The only example of vicarious punishment in biblical times took place during the Day of Atonement when a goat was sent away into the wilderness, carrying people's sins (See, Lev. 16). This practice disappeared from Judaism with the destruction of the Temple in Jerusalem.

## God the Redeemer and Savior

The Jewish understanding of the concepts of redemption (from the Hebrew root *ga-al* or *padah*) and salvation (from the root, *yesha'*) is very different from Christianity. In Christianity these terms are often used to indicate redemption from sin and its consequences. In the New Testament, the death of Jesus is even taken to be a redemptive act (e.g., Matthew, 20:28). In the dominant Jewish thought, on the other hand, these expressions refer to the ability to overcome any situation that destroys human life in this world.

In the Bible, a "redeemer" is primarily a person who rescues real property, an animal, or even another human being from his oppressor by paying a sum of money. For instance, the Book of Leviticus instructs us, "If your kinsman is in straits and has to sell part of his holding, his nearest redeemer (*goalo*) shall come and redeem what his kinsman has sold" (25:25). By extension, the role of "redeemer" is given to God who rescues the Israelites from Egypt (Ex. 6:6) or from any other trouble (Ps. 25:22). Similarly, in the Bible, the word *yeshua'h* ("salvation") basically means "victory." Thus, for instance, a military leader is often called a *moshia'* (e.g., "a champion;" see, Judges, 3:9). By extension, God is the ultimate "savior" (Ps. 3:8). In the rabbinic literature, *geulah* refers to national redemption here on earth. In modern Jewish thought, it has a wider connotation, and could mean, for example, self-fulfillment, eventual triumph of good over evil, social reforms, even the establishment of the State of Israel.

## God and Prayer

A prayer is a human attempt to reach the divine. In English, the verb "to pray" comes from Old French and ultimately Latin and means, "to obtain by begging," whereas in Hebrew *lehitpallel*, a reflective verb, refers to "judging oneself."

People have prayed from the beginning of time, and developed various types of worship. In the Biblical time, the major avenue of worship was the offering before God of animals, libations, or certain meals. After the Second Temple was destroyed in 70 CE, the Rabbis replaced sacrifices with prayers, and they began to create and compile different types of oral prayers. Eventually these were written down in prayerbooks.

There are three major types of prayer in the Jewish liturgy: a) Gratitude: These express thanks to God for one's own well-being; b) Praise: These laud God for being God and for all the greatness that God displays; c) Petition: Through these prayers, the worshiper asks God something specific.

Though prayer is one of the basic human needs, it must overcome a number of impediments today. How much praise of God is appropriate or necessary? Petitionary prayers, in particular, present serious challenges. For example,

1. Some people expect an immediate answer to their prayers, and when the response fails to materialize, they become disappointed. We find a reflection of this feeling in the Bible, when the Psalmist cries, "As for me, I cry out to You, O Eternal. Each morning my prayer greets you. Why, O Eternal, do you reject me? Do you hide Your face from me?" (Ps. 88:14-15). Similarly, the prophet Habakkuk said, "How long, O Eternal, shall I cry out, and You do not listen?" (1:2).

2. The prayer text itself is at times not gender-free, non-inclusive, or is archaic, and does not reflect our present needs.

3. Often, we do not say what we mean in our prayers or mean what we pray.

4. If one prays for a miracle, he/she may be highly disappointed if the miracle does not occur.

5. If we equate nobility of expression with profundity of thought, we may leave the worship empty.

6. Sometimes, the seating, the setting, the music, or the sermon becomes a block to concentration and meditation.

7. Also, if one assumes that authentic prayer issues from a belief in God, however conceived, the lack of such a belief becomes a serious impediment to prayer. The Jewish philosopher Abraham J. Heschel (1907–1972) once expressed this idea by stating, "The issue of prayer is not prayer, the issue of prayer is God." However, it is also possible to develop a God concept while struggling with prayer. Thus, Rabbi Eric Yoffie, the former president of the Union for Reform Judaism, declared, "To those who say, 'first theology, and then prayer,' I would respond, 'no, first prayer, and the theology will take care of itself.'"[9]

For an authentic prayer, the setting has to be appropriate, the music sublime, and the text inspiring. It must enable the individual to transcend him/herself in order to connect with something bigger than him/herself, by becoming part of a wider community. Prayers need to be read not as legal briefs but as poetry, evoking higher feelings. Prayers can be viewed not only as dialogues with God but also as self-expression, during which one expresses his/her religious thoughts, aspirations, and hopes. Furthermore, prayers should not be uttered to ask for the impossible. In other words, prayers for miracles are worthless. They raise expectations that are unlikely to be fulfilled.

Some people believe that prayers can have positive results in the physical world. Others, using more rational thinking, maintain that prayers at best can transform the person who prays. They give the individual a deeper insight into him/herself about the world and society. A wise person quipped, "Who rise from prayer better persons, their prayer is answered."[10]

## God's Kingdom; Messianic Age

In Jewish thought, the expectation is that at the end of time, God's kingdom will be manifest with the establishment of wholeness ("Shalom" in Hebrew) in the universe. According to the Rabbis, this period will be ushered in by the arrival of the Messiah.

The term "Messiah" (*mashiah*, in Hebrew) means "anointed." (In Greek, the word is translated as "Christos," from which the word Christ is derived.) In biblical times, many people—kings, priests, prophets—were anointed for a special role by pouring a bit of olive oil on their head. The altar, too, was anointed. At times, even some non-Israelites, like Cyrus, the Persian king (sixth century BCE), were called "Messiah" (Isa. 45:1). Later, the term was associated with a descendent of King David who, in the distant future, will save Israel and humanity from all oppressors. When exactly this extended meaning of the Messiah began is far from clear, but it appears to have been popular in late biblical and early rabbinic times when it became a cardinal belief among Jews.

Even today, many Jews expect the arrival of a personal Messiah at the end of time. In the daily liturgy, Orthodox Jews, "Blessed are You, O God…who in love will bring a redeemer (*goel*) to their children's children for Your Name's sake." Not even the emergence of "false messiahs" is Jewish life—such as Bar Kohba (second century CE) or Sabbetay Zevi (seventeenth century Ottoman Empire)—dimmed in the hope that when the Messiah comes, all Jews will be redeemed from oppression, and humanity will enter into a period of real peace. Christians, on the other hand, believe that the Messiah, in the person of Jesus, has already come once, but will come again at the end of time.

Whereas Orthodox Jews expect that the Messiah, a descendent of King David, will be a real human being, Reform Jews pray for the coming of the "Messianic Age" as the result of our common efforts to benefit all humanity. This hope was expressed in many pronouncements in Reform Jewish history. Thus, as early as 1885, the Pittsburgh Platform stated, "We recognize in the modern era of universal culture of heart and intellect the approach of the realization of Israel's great Messianic hope for the establishment of the kingdom of truth, justice and peace among men." About 50 years later, the Columbus Platform of 1937 proclaimed, "Throughout the ages it has been Israel's mission to witness to the Divine in the face of every form of paganism and materialism. We regard it as our historic task to cooperate with all men in the establishment of the kingdom of God, of universal brotherhood, Justice, truth and peace on earth. This is our Messianic goal." The Centenary Perspective of 1976 contained a similar statement: "Throughout our long history our people has been inseparable from its religion with its messianic hope that humanity will be redeemed." In the Centenary Platform of 1997 we find, "We believe that the renewal and perpetuation of Jewish national life in *Eretz Yisrael* ["the Land of Israel"] is a necessary condition for the realization of the physical and spiritual redemption of the Jewish people and of all humanity. While that day of redemption remains but a distant yearning, we express the fervent hope that *Medinat Yisrael* ["the State of Israel"], living in peace with its neighbors, will hasten the redemption of *A'm Yisrael* ["People of Israel"], and the fulfillment of our messianic dream of universal peace under the sovereignty of God."

However, not everyone in the Jewish community supports the idea of Messianism. Religious humanists, for example, consider the concept dangerous. Thus, Rabbi Sherwin Wine, the founder of Humanistic Judaism, a small group in the American Jewish scene, declared in 1999, "Listening to the Jesus people [Messianic Jews] or the Lubavicher Rebbe people, it's the same thing. There is a figure sent by God who is going to rescue us. Therefore, I find all messianic thinking dangerous. I think it's one of the dangerous ideas that came out of the Jewish past. Because messianism is utopianism, and utopianism is a very dangerous thing. ... If you want utopian goals, then you're going to be disappointed and frustrated all the time. The way to live the life of courage is to have goals that are realistic and appropriate."[11]

---

### Selected Texts About Some Jewish Concepts Of God: In The Bible

The patriarch discovers the reality of God on his way to Haran, in southeastern Anatolia:

Jacob left Beer-sheba, and set out for Haran. He came upon a certain place and stopped there for the night, for the sun had set. Taking one of the stones of that place, he put it under his head and lay down in that place. He had a dream; a stairway [or, "ramp"] was set on the ground and its top reached to the sky, and angels of God were going up and down on it. And the Lord was standing beside him and He said: "I am the Lord, the God of your father Abraham and the God of Isaac: the ground on which you are lying I will give to you and to your offspring. Your descendants shall be as the dust of the earth; you shall spread out to the west and to the east, and to the north and to the south. All the families of the earth shall bless themselves by you and your descendants. Remember, I am with you: I will protect you wherever you go and bring you back to this land. I will not leave you until I have done what I have promised you." Jacob awoke from his sleep and said: "Surely the Lord is present in this place, and I did not know it!" (Gen. 28:10-16, NJPS).

I. The Bible provides different images of God

1. God as the power of nature:

He makes clouds rise from the end of the earth;
He makes lightning for the rain;
He releases the wind from His vaults. (Ps. 135:7)

2. God creates nature through a creative word:

For He spoke, and it was;
He commanded, and it endured. (Ps. 33:9).

3. God as a warrior:

The Lord, the Warrior;
Lord is His name. (Ex. 15:3)

4. God as caring shepherd and a loving parent:

The Lord is my shepherd, I shall not want. (Ps. 23:1)

As a father has compassion for his children,
so the Lord has compassion for those who fear Him. (Ps. 103:13)

5. God as master of history:

The Lord freed us from Egypt by a mighty hand.
He brought us to this place and gave us this land. (Deut. 26:8-9)

You alone have I singled out
Of all the families of the earth;
That is why I will call you to account
For all your iniquities. (Amos 3:2)

6. God demands ethical behavior:

I desire goodness (*hesed*), not sacrifice. (Hos. 6:6)

He has told you, O man, what is good
And what the Lord requires of you:
Only to do justice
And to love goodness
And to walk modestly with your God. (Mic. 6:8)

II. Rabbinic literature also contains various perceptions of the divine

1. Proof for the existence of God:

"God created" (Gen. I:I). It happened that a heretic came to Rabbi Akiva [second century CE] and asked: "This world—who created it?" R. Akiva replied: "The Holy One, blessed be He." The heretic said: "Show me clear proof." R. Akiva replied, "Come back to me tomorrow." The next day, when the heretic came, R Akiva asked him, "What are you wearing?" The heretic replied, "A garment." R. Akiva asked, "Who made it?" The heretic, "A weaver." "I don't believe you," said R. Akiva; "show me clear proof." The heretic: "What can I show you? Don't you know that a weaver made it?" R. Akiva then asked, "And you, do you not know that the Holy One made His world?" After the heretic departed, R. Akiva's disciples asked him, "But is that the clear proof?" He replied, "My children, even as a house proclaims its builder, a garment its weaver, or a door its carpenter, so does the world proclaim the Holy One, blessed be He, that created it."[12]

2. God is everywhere:

A heathen once asked Rabbi Joshua b. Korhah: 'Why did God choose a thornbush from which to speak to Moses?' [See, Ex. 3:1-6]. He replied: '... To teach you that no place is devoid of God's presence, not even a thorn-bush.' (Gen. R. 3:5, Soncino)

3. Our responsibility:

What means the text, *'Ye shall walk after the Lord your God'*? [Deut. 13:5] Is it, then, possible for a human being to walk after the Shekhinah; for has it not been said, *'For the Lord thy God is a devouring fire?'* [Deut. 4:24] But [the meaning is] to walk after the attributes of the Holy One, blessed be He. As He clothes the naked ... so do thou also clothe the naked. The Holy One, blessed be He, visited the sick ... comforted the mourners ... buried the dead ... so do thou also ... (BT Sota 14a, Soncino)

III. In Medieval Times

1. MAIMONIDES (1135–1204)

The Jewish philosopher Maimonides, born in Cordoba, Spain, and buried in Tiberias, was a follower of Aristotle. He considered God as a "Mind" who is the prime mover of all existence:

The First Fundamental Principle: To believe in the existence of the Creator; that there is an Existence complete in all the senses of the word "existence." He is the cause of all existence. In Him all else subsists and From Him derives … He is sufficient to Himself. All else, whether angels or celestials and whatever is in them or below them, needs Him to exist. … God is one, the cause of all oneness … He is incorporeal … absolutely eternal. (Helek: Sanhedrin, Ch. 10, Twersky)

It is as if you say: this stone, which was in motion, was moved by a staff: the staff was moved by a hand; the hand by tendons; the tendons by muscles; the muscles by nerves; the nerves by natural heat; and the natural heat by the form that subsists therein, and this form being undoubtedly the first mover. (Guide, II/1)

Human reason cannot fully conceive God in His true essence, because of the perfection of God's essence and the imperfection of our own reason. (Avot, Eight Chapters, VIII).

## 2. ISAAC LURIA (1534–1572)

A master of Kabbalah, Isaac Luria was born in Israel and taught in Safed. He is the founder of a Jewish mystical school called Lurianic Kabbalah. His view of the creation of the world rests on three stages: 1. *Tzimtzum* ("contraction"); 2. *Shevirat ha-kelim* ("breaking of the vessels"); and, 3. *Tikkun O'lam* ("restoration of wholeness"):

Know that before the emanations were emanated and the creatures created, the simple supernal light [of the *En Sof*] filled all there was and there was no empty area whatever, that is, an empty atmosphere and a vacuum. All was simple infinite light. It had no beginning and no end. All was simple light in total sameness.

When in His simple will it was resolved to create worlds and emanate emanations He contracted Himself within the middle point in Himself, in the very center. And He contracted that light, and it was withdrawn to the sides around the middle point. Then there was left an empty space, an atmosphere, and a vacuum extending from the precise point of the center.

After this contraction … there was left a vacuum … an area in which there could be emanations, the beings created and formed and made. (Hayyim Vital, Etz Ha-Hayyim, 1; quoted in *The Jewish Mystical Tradition*, B. Bokser, NY: Pilgrim, 1981, p.143/4).

IV. Modern Times

## 1. MARTIN BUBER (1878–1965)

*This German-Jewish philosopher believed that one can relate to another in two different ways: I-It, is a connection of use and evaluation; whereas I-Thou is a relationship of total acceptance. It is during this I-Thou meeting that one feels the presence of God:*

The attitude of man is twofold, in accordance with his twofold nature of the primary words which he speaks. … The one primary word is the combination I-Thou. The other primary word is the combination I-It. (1 and Thou, NY: Scribners, 1958, Smith, p. 3)

Every particular Thou is a glimpse through to the eternal Thou; by means of every particular Thou the primary word addresses the eternal Thou … the inborn Thou is realized in each relation and consummated in none. It is consummated only in the direct relation with the Thou that by its nature cannot become It. (Ibid., p. 75)

## 2. MORDECAI KAPLAN (1881–1983)

*Kaplan was the founder of the Reconstructionist Jewish movement in the United States. He was a process theologian, and considered God as the totality of forces that help us become the best of what we can be.*

To believe in God means to accept life on the assumption that it harbors conditions in the outer world and drives in the human spirit which together impel man to transcend himself. To believe in God means to take for granted that it is man's destiny to rise above the brute and to eliminate all forms of violence and exploitation from human society. In brief, God is the Power in the cosmos that gives human life the direction that enables the human being to reflect the image of God. (*Judaism Without Supernaturalism*, NY: Reconstructionist, 1958, p. 111/2)

(God is) the Power that makes for human salvation. (ibid., p. 114/5)

## 3. ERICH FROMM (1900–1980)

*A prominent psychoanalyst and philosopher, Fromm was a religious humanist who believed that God is an idea, not a reality, and stood for one's own highest image of oneself.*

Man's aim in humanistic religion is to achieve the greatest strength, not the greatest powerlessness; virtue is self-realization, not obedience. Faith is certainty of conviction based on one's experience of thought and feeling, not assent to propositions on credit of the proposer.

Inasmuch as humanistic religions are theistic, God is a symbol of man's own powers which he tries to realize in his life, and is not a symbol of force and domination, having power over man. (*Psychoanalysis and Religion*, New Haven: Yale, 1959, p. 37)

4. ROLAND B. GITTELSOHN (1910–1996).

*A well-known religious naturalist, Gittelsohn was a Rabbi in Boston:*

God is:
1. The Spiritual Power which created and sustains nature.
2. The Energizing Force which has been slowly working its way through evolution toward fulfillment of a plan.
3. The Moral Power which impels and governs the operation of Moral Natural Law. We see a portion of this Power within ourselves in the form of conscience.
There is also a fourth possible interpretation of God…. We can also conceive Him as a Goal…. God can be considered as a combination of all our ethical goals. At one and the same time He can be the Moral Power impelling us to improve and the Ethical Goal toward which our improvement is aimed. (*Wings of the Morning*, NY: UAHC, 1969, p. 166/7)

5. HAROLD S. KUSHNER

*Rabbi Harold Kushner of Natick, MA, is a prolific writer and speaker. He probably is a good representative of limited theism, which proclaims the personhood of God without being all-powerful:*

I believe in God … I recognize His limitations. He is limited in what He can do by laws of nature and by the evolution of human nature and human moral freedom.

God does not cause our misfortunes. Some are caused by bad luck, some are being human and being mortal, living in a world of inflexible natural laws. (*When Bad Things Happen to Good People*, NY: Schocken, 1981, p. 134)

God may not prevent the calamity, but He gives us the strength and the perseverance to overcome it. (ibid., p. 141)

For the religious mind and soul, the issue has never been the *existence* of God but the *importance* of God, the difference that God makes in the way we live. (*Who Needs God?* NY: Summit, 1989, p. 23)

## 6. MARCIA FALK

*A highly respected poet and thinker, Falk is a humanist as well as a feminist:*

Let us bless the source of life
that brings forth bread from the earth.
(*The Book of Blessings*, San Francisco: Harper, 1996, p. 18)

Hear, o Israel—
The divine abounds everywhere
And dwells in everything; the many are One. (ibid., p. 24)

May our hearts be lifted,
our spirits refreshed,
as we light the Sabbath candles. (ibid., p. 60)

Let us bless the flow of life
That revives us, sustains us,
and brings us to this day. (ibid., p. 368)

Let us acknowledge the source of life
source of all nourishment.
May we protect the bountiful earth
that it may continue to sustain us,
and let us seek sustenance
for all who dwell in the world. (ibid., p. 380)

# ENDNOTES

1. Zohar, Vayikra, 73.
2. For more on the biblical view of God, see, Rifat Sonsino and Daniel B. Syme, *Finding God: Selected Responses*. New York: UAHC Press (now URJ), 2002.
3. Michael Benedikt, *God Is the Good We Do*. New York: Bottino, 2007. For God concepts in Judaism, see Sonsino, op.cit; Also, Sonsino, *The Many Faces of God: A Reader of Modern Jewish Theologies*. New York: URJ Press, 2004.

4. On God's various names, see Louis Jacobs, *A Jewish Theology*. New York; Behrman, 1973, 136–151.

5. On God's proper name, see, Rifat Sonsino, *Did Moses Really Have Horns?*, 12–24.

6. On the issues regarding the location and content of the covenant, see Sonsino, *Did Moses Really Have Horns?*, 82–96.

7. See also, the article, "Good and Evil," in the Encylopaedia Judaica, 2007, Vol. 2, 752ff.

8. This is in contradiction to the generational extension of punishment recorded in Ex. 34:7 or Num. 14:18, and reflected in later texts, such as Deut. 24:16; Ezek. 18:20; cf. BT Makkot 24a, where the principle of individual responsibility is established.

9. Eric H. Yoffie, "Remarks to the UAHC Executive Committee," New York: Union of American Hebrew Congregations [today, Union for Reform Judaism], Feb. 7, 2000, 3.

10. *Gates of Prayer*. New York: Central Conference of American Rabbis, 1975, 8.

11. Moment Magazine, Feb, 1999.

12. Tem.3; Bialik and Ravnitzky, *The Book of Legends*. New York: Schocken, 1992, 6:6.

# BASIC AFFIRMATIONS—PART TWO

## II. SECOND PILLAR: TORAH

In Jewish teachings, Torah, basically meaning "instruction," (see Preface) is imparted through sacred texts. Here below are the major sacred books created by Jews over the centuries:

### The Hebrew Bible

The Bible is one of the main pillars of Western culture. Through translation into over hundreds of languages, it has had a tremendous impact on language, literature, and religious beliefs. For Jews, the Bible is the repository of the culture of the biblical Israelites and the fountainhead of our religious ideology and practice today. A quick survey of the Biblical texts show that, contrary to popular belief, it is not a monolithic document, but an anthology of various books representing different points of view on a variety of subjects, having been composed and edited by mostly unknown individuals. They are primarily religious documents, not historical texts, which proclaim a belief in the existence of one invisible and spiritual God conceived as the power behind nature and history. The Bible covers a long period of time: from Creation to the second century BCE (Dan. 7:1-8).

The term "Bible" comes from the Greek, *biblia* (meaning "books"), and was adopted by the Greek-speaking Jews of the second century BCE. What to call this collection of sacred books is not an easy matter. Jews do not use the expression "Old Testament," because this assumes the religious validity of the New Testament, which Jews deny. The term "Sacred Scriptures" is too general and "Hebrew Scriptures" is only party correct, because the Bible also contains texts in Aramaic, such as Daniel and Ezra. The best term is TANAK, with each Hebrew consonant standing for the first letter of one the three divisions: T(orah), N(eviim—the Prophets), and K(etuvim—The Writings). The TANAK contains 24 books in all.

Torah: Torah: This compilation (also called "Torah," for short) is made up of the first five books attributed to Moses (thus the term, "Pentateuch"): Genesis, Exodus, Leviticus, Numbers, and Deuteronomy. They cover the historical period from Creation to the death of Moses. The Bible itself (Ex. 24:4; cf. Lev. 26:46) and ancient Rabbis maintained that it was authored by Moses (BT BB 14b). The sages even taught that a person does not have a share in the world-to-come if he/she denies that Torah comes from heaven (M Sanh. 10:1). However, modern biblical scholarship, based on a critical analysis of the texts, which reveal a number of duplications, contradictions, and historical anachronisms, assumes that it was written over a long period of time and reflects many schools of thought in ancient Israel. Most likely it was edited during post-Exilic times. (See below, Excursus.)

The basic theory of how the Pentateuch was put together was proposed by the German Biblical scholar Julius Wellhausen (1844–1918), who argued that four distinct sources lie behind our present text. The earliest southern source, called J (after the name *YHVH*—Germans use J instead of Y), originated around 850 BCE. The second source, a document called E (after the name Elohim for God) is of northern origin, about 750 BCE. These two sources were combined by a redactor around 650 BCE. After the Deuteronomic reformation around 621 BCE, the third source was composed, namely D (for Deuteronomy). A redactor combined all three sources around 550 BCE. Finally, the priests (the authors of so-called P source) added their own contributions, especially in the area of temple ritual, and gave form to the Pentateuch around 400 BCE. Recent scholarship considerably altered this theory. However, the basic assumption that various sources or schools of thought are at the basis of the Pentateuch still remains as a starting point for all modern scholars.

Neviim: The Prophets. This section is sub-divided into two: Early and Later Prophets. Early Prophets contains some historical information covering the period between the Conquest of Canaan and the destruction of the First Temple in 586 BCE. The reason this section is called "Prophets" is that it contains references to a number of pre-classical prophets who lived during this period. Later Prophets includes the three great prophets, namely Isaiah, Jeremiah, and Ezekiel, and the Twelve Minor prophets. In the opinion of many biblical scholars, this section was completed around 200 BCE.

Ketuvim: The Writings. Contains a number of late texts representing a variety of literary genres, and includes the following books: Psalms, Proverbs, Job, The Song of Songs, Ruth, Lamentations, Ecclesiastes, Esther, Daniel, Ezra, Nehemiah, and I and II Chronicles. The third section of the Bible was finalized by the ancient sages in the first century CE.[1]

This tri-partite division represents a Jewish division. Christians have adopted a different one and place the Prophets at the end of the Bible, as the third division. This is based on the theological assumption that the prophetic messages of the Tanak were fulfilled in the life and personality of Jesus. Furthermore, whereas the Hebrew Bible leaves out the Apocrypha (a collection of texts that emerged during the inter-testamental period), the Catholics include the Apocrypha in their Sacred Bible along with the New Testament. The Protestants include the "Old" Testament and the New Testament, but leave out the Apocrypha.

---

### Excursus: A Few Problematic Texts Regarding Mosaic Authorship Of The Pentateuch

#### A. Post-Mosaic Passages In The Pentateuch

1. Abram took his wife Sarai, his brother's son Lot, all the possessions that they had accumulated, and the persons they had acquired in Haran, and they set out for the land of Canaan. When they came to the land of Canaan, Abram passed through the land as far as the sacred place at Shechem, by the terebinth of Moreh. The Canaanites were then in the land. (Gen. 12:5-6)
*Note: The author of this sentence lived at a time when the Canaanites were no longer living in the land; that is, after the times of Moses. Hence, Moses could not have written it, because the Canaanites were indeed present in the land during his lifetime.*

2. The following are the kings who reigned in the land of Edom before any king reigned over the Israelites. (Gen. 36:6)
*Note: Moses did not know Jewish kings ruling over Israel. They emerged long after his death. Traditional sources claim that they knew this fact by virtue of his prophetic skills.*

3. So there, in the land of Moab, Moses, the servant of the LORD, died as the LORD had said; and he was buried in the ravine opposite Beth-peor in the land of Moab, but to this day no one knows the place of his burial. (Deut. 34:5-6)
*Note: It is inconceivable that Moses would be writing about his own death. Traditional sources had to admit that this sentence was written by someone else, perhaps by Joshua, Moses's successor.*

4. These are the words which Moses spoke to all Israel beyond the Jordan in the desert, in the Arabah. (Deut. 1:1)

*Note: This passage is written from the perspective of Canaan looking west over the Jordan River, a river Moses did not cross.*

## B. Contradictions

1. NOAH: Of all other living creatures you shall bring <u>two</u> into the ark, one male and one female, that you may keep them alive with you. (Gen. 6:19)

Of every clean animal, take with you <u>seven</u> pairs, a male and its mate; and of the unclean animals, one pair, a male and its mate; likewise, of every clean bird of the air, seven pairs, a male and a female, and of all the unclean birds, one pair, a male and a female. (Gen. 7:2)
*Note: Is it "two" or "seven"?*

2. Where were the Ten Commandments given?
When the LORD came down to the top of Mount <u>Sinai</u>, he summoned Moses to the top of the mountain, and Moses went up to him. (Ex. 19:20)

The LORD, our God, made a covenant with us at <u>Horeb</u>. (Deut. 5:2)
*Note: Is it at Mt. Sinai or at Mt. Horeb? Are they one and the same, or two different mountains?*

3. Moses in the 3rd person:
Now, Moses himself was by far the meekest man on the face of the earth. (Num. 12:3)
*Note: No person writes this about himself!*

## C. Duplications

1. There are two parallel creation stories in the Pentateuch, each with a different name for God: Elohim in Gen. 1 and *YHVH* in Gen. 2. Why?

2. Two similar covenants are given to Abraham (Gen. 15 and 17). Why?

3. The Pentateuch contains two sets of the Decalogue (Ex. 20 and Deut. 5), with some considerable differences between them. Why?

These are among the major observations that led modern biblical scholars to argue that the Pentateuch was edited long after the death of Moses.

## 2. The Mishnah

When the Pharisees emerged in the historical scene in the late second century BCE, they advocated the belief that Torah was revealed on Mt. Sinai in two different forms: *Torah she-bikhtav* (The Written Torah) and its interpretation in the form of *Torah she-bea'l peh* (The Oral Torah). For a long period of time these oral teachings were transmitted from teacher to student in an oral fashion. However, some Rabbis, like Rabbi Akiba (d. 135 CE), started to collect a few of these instructions, and by the time of the Patriarch Judah Hanasi (early third century CE), it was decided to write them down in order to preserve them. A few texts were added later on after his death. This collection is called the *Mishnah*.

The *Mishnah* is divided into six major volumes: *Zeraim* ("Seeds"), *Moed* ("Festivals"), *Nashim* ("Women"), *Nezikin* ("Damages"), *Kodashim* ("Holy Things"), and *Tohorot* ("Purifications"). The collection is primarily made up of legal matters but it does contain a tractate dealing with religious ethics (namely, Avot in *Nezikin*). The text was produced in Judea primarily in Hebrew with a number of words in Greek, reflecting the Greek domination of the country at the time. All together it contains sixty-three tractates. The sages mentioned in the *Mishnah* are called *Tannaim*, and their period Tannaitic. Around the year 300 CE, a number of parallel and, at times, supplementary texts (called *Baraytot*) were compiled in a collection named Tosefta.[2]

---

### Examples Of Mishnaic Texts:

1. The Oral Torah
Moses received the (oral) Torah from Sinai, and he delivered it to Joshua, and Joshua to the elders, and the elders to the prophets, and the prophets delivered it to the men of the Great Synagogue. They said three things: Be deliberate in judgment; and raise up many disciples; and make a fence to the Torah. (M Avot 1:1)

2. Sound Rabbinic Advice
Hillel used to say: If I am not for myself who is for me? and being for my own self what am I? If not now when? (Av.1:15)

Hillel said: Do not separate yourself from the community; and do not trust in yourself until the day of your death. Do not judge your fellow until you are in his place. Do not say something that cannot be understood but will be understood in the end. Say not: When I have time I will study because you may never have the time. (Av. 2:5)

Ben Zoma said: Who is wise? He who learns from all men, as it is written (Psalm 119:99) "I have gained understanding from all my teachers."

---

Who is mighty? He who subdues his passions, as it is written (Proverbs 16:32) "One who is slow to anger is better than the mighty, and one whose temper is controlled than one who captures a city."

Who is rich? He who rejoices in his portion, as it is written (Psalm 128:2) "You shall eat the fruit of the labor of your hands; you shall be happy, and it shall go well with you." "You shall be" refers to this world; and "it shall be well with you" refers to the world to come.

Who is honored? He that honors his fellow men as it is written" (I Samuel 2:30). "For those who honor me I will honor, and those who despise me shall be treated with contempt."(Av. 4:1)

3. Reverence for a holy place

No man is to behave in an irreverent manner when near the eastern gate [of the Temple], for it is in the direction of the Sanctum Sanctorum. No man is to go on the mountain of the Temple [Moriah] with his stick, his shoes, or with his purse [girdle of money], nor yet with dust-covered feet; nor is he to make it a thoroughfare [to lessen the distance] [short cut], much less is he permitted to spit thereon. All the blessings pronounced in the Temple concluded with the set form, [Blessed be the Lord God of Israel] 'from eternity.' But since the heretics perversely taught, there is but one state of existence [namely, no world-to-come], it was directed that men should close their benedictions with the form [Blessed be the Lord God of Israel] 'from eternity to eternity.'"(Ber. 9:5)

4. Passover

A person discharges his obligation on Passover with the following articles made in unleavened form: wheat, barley, spelt, oats, and rye. (Pes. 2:5)

5. The Day of Atonement

On the Day of Atonement, it is forbidden to eat and to drink, to wash, to anoint, to lace on [leather] shoes, and to indulge in sexual intercourse. A king and a bride [until the 30th day after her nuptials] may wash their faces; and a woman after child birth may lace [put] on [leather] shoes. Such is the dictum of Rabbi Eleazar: but the sages prohibit it. (Yoma 8:1)

## 3. The Talmud

The sages continued to comment upon the Mishnah and the Tosefta. These interpretations, written in Hebrew and in colloquial Aramaic, are called Gemara ("the commentary"). In time, the Mishnah and the Gemara were combined, and this formed the Talmud.

On the surface, the Gemara gives the impression that all the discussions are taking place around the table at a given historical times, but very often the opinion of one sage is recorded as a reaction to the teaching of another who lived centuries before. The teachers of the Talmud were not ordained Rabbis like their predecessors in the Mishnah. They called themselves Rav ("Master"), but they were no less erudite and no less influential.

There are two versions of this enormous collection: The Talmud of the Land of Israel, also called Jerusalem Talmud, was completed around 450 CE, and the Babylonian Talmud around 500 CE. The teachers who lived during the Talmudic period are called Amoraim.

The Jerusalem Talmud is much shorter than the Babylonian Talmud. The first deals more with agricultural matters whereas the second, reflecting the social realities of the diaspora, covers more commercial issues. In case there is a discrepancy between the two texts, most Jews follow the teachings of the Babylonian Talmud.

## Examples Of Talmudic Teachings

1. Rabbinic Decision Making
On that day Rabbi Eliezer brought forward every imaginable argument, but they did not accept them. Said he to them: 'If the *halakhah* ["Jewish Law"] agrees with me, let this carob-tree prove it!' Thereupon the carob-tree was torn a hundred cubits out of its place—others affirm, four hundred cubits. 'No proof can be brought from a carob-tree,' they retorted. Again he said to them: 'If the *halakhah* agrees with me, let the stream of water prove it!' Whereupon the stream of water flowed backwards—'No proof can be brought from a stream of water,' they rejoined. Again he urged: 'If the *halakhah* agrees with me, let the walls of the schoolhouse prove it,' whereupon the walls inclined to fall. But R. Joshua rebuked them, saying: 'When scholars are engaged in a halakhic dispute, what have ye to interfere?' Hence they did not fall, in honor of Rabbi Joshua, nor did they resume the upright, in honor of Rabbi Eliezer; and they are still standing thus inclined. Again he said to them: 'If the *halakhah* agrees with me, let it be proved from Heaven!' Whereupon a Heavenly Voice cried out: 'Why do ye dispute with Rabbi Eliezer, seeing that in all matters the *halakhah* agrees with him!' But Rabbi Joshua arose and exclaimed: 'It is not in heaven' [Deut.30:12]. What did he mean by this?—Said Rabbi Jeremiah: That the Torah had already been given at Mount Sinai; we pay no attention to a Heavenly Voice, because Thou hast long since written in the Torah at Mount Sinai, 'After the majority must one incline.' (BT BM 59b, Soncino)
*Note: This Talmudic passage argues that legal matters are decided by majority vote. Rabbis Eliezer ben Horkanos and Judah ben Hananiah were students of Rabban Yohanan ben Zakkai of Yavneh. They lived in the second century CE. Rabbi Jeremiah lived in the fourth century CE.*

2. Whose Life Comes First?
If two are travelling on a journey [far from civilization], and one has a pitcher of water, if both drink, they will [both] die, but if one only drinks, he can reach civilization,—The

Son of Patura taught: It is better that both should drink and die, rather than that one should behold his companion's death. Until Rabbi Akiba came and taught: 'that thy brother may live with thee': thy life takes precedence over his life. (BT BM 62a)

### 3. Excessive Praise of God

A certain [prayer reader] went down in the presence of Rabbi Hanina and said, "O God, the great, mighty, terrible, majestic, powerful, awful, strong, fearless, sure and honored." He waited till he had finished, and when he had finished he said to him, Have you concluded all the praise of your Master? Why do we want all this? Even with these three that we do say, had not Moses our Master mentioned them in the Law and had not the Men of the Great Synagogue come and inserted them in the Tefillah, we should not have been able to mention them, and you say all these and still go on! It is as if an earthly king had a million *denarii* of gold, and someone praised him as possessing silver ones. Would it not be an insult to him? (BT Ber. 33b)

### 4. Who Wrote the Bible?

Who wrote the Scriptures? — Moses wrote his own book and the portion of Balaam and Job. Joshua wrote the book which bears his name and [the last] eight verses of the Pentateuch. Samuel wrote the book which bears his name and the Book of Judges and Ruth. David wrote the Book of Psalms, including in it the work of the elders, namely, Adam, Melchizedek, Abraham, Moses, Heman, Yeduthun, Asaph, and the three sons of Korah.[1] Jeremiah wrote the book which bears his name, the Book of Kings, and Lamentations. Hezekiah and his colleagues wrote Isaiah, Proverbs, the Song of Songs and Ecclesiastes. The Men of the Great Assembly wrote Ezekiel, the Twelve Minor Prophets, Daniel and the Scroll of Esther. Ezra wrote the book that bears his name and the genealogies of the Book of Chronicles up to his own time. This confirms the opinion of Rab, since Rab Judah has said in the name of Rab: Ezra did not leave Babylon to go up to Eretz Yisrael [Land of Israel] until he had written his own genealogy. Who then finished it [the Book of Chronicles]? — Nehemiah the son of Hachaliah. (BT BB 14b)
Note: This is a Talmudic assumption about the composition of the Bible, which remains normative among many Jews who read the text literally. It differs significantly from the position of the majority of the modern Biblical scholars today.

### 5. Love Your Neighbor

It happened that a certain gentile came before Shammai [i.e., school of thought in the first century CE) and said to him, 'Make me a proselyte, on condition that you teach me the whole Torah while I stand on one foot.' Thereupon he repulsed him with the builder's cubit which was in his hand. When he went before Hillel, he said to him, 'What is hateful to you, do not to your neighbor: that is the whole Torah, while the rest is the commentary thereof; go and learn it.' (BT Shab. 31a).

6. Each Person Is Unique

A favorite saying of the Rabbis of Jabneh was: I am God's creature and my fellow is God's creature. My work is in the town and his work is in the country. I rise early for my work and he rises early for his work. Just as he does not presume to do my work, so I do not presume to do his work. Will you say, I do much and he does little? We have learnt: One may do much or one may do little; it is all one, provided he directs his heart to heaven. (BT Ber. 17a)

# 4. The Midrash

In Hebrew, the word Midrash refers to scriptural exegesis. The collection of Midrashim (pl. of Midrash) contains stories, homilies, folklore, and exegesis of scriptural verses.

There are two types of Midrash: Midrash Halakhah-Midrash that deals with legal matters, and Midrash Aggadah, Midrash that covers non-legal issues. The most important Halakhic Midrashim are the *Mekilta* (on Exodus), the *Sifra* (on Leviticus), the *Sifre* (on Numbers), and *Sifre Devarim* (on Deuteronomy). Among the Aggadic Midrashim, one could mention the *Tanhuma, Pesikta Rabbati, Pirke de Rabbi Eliezer, Midrash Tehillim,* and *Midrash Rabbah.* These collections were produced between 200 CE and medieval times.

## Examples From Midrashic Literature

1. Truth vs. Peace

"Then God said, Let us make man in our likeness" [Gen. 1:26], and let there be a creature not only the product of earth, but also gifted with heavenly, spiritual elements, which will bestow on him reason, intellect and understanding.' Truth then appeared, falling before God's throne, and in all humility exclaimed: 'Deign, O God, to refrain from calling into being a creature who is beset with the vice of lying, who will tread truth under his feet.' Peace came forth to support this petition. 'Wherefore, O Lord, shall this creature appear on earth, a creature so full of strife and contention, to disturb the peace and harmony of Thy creation? He will carry the flame of quarrel and ill-will in his trail; he will bring about war and destruction in his eagerness for gain and conquest.'

Whilst they were pleading against the creation of man, there was heard, arising from another part of the heavens, the soft voice of Charity: "Sovereign of the Universe," the voice exclaimed, in all its mildness, "vouchsafe Thou to create a being in Thy likeness, for it will be a noble creature striving to imitate Thy attributes by its actions. I see man now in Spirit, that being with God's breath in his nostrils, seeking to perform his great mission, to do his noble work. I see him now in spirit, approaching the humble hut, seeking out those who are distressed and wretched to comfort them, drying the tears of the afflicted and despondent, raising up them that are bowed down in spirit, reaching his helping hand to those who are in need of help, speaking peace to the heart of the widow, and giving shelter to the fatherless. Such a creature cannot fail to be a glory to His Maker." The Creator approved of the pleadings of Charity, called man into being, and cast Truth down to the earth to flourish there; as the Psalmist says (Ps. 85:12): "Truth shall spring out of the earth; and righteousness shall look down from heaven to abide with man"; and He dignified Truth by making her His own seal. (Gen. R. 8, Rapaport).[3]

2. Honoring parents
"Honor your father and your mother" [Ex. 20:12]. I might understand it to mean only with words but Scripture says, "Honor the Lord with your substance" [Prov. 3:9]. Hence it must mean, with food, drink, and with clean garments." (Mekilta, Bahodesh, Ch. 8, Lauterbach).

3. Meaning of the verb "remember" (the Sabbath day, in the Ten Commandments)
"How then am I to interpret 'remember'? It means that you should repeat with your mouth [the teachings concerning the Sabbath day]. (Sifra, Behukotay, 1, Neusner).

4. I have come back to my garden, my sister, my bride" [S. of S. 5:1]. Said Rabbi Hanina: The Torah teaches you proper conduct. Specifically, a groom should not go into the marriage canopy until the bride gives him permission to do so. "Let my beloved come into my garden" (S. of S. 4:16), after which, "I have come back to my garden, my sister, my bride" [S. of S. 5:1] (Pesikta de Rav Kahana, 1, Neusner).

# 5. The Zohar

The *Zohar* is considered to be the masterpiece of Spanish mysticism. It is often called the Bible of the *Kabbalah*. It is widely assumed that it was authored by Moses de Leon in Guadalajara, a small town close to Madrid, around 1200 CE. The book was attributed to an early sage, Rabbi Shimon bar Yohai, who lived in the second century CE.

Written in Aramaic, the *Zohar* appears as a mystical commentary on various portions of the Pentateuch. Its aim is to explain the Mitzvot and encourage their performance for mystical purposes. Among others, it deals with the hidden meanings of the texts, the mysteries of the soul, the powers attributed to the Hebrew alphabet, the profound nature of God, and the kabbalistic significance of the Decalogue.[4]

---

### Selected Zoharic texts

1. God

B'RESHIT. "In the beginning" was En Sof ("No End"), the Divine, the self-existent infinite begin, without likeness or reflection, the incomprehensible, the unknowable One, the blessed and only Potentate, the King of Kings and Lord of Lords, who only hath immortality, dwelling in Light which no man can approach unto, whom no man hath seen or can see, before whom the great archangel with face beneath his wings bends in lowly reverence and adoration, crying, "Holy! Holy! Holy! who art and was and evermore shall be." (Gen 1:1, Nurho de Manhar).

2. The hidden light

"And God said: 'Let there be light'" [Gen. 1:3]. This first light, God made before He made the sun and stars. He showed it to David, who burst into song. This was the light Moses saw on Sinai! At the creation, the universe from end to end radiated light—but it was withdrawn...And now it is stored away for the righteous, until all the worlds will be in harmony again and all will be united and whole. But until this future world is established, this light, coming out of darkness and formed by the Most Secret, is hidden: "Light is sown for the righteous" Ps. 97:11]. (Zohar, 1; 13b; Gates of Prayer, 1975, 168).

3. Creation

With 'beginning' [i.e., 'Wisdom'], the unknown concealed one [i.e., God] created the palace, a palace called God [i.e., God is omnipresent; everything is God]. The secret is: 'With Beginning.—created God. (Zohar, 1:15a, Matt, 52).

---

## 6. The Codes

The rabbinic discussions of the Talmud did not always resolve legal matters. So there was a necessity to formulate the law the way in which it was to be carried out. The collection of legal codes met this need. One of the earliest codes was prepared by Moses Maimonides in the late 12th cent., called *Mishneh Torah* (also named, *Yad Ha-hazakah*), consisting of fourteen books.

The second major collection of rabbinic laws was by Jacob ben Asher (Toledo, Spain, 15th cent.) called *Arba'ah Turim* ("Four Rows"). This was divided into four sub-sections: *Orah Hayyim* ("The Path of Life"), dealing with liturgy and festivals; *Yore Dea'h* ("The Teachings of Knowledge"), dealing with a variety of ritual matters, such as kashrut, or charity; *Even Hae'zer* ("The Stone of Help"), dealing with marriage and divorce; and *Hoshen Mishpat* ("The Breastplace of Judgment"), dealing with civil law.

The third collection was prepared by Joseph Caro (Safed, 16ᵗʰ cent.) called *Shulhan Arukh* ("The Set Table"). This book is also divided into four sections, and follows the same structure as ben Asher's book. Caro, a Sephardic Rabbi and mystic, codified Jewish Law for many generations to come. Moses ben Israel Isserless, a Polish Rabbi, used the same format, and added a *Mappah* ("Cover") reflecting the practices of Ashkenazic Jewry.

In more recent times, Rabbi Solomon Ganzfried (nineteenth century Hungary) edited an abridged version of the *Shulhan Arukh*, called *Kitzur Shulhan Arukh*, covering the most important aspects of all the legal material.

---

### Examples From The Codes

1. Sabbath and medical emergencies

Halakhah 1: The [laws of] the Sabbath are suspended in the face of a danger to life, as are [the obligations of] the other mitzvot. Therefore, we may perform—according to the directives of a professional physician of that locale—everything that is necessary for the benefit of a sick person whose life is in danger.

When there is a doubt whether or not the Sabbath laws must be violated on a person's behalf, one should violate the Sabbath laws on his behalf, for the Sabbath laws are suspended even when there is merely a question of danger to a person's life. [The same principles apply] when one physician says the Sabbath laws should be violated on a person's behalf and another physician states that this is not necessary. (Maimonides, Mishneh Torah, Shabbat, 2)


2. Obligation to set up a Synagogue

The residents of a town must build a synagogue and buy Torah scrolls and other holy books. When possible, the synagogue should be built at the highest point of the town, and should be taller than any other inhabited building. The entrance of the synagogue should be opposite the side that the congregation faces to pray, and nothing should be built near the synagogue's windows. The Ark (where the Torah scrolls are kept) should be on the side that the congregation faces, and the platform (BIMAH) from which the Torah is read should be built in the center. The leader faces the Ark; the elders sit along that side, facing the congregation. (From Caro's Shulhan Arukh, Orakh Hayyim, 150)


3. Respect for holy books

Sacred books should not be thrown around, be they even merely books of law and Aggada, nor should they be placed wrong side up; should we find them inverted, we must put them back up in the proper position. (The Scroll and Other Holy Books, Ch. 28/6, Ganzfried).

## 7. Rabbinic Commentaries

Ancient Rabbis argued that biblical texts can be studied on four different levels, identified with the acronym PARDES (meaning, "orchard"): *peshat* is the simple reading of
the texts; *remez* stands for the internal meaning, the allegorical that points to something
higher; *derash*, is the homiletical approach; and *sod* deals with the mysterious and mystical
interpretation. Using these tools of interpretation, Rabbis wrote commentaries on the
Torah, *Mishnah*, and Talmud to elucidate each verse.

Biblical translations into languages other than Hebrew are also considered commentaries, because they depend on the understanding of the text by those who actually did
the translation. Among the early Jewish translations of the Torah is Targum Onkelos, an
Aramaic translation attributed to Onkelos, a proselyte to Judaism around the first century
CE.

From medieval times on a number of rabbinic commentators appeared in the Jewish
scene. The *Rishonim*, the early commentators, lived from the 10th to 15th centuries; the
*Aharonim*, the later commentators, lived after the 16th centuries. Among these prominent
commentators are Moshe ben Nahman (Nahmanides) (1194–1270), a Spanish Talmudic
scholar from Catalonia; Abraham Ibn Ezra (1093–1167), a Spanish-born grammarian
and scholar; Ovadia Sforno (1475–1550), an Italian physician and commentator; Samuel
ben Meir (called Rashbam) (1085–1174), a French scholar; and M̲eïr L̲eibush b̲en J̲ehiel
M̲ichel Weiser (called Malbim) of Volhynia (1809–1879), who paid attention to the
significance of every single word in the Tanak, arguing that there are no real synonyms in
the Bible.

In medieval times, one of the most popular commentators was Rabbi Shelomo ben
Yitzhak of Troyes, France (1040–1105), known as RASHI for short. He studied in
Germany and upon his return to Troyes, he earned his living growing grapes. He also
established a school where he taught and wrote commentaries on the Torah and Talmud,
using the Peshat method. His views often reflect the teachings of the Midrash. In order to
elucidate some obscure words in Scriptures, he also provided his readers with the equivalent French words of his time.

---

### From Rashi's Commentaries

"*Let us make man*" (Gen. 1:26). Scripture teaches courtesy and the attribute of humility,
namely that the greater one consult and ask permission of a smaller one. Had it been
written "I will make man," we would not have learned that He consulted with His [heav-
enly] court, but only with Himself. The response to the heretics is written alongside:
"God created man" and it does not say "They (the angels) created.

---

> *"We came to the land you sent us; it does flow with milk and honey"* (Num. 13:27). They (the spies whom Moses sent to reconnoiter Canaan) stated this, because even though they intended to tell lies (about the Holy Land), they had to strengthen their false reports with some true facts..
>
> *"So Moses the servant of the Lord died there"* (Deut. 34:5). Is it possible that Moses died and then wrote, "And Moses died there"? No, it is not possible; so the answer must be that Moses wrote everything in the Torah up to these verses, and Joshua wrote the rest.

## 8. THE PRAYERBOOK

After the destruction of the Second Temple in the year 70 CE, the sacrificial service came to an end. Even though certain prayers were used during the biblical times in local temples, and, later on in the seventh century BCE, only in the Temple of Jerusalem, their role was secondary to sacrifices. The collapse of the sacrificial system compelled the sages to look for new venues of communion with the divine, and they began to write new prayers for all occasions as the only medium of worship. At the beginning, these prayers circulated orally, but soon they were written down, and eventually collected and edited. The first systematic prayerbook was prepared by Rav Amram ben Sheshna Gaon of the Academy of Sura, Babylonia in 870 CE. Later on, Saadia Gaon in the $10^{th}$ century compiled an updated prayerbook that remains as the model for the present times. In 1208 the French Rabbis introduced the Mahzor Vitri, reflecting the customs of Ashkenazic Jews. The prayerbook used by Jews today carry two different names: The Siddur is for daily and Sabbath services, whereas the Mahzor is for the festivals.

In the Reform movement a number of Rabbis created their own prayerbooks. In America, the first Reform prayerbook was published by the Charleston Congregation in 1830. Rabbi Isaac Meyer Wise published his *Minhag America* 1859 (withdrawn in 1894). However, the most significant prayerbook of the Reform movement of America was the *Union Prayer Book* (UPB), which was edited and published by the Central Conference of American Rabbis (CCAR) in 1892–4. This was partly based on *Olat Tamid*, a prayerbook written by Rabbi David Einhorn (1809–1879) of Baltimore. The UPB, containing prayers both in Hebrew and English, went through a number of revisions until 1975 when the CCAR published its *Gates of Prayer*. In order to meet the present conditions, however, this prayerbook was supplanted by the new *Mishkan T'filah: A Reform Siddur* (2008), which is egalitarian and gender-free; it also contains transliteration of all the Hebrew prayers.

The ancient Rabbis have identified the basic rubrics of the Jewish service as follows: a) The Shema (Deut. 6:4) and its blessings, which include the three major themes: Creation,

Revelation, and Redemption; b) The 18 petitionary prayers called *tefilah*, to which a 19th was added later on; c) The Concluding prayers, ending with the doxology, the *kaddish*. Depending on the occasion, other prayer texts are inserted in different parts of the service.

A portion of the Torah (i.e., the Pentateuch) is usually read on Saturday mornings and Saturday afternoons as well as on Monday and Thursday mornings (which were market days in ancient times). On Shabbat a Haftarah (a prophetic portion) is added. The Torah is also read during the Jewish festivals, with their own schedule. Even in our own time, the new prayerbooks follow the same patterns. Obviously, a number of creative prayers and hymns have been added throughout the centuries.

The prayerbook of the Sephardic Jews, though preserving the same framework, varies considerably from the Ashkenazic prayerbooks, especially during the High Holydays.

In Orthodox Judaism the presence of ten men is required to have a congregational service. This is called a *minyan* ("counting"). Non-Orthodox Jews are less demanding in this area, and even those who require ten individuals for a congregational service count women in the *minyan*.

## 9. Responsa Literature

Lacking a centralized religious authority that can speak on behalf of Judaism, many Jews turn to respected rabbinic sages of their time for answers that cannot be found in our sacred texts. These questions and responses are called *sheelot uteshuvot*, and, even though they are not binding, they carry a great weight in the Jewish community. These Responsa provide guidance in practical matters. Each decider (*posek*, in Hebrew) attempts to find the answer to these contemporary situations by sifting through precedents found in classical texts, and, using personal judgment, adapts them to present conditions. Many of these Responsa have been collected and published through the centuries.

In the Reform Jewish community, one of the great deciders was Rabbi Solomon B. Freehof (1892–1990) of Pittsburgh, Pennsylvania, whose Responsa have been published in many volumes (from 1960 to 1980). He was followed by Rabbis Walter Jacob, W. Gunther Plaut, and Mark Washofsky as chairs of the Central Conference of American Rabbis' (CCAR) Responsa Committee. In the Conservative Jewish Movement, this role is played by the Committee on Jewish Law and Standards. Various Orthodox Jewish Responsa are also available.

# From The Reform Responsa

## 1. A Jewish teacher married to a non-Jew

QUESTION: A Jewish woman, who is married to a Christian man, has applied for a teaching position in our religious school. Should our synagogue even consider her (or anyone in a mixed marriage) as an eligible candidate to teach our children Judaism?

Answer:

Our synagogues are entitled and indeed required to ask that those who teach our children be "good Jews," "positive Judaic role models." And since marriage choice has a great deal to do with the quality of one's Judaic commitments, you are certainly entitled to consider this applicant's marriage to a non-Jew as part of your determination of her fitness to teach. From our perspective, though, a point of view shaped by the experience of our contemporary North American Reform Jewish communities, we do not believe that the fact of her mixed marriage is an automatic indicator of her *lack* of fitness. The important concern is whether her personal practice and family life are characterized by Jewish depth and quality. If such is the case, then she might well prove to be a qualified and talented teacher for you. By hiring her, you may be doing a favor to your students, and you may help to fulfill the *mitzvah* of bringing this person and her family ever closer to Jewish life. (CCAR. #5758.14., 2005).

## 2. Tattooing

QUESTION: A congregant plans reconstructive breast surgery following a radical mastectomy. Her surgeon will tattoo an areola on the reconstructed breast. She wishes to know whether this would violate the traditional Jewish prohibition against tattooing. Is there a distinction to be drawn when the tattooing does not occur as a result of a medical procedure? What should be our response to the phenomenon of tattooing and body-piercing for the sake of adornment or self-expression?

Answer:

Tattooing is certainly permissible as an element of reconstructive surgery. Yet Judaism requires that our bodies be treated with honor and respect. Therefore, while we recognize the importance of personal adornment, as Jews we must pursue it in the light of the historical Jewish emphasis on the integrity and holiness of the human form. Tattooing and body-piercing, when not part of a legitimate medical procedure, are most difficult to reconcile with that emphasis. They are chavalah, pointless destruction of the human form; we do not and cannot regard them as "adornments." Unless and until we are otherwise persuaded, we should continue to teach that Judaism forbids these practices as the negation of holiness, the pointless and unacceptable disfigurement of the human body. (CCAR #5759.4)

## 3. Cremation

QUESTION: A man, who is approaching death, has instructed that his body be cremated. His children are very uncomfortable with this request. They ask whether, under Jewish tradition, they are obliged to honor it, or are they entitled to bury him intact, in contradiction to his express wishes? Rabbi Solomon B. Freehof has ruled that in such a case we apply the Talmudic dictum "it is a mitzvah to fulfill the wishes of the deceased" (B. Gitin 40a and elsewhere). I wonder, however, if a more nuanced approach is better suited to a case such as this, where the children have strong religious objections to their father's instruction?

Answer:

How should the children of whom our she'elah speaks respond to their father's request? Considering all the above, we would counsel the following.

a. The North American Reform movement does not regard cremation as a "sin." The 1892 resolution of the CCAR calls upon rabbis to officiate at cremation services, and despite our reservations concerning cremation, we hold that the procedure does not "contravene the law." Therefore, the children are not forbidden to honor this request, and they may arrange for cremation in response to the mitzvah to honor our parents and to the dictum that we should seek to fulfill the wishes of the deceased.

b. Nonetheless, the children are not obligated to honor their father's request. The CCAR discourages the choice of cremation; it supports the choice of traditional burial; and Reform thought today recognizes the right of our people to adopt traditional standards of religious practice that previous generations of Reform Jews may have abandoned. The commandment to honor one's parents does not apply in such a case, for a parent is not entitled to compel his or her children to violate their sincerely held Judaic religious principles. Thus, when a Reform Jew has serious and substantive religious objections to cremation, he or she may refuse a loved one's request for it.

c. By "traditional burial," we do not mean to endorse many of the practices that, although associated with burial in the public mind, would be deemed as excessive or inappropriate by many of us. Among these are such elaborate and unnecessary steps as embalming, expensive caskets, and the like. Jewish tradition emphasizes simplicity and modesty in burial practices; individuals should not feel driven to choose cremation in order to avoid the expense and elaborate display that all too often accompany contemporary burial.

d. It is essential that families speak about such matters openly, honestly, and before the approach of death. When the child fails explicitly to say "no" to a parent's request for cremation, the parent will justifiably think that the child has agreed to carry out that instruction. In such a case, the child quite likely has made an implied promise to the parent and thus bears an ethical responsibility to keep it. Therefore, if the children have objections to cremation, they should make their feelings known to their parents sooner— much sooner—rather than later. (CCAR, #5766.2)

# Endnotes

1. For more details about the composition of the Tanak, see, Richard E. Friedman, *Who Wrote the Bible?* New York: Summit, 1997. There are many introductions to the Hebrew Bible. A good one is by Bernard W. Anderson, et al., *Understanding of the Old Testament.* Pearson, Prentice Hall, 5th Ed., 2007.

2. There are two good translations of the Mishnah in English: Herbert Danby, *The Mishnah,* Oxford University, 1933, and Jacob Neusner, *The Mishnah,* Yale University Press, 1988.

3. For an English translation of Midrash Rabbah, see, H. Freedman and M. Simon, *Midrash Rabbah* (10 Vol) (Soncino, 1992).

4. For an English translation of the entire Zohar, see Daniel Matt, *The Zohar.* Stanford University Press, 2007.

# BASIC AFFIRMATIONS—PART THREE

## III. THE THIRD PILLAR: ISRAEL

The word "Israel" refers both to the people as well as to the land of Israel. We shall discuss these concepts one after the other. (See Preface.)

### Israel, The People

In the Hebrew Bible, the word "Israel" often refers to the "people of Israel." For instance, "The Eternal brought Israel from Egypt" (Ex. 18:1), or "Hear, O Israel" (Deut. 6:4). It is based on the tradition that the patriarch Jacob's name was changed from "Jacob" to "Israel" (Gen. 32:28; 35:9). The term "Jew" originally comes from Judah, one of the sons of Jacob, the third patriarch, and then from the name given to the Southern Kingdom (centered on the tribe of Judah, one of Jacob's sons) that emerged in the tenth century BCE after the split of the monarchy in the days of King Solomon's son, King Rehoboam.

### Who Is A Jew?

In biblical times, identity followed the father. Thus, for example, the child of a male priest, a Kohen, is a Kohen (e.g., Lev. 1:7; Num. 3:3; Lev. 22:12-13).[1] Also, the genealogies listed in Num.1:2 ff. follow *levet avotam* ("the household of the fathers"). Similarly, King Solomon's son, Rehoboam, became king after his father's death, even though his mother was Naamah the Ammonitess (I K. 14:24). However, in a major shift, rabbinic Jewish law, the Halakhah, considers the child of a Jewish mother as Jewish (BT Yev. 45b; Shulhan Arukh, Even ha-Ezer, 4.5), whether the father is a Jew or a Gentile.

When exactly this change took place or why is not at all clear. It has been suggested that this rabbinic practice may have had its origin in the post-Exilic days of Ezra (e.g., Ezra 10:3), when Jews were asked to send their non-Jewish wives away, or during the Roman period at the end of the biblical period, when oppression of foreign powers, Greek or Roman, was so intense that a number of Jewish women were being raped by foreign soldiers, and therefore the father's identity could not be verified but the mother's identity was known to the Jewish community.[2]

In modern times, the question became more pressing when the State of Israel was established in 1948. In order to deal with the question of identity of thousands of Jews who immigrated to Israel, the government decided in 1958 that anyone who declared himself to be Jewish would be registered as such. However, upon objections from many traditional quarters, David Ben Gurion, then prime minister, wrote to Jewish leaders around the world asking for their help in clarifying the issue, and received numerous responses, some of them contradictory. Subsequently, in 1966 the Israeli Supreme Court took up the issue to resolve the Brother Daniel Case: Oswald Rufeisen was a young Jewish boy in Poland, who had been active in the Zionist Youth movement. He was hidden in a Catholic monastery during the Nazi period, and eventually converted to Catholicism, and became a priest, taking the name Daniel. Shortly thereafter, Daniel's order asked him to go to Israel and continue his work there. When he applied for an immigrant visa under the Law of Return, which grants automatic citizenship to Jews, the government denied his request. In a 3-1 decision, the Supreme Court ruled that "An apostate cannot possibly identify himself completely with a people." However, Justice Cohen, in his minority opinion, stated, "I accept only the definition of a Jew, [namely], a Jew who in good faith declared himself to be Jewish."

The question was revisited in 1970 during the Shallit Case: Commander Binyamin Shallit, an Israeli naval officer, married a non-Jewish woman from Scotland, and wanted to register their children as Jewish in Israel. This time, the Israeli Supreme Court voted 5-4 in favor of registering the Shallit children as Jews, with the provision that such registration would have no bearing on matters of marriage and divorce. However, the Israel Knesset overturned the Supreme Court's decision and defined a Jew as, "One who is born of a Jewish mother or who converted to Judaism and who is not of another faith," thus confirming the position of the traditional Jewish law. One of the right-wing Orthodox groups, the Agudah, requested that the words "and converted to Judaism according to the Halakhah" be added, but both Reform and Conservative Jews objected, and they were not included in the law.

In 1983, Reform Rabbis of the United States voted the Patrilineal Resolution that changed the definition of a Jew since early rabbinic times, because of increasing number of intermarriages occurring in the modern world. Through this stand, the Reform movement in the USA reverted to the biblical definition of "Who is a Jew? (called "Patrilineal Descent"), but took an extra step by saying that, in our time, children could derive their Jewish identity either from the father or the mother. It stated:

> The Central Conference of American Rabbis declares that the child of one Jewish parent is under the presumption of Jewish descent. This presumption of the Jewish status of the offspring of any mixed marriage is to be established through appropriate and timely public and formal acts of identification with the Jewish faith and people. The performance of these *mitzvot* serves to commit those who participate in them, both parent and child, to Jewish life. Depending on circumstances, *mitzvot* leading toward a positive and exclusive Jewish identity will include entry into the covenant, acquisition of a Hebrew name, Torah study, Bar/Bat Mitzvah, and *Kabbalat Torah* (Confirmation).For those beyond childhood claiming Jewish identity, other public acts or declarations may be added or substituted after consultation with their rabbi.

It needs to be noted that this lineal resolution (not matrilineal or patrilineal) was accepted as valid by the overwhelming majority of Reform Jews in North America, but was rejected by many other Reform Jews in the rest of the world, including the Israeli Reform establishment, which still operates under the Halakhic understanding of Jewish identity based on matrilineal descent.

---

### *Patrilineal and Matrilineal Descent CCAR Responsa, Oct. 1983*

QUESTION: What are the origins of matrilineal descent in the Jewish tradition; what halakhic justification is there for the recent Central Conference of American Rabbis' resolution on matrilineal and patrilineal descent which also adds various requirements for the establishment of Jewish status?

ANSWER: We shall deal first with the question of matrilineal and patrilineal descent. Subsequently we shall turn to the required positive "acts of identification."
It is clear that for the last two thousand years the Jewish identity of a child has been determined by matrilineal descent. In other words, the child of a Jewish mother was Jewish irrespective of the father (Deut. 7.3, 4; M. Kid. 3.12; Kid. 70a, 75b; Yeb. 16b, 23a, 44a, 45b; A. Z. 59a; J. Yeb. 5.15 (6c), 7.5 (8b); J. Kid. 3.12 (64d); Yad Issurei Biah 15.3 f; etc.). The Talmudic discussion and that of the later codes indicate the reasoning behind this rule.
The rabbinic decision that the child follow the religion of the mother solves the problem for offspring from illicit intercourse of unions which are not recognized, or in which

paternity could not be established, or in which the father disappeared. This practice may have originated in the period of Ezra (Ezra 10.3; Neh. 13.23 ff) and may parallel that of Pericles of Athens who sought to limit citizenship to descendants of Athenian mothers (G. F. Moore, Judaism, Vol. 1, p. 20). It may also have represented temporary, emergency legislation of that period. We hear nothing about such a permanent change till early rabbinic times, then the union between a Jew and a non-Jew was considered to have no legal status (*lo tafsei qiddushin*). At one stage in the Talmudic discussions, an authority, Jacob of Kefar Neburya, considered a child of such a union Jewish, but subsequently retracted his opinion when faced with a verse from Ezra quoted by R. Haggai (J. Kid. 64d; J. Yeb. 4a; see Shaye J. D. Cohen, "The Origin of the Matrilineal Principle in Rabbinic Law," Judaism, Winter, 1984, note 54). R. Judah in the name of R. Assi considered a union between a Jew and non-Jew valid in "his time" as the non-Jew might be a descendent of the lost ten tribes (Yeb. 16b). Many authorities considered children of all such unions as mamzerim. They felt that the danger lay with non-Jewish women who could not be trusted to establish the Jewish paternity of their child, though that was contested by others.

The statement which grants the status of the mother to the child saves that child from the status of mamzerut [see the note below] or other similar disabling category. There was considerable disagreement before the decision later universally accepted was reached (Kid. 66b ff; Shulhan Arukh Even Haezer 4.19 and commentaries). The discussions demonstrate that this decision represented rabbinic reaction to specific problems.

We should contrast the rabbinic position to the view of the earlier Biblical and post-Biblical period. Patrilineal descent was the primary way of determining the status of children in this period. The Biblical traditions and their early rabbinic commentaries take it for granted that the paternal line was decisive in the tracing of descent, tribal identity, or priestly status. A glance at the Biblical genealogies makes this clear. In inter-tribal marriage paternal descent was likewise decisive (Nu. 1.2, *l'mishpehotam l'veit avotam*); the line of the father was recognized while the line of the mother was not (*mishpahat av keruyah mishpahah, mishpahat em enah keruyah mishpahah*, B. B. 109b; Yeb. 54b; Yad Hil. Nahalot 1.6, etc.).

We should also recognize that later rabbinic tradition did not shift to the matrilineal line when conditions did not demand it. Therefore, the rabbinic tradition remained patrilineal in the descent of the priesthood; it was and remains the male kohen who determines the status of his children. The child is a kohen even if the father married a Levite or an Israelite. Thus lineage was and continues to be determined by the male alone whenever the marriage is otherwise proper (M. Kid. 3.12; Kid. 29a; Shulhan Arukh Yoreh Deah 245.1).

If a marriage is valid but originally forbidden, (marriage with someone improperly divorced, etc.), then the tainted parent, whether mother or father, determines lineage (Kid. 66b; Shulhan Arukh Even Haezer 4.18). The same rule applies to children born out of wedlock if both parents are known.

Matrilineal descent, although generally accepted for the union of a Jew and a non-Jew, has rested on an uncertain basis. Some have deduced it from Deuteronomy 7.4, others from Ezra 9 and 10. Still others feel that the dominant influence of the mother during the formative years accounted for this principle. A few modern scholars felt that the rabbinic statement followed the Roman Paulus (Digest 2.4 f), who stated that the maternity was always known while paternity was doubtful; this, however, could be extended to the offspring of any parents. Shaye Cohen has also suggested that the rabbis may have abhorred this type of mixture of people as they felt negatively toward mixtures of animals and materials. A full discussion of this and other material may be found in Aptowtizer's "Spuren des Matriarchats im jüdischen Schriftum," *Hebrew Union College Annual*, Vols. 4 and 5 and Shaye J. D. Cohen's "The Origin of the Matrilineal Principle in Rabbinic Law," *Judaism*, Winter, 1984.

We should note that the Karaites considered the offspring of a Jewish father and a Gentile mother to be a Jew. It is, however, not clear from the sources available to me whether the conversion of the mother to Judaism may not have been implied (B. Revel, "The Karaite Halakhah," *Jewish Quarterly Review* III, pp. 375 f.) The matter continues to be debated.

These discussions show us that our tradition responded to particular needs. It changed the laws of descent to meet the problems of a specific age and if those problems persisted, then the changes remained in effect.

The previous cited material has dealt with situations entirely different from those which have arisen in the last century and a half. Unions between Jews and non-Jews during earlier times remained rare. Furthermore, the cultural and sociological relationship with the people among whom we lived did not approach the freedom and equality which most Jews in the Western World now enjoy.

We in the twentieth century have been faced with an increasing number of mixed marriages, with changes in the structure of the family, and with the development of a new relationship between men and women. This has been reflected in the carefully worded statement by the Committee on Patrilineal Descent (W. Jacob, American Reform Responsa, Appendix).

We may elaborate further with the following statements which reflect the previously cited historical background, the introduction to the resolution as well as other concerns. We shall turn first to the question of descent and then to the required "acts of identification."

1. In the Biblical period, till the time of Ezra or beyond, patrilineal descent determined the status of a child, so the children of the kings of Israel married to non-Jewish wives were unquestionably Jewish. This was equally true of other figures. Furthermore, our tradition has generally determined lineage (yihus) through the father, i.e., in all valid but originally forbidden marriages. This was also true for priestly, Levitical and Israelite lineage which was and continues to be traced through the paternal line (Nu. 1.2, 18; Yad Hil. Issurei Biah 19.15; Shulhan Arukh Even Haezer 8.1). If a marriage was valid, but originally forbidden, then the tainted parent (mother or father) determines status (Kid.

66b; Shulhan Arukh Even Haezer 4.18). The same rule applies to children born out of wedlock if both parents are known.

Yihus was considered significant, especially in the Biblical period, and long genealogical lines were recorded; an effort was made in the time of Ezra and, subsequently, to guarantee pure lines of descent and precise records were maintained (Ezra 2:59 ff; genealogies of I, II Chronicles). An echo of that practice of recording genealogies remained in the Mishnah and Talmud despite the difficulties caused by the wars of the first and second century which led to the destruction of many records (M. Kid. 4.1; Kid. 28a, 70a ff). In the Biblical period and in specific later instances, lineage was determined by the father.

2. Mishnaic and Talmudic authorities changed the Biblical laws of descent, as shown earlier in this responsum, as well as many others when social or religious conditions warranted it. Family law was changed in many other ways as demonstrated by the laws of marriage. For example, the Talmudic authorities validated the marriage of Boaz to Ruth, the Moabites, despite the strict ruling against such marriages (Deut. 23.4); they indicated that the Biblical rule applied only to males, not to females (Yeb. 76b ff). Earlier the Mishnah (Yad. 4.4) claimed that the various ethnic groups had been so intermingled by the invasion of Sennacherib that none of the prohibitions against marriage with neighboring people remained valid. In this instance and others similar to them, we are dealing with clear Biblical injunctions which have been revised by the rabbinic tradition. We have followed these examples in our own twentieth century revision.

3. The Reform movement has espoused the equality of men and women, virtually since its inception (J. R. Marcus, Israel Jacobson, p. 146; W. G. Plaut, The Rise of Reform Judaism, pp. 252 ff). As equality has been applied to every facet of Reform Jewish life, it should be applied in this instance.

4. We, and virtually all Jews, recognize a civil marriage between a Jew and a Gentile as a marriage although not *kiddushin*, and have done so since the French Sanhedrin of 1807 (Tama, Transactions of the Parisian Sanhedrin. Tr. F. Kerwan, p. 155 f; Plaut, op. cit., p. 219). We are morally obliged to make provisions for the offsprings of such a union when either the father or mother seeks to have their children recognized and educated as a Jew.

5. We agree with the Israeli courts and their decisions on the matter of status for purposes of *leam*, the registration of the nationality of immigrants and the right to immigrate under the Law of Return. Such rulings are secular in nature and do not bind the Israeli rabbinic courts or us, yet they have far reaching implications for all Jews. In the Brother Daniel case of 1962, this apostate was not judged to be Jewish although he had a Jewish mother (1962 - 16 - P.D. 2428). The court decided that a Jew who practiced another religion would not be considered Jewish despite his descent from a Jewish mother. "Acts of religious identification" were determinative for secular purposes of the State of Israel. The court recognized that this had no effect on the rabbinic courts; nonetheless, it marked a radical change which deals with new conditions.

Earlier in March, 1958, the Minister of Interior, Israel Bar-Yehuda, issued a directive which stated that "any person declaring in good faith that he is a Jew, shall be registered as a Jew." No inquiry about parents was authorized. In the case of children, "if both parents declare that the child is Jewish, the declaration shall be regarded as though it were legal declaration of the child itself" (S. Z. Abramov, Perpetual Dilemma, p. 290; Schlesinger v. Minister of Interior 1963 - I - 17 P.D. 225; Shalit v. Minister of Interior 1968-II-231P.D. 477–608). This was for the purposes of immigration and Israeli registration. It represented the farthest stance away from halakhah which any official body in the State of Israel has taken in this matter. It remained law until challenged and later legislation replaced it. There have been a number of other decisions which have dealt with this matter.

The current law, passed in 1970 after a government crisis over the question of "Who is a Jew," reads, "for the purpose of this law, Jew means a person born to a Jewish mother, or who has become converted to Judaism, and who is not a member of another religion" (Law of Return. Amendment, March, 1970, #4b; M. D. Goldman, Israel Nationality Law, p. 142; Israel Law Journal, Vol. 5, #2, p. 264). Orthodox efforts to change this to read "converted according to halakhah" have been defeated on various occasions. We should note that although the definition of a Jew was narrowed, another section of the law broadened the effect of the Law of Return and included "the child and grandchild of a Jew, the spouse of a Jew and the spouse of the child and grandchild of a Jew—with the exception of a person who was a Jew and willingly changed his religion" (Law of Return Amendment #2, #4a, March, 1970). This meant that a dual definition (descendants from Jewish mothers or fathers) has remained operative for immigration into the State of Israel.

The decision of an Israeli Court is a secular decision. It is, of course, not determinative for us as American Reform Jews, but we should note that their line of reasoning is somewhat similar to ours. We also see flexibility to meet new problems expressed in these decisions.

For the reasons cited in the introduction to the Resolution, those stated above and others, we have equated matrilineal and patrilineal descent in the determination of Jewish identity of a child of a mixed marriage.

Now let us turn to the section of the resolution which deals with "positive acts of identification." There are both traditional and modern considerations for requiring such acts and not relying on birth alone.

The clause which deals with the "appropriate and timely acts of identification with the Jewish faith and people ..." has gone beyond the traditional requirements for consideration as a Jew. Here we have become stricter than traditional Judaism. We have done so as the normal life of Jews has changed during the last two centuries.

In earlier periods of our history, individuals whose status was doubtful were limited in number. The question became significant only during the period of the Marranos. When such individuals identified themselves and lived as part of the Jewish community, they joined a semi-autonomous corporate community largely cut off from the surrounding world. Its entire way of life was Jewish. Emancipation changed this condition. It is difficult for those of doubtful status to integrate in an effortless way as was possible in earlier periods of our history. They and virtually all Jews live in two worlds.

We are dealing with a large number of individuals in our open American society as well as in all western lands. The Jewish status of a potentially large number of immigrants from the Soviet Union is also doubtful.

In order to overcome these problems as well as others, we now require "appropriate and timely public and formal acts..." The requirement has been worded to permit some flexibility for individual circumstances. With time and experience, custom will designate certain acts as appropriate and others not. It would be wrong, however, to set limits now at the beginning of the process.

We are aware that we have made more stringent requirements than our tradition. We believe that this will lead to a firmer commitment to Judaism on the part of these individuals and that it will enable them to become fully integrated into the Jewish community. We have taken this step for the following additional reasons:

1. We do not view birth as a determining factor in the religious identification of children of a mixed marriage.
2. We distinguish between descent and identification.
3. The mobility of American Jews has diminished the influence of the extended family upon such a child. This means that a significant informal bond with Judaism which played a role in the past does not exist for our generation.
4. Education has always been a strong factor in Jewish identity. In the recent past we could assume a minimal Jewish education for most children. In our time almost half the American Jewish community remains unaffiliated, and their children receive no Jewish education.

For those reasons the Central Conference of American Rabbis has declared: "The Central Conference of American Rabbis declares that the child of one Jewish parent is under the presumption of Jewish descent. This presumption of the Jewish status of the offspring of any mixed marriage is to be established through appropriate and timely public and formal acts of identification with the Jewish faith and people. The performance of these mitzvot serves to commit those who participate in them, both parents and child, to Jewish life. Depending on circumstances, mitzvot leading toward a positive and exclusive Jewish identity will include entry into the covenant, acquisition of a Hebrew name, Torah study, Bar/Bat Mitzvah, and Kabbalat Torah (Confirmation). For those beyond childhood claiming Jewish identity, other public acts or declarations may be added or substituted after consultation with their rabbi."

*Note: In Jewish law, a "mamzer" is a child born of an adulterous or incestuous relation. "Mamzerut" deals with issues relating to a mamzer.*

## Jewish Population In The World

It is not easy to estimate the number of Jews in the world today, because in most countries personal identity cards do not list religion and/or ethnic background. So we are left with educated guesses based on affiliation with religious institutions or charitable causes as well as governmental information. It is estimated that the world Jewish population in 2012 stands at 13,746,100 (cf. www.jpeopleworld.org), with Israel having 5,978,600 (cf. www.jewishvirtuallibrary.com) and the United States about five and a half million Jews. The rest are spread out throughout the world.

## Conversion To Judaism

### Welcoming Non-Jews

*The Gates of Mitzvah*, a Reform Jewish publication that deals with life-cycle events, states, "It is a *mitzvah* to admit into the Jewish community any person who wishes sincerely to adopt Judaism and who is willing to study it and accept its *mitzvot*."[3] In rabbinic literature a male convert is called a *ger* (a female is called a *giyoret*), a term that in the biblical times meant a "resident alien" who came to live among the Israelites. Judaism accepts proselytes, and has welcomed them since early biblical times. Even King David was allegedly a descendent of Ruth, the Moabite, who became part of the Jewish people by uttering these famous words: "Your people shall be my people, and your God my God" (Ruth 1:16).

In the early rabbinic period, proselytism continued—and apparently in large scale. The New Testament states that "you [Pharisees] encompass sea and land to make one proselyte" (Math. 23:15), and most sages facilitated the conversion process to Judaism. Thus, they taught, "one should take care not to impose [upon the candidate] too many commandments nor go into many fine details about these obligations" (BT Yev. 47a/b). Similarly, it is said that the great sage Hillel (end of the first century BCE) easily admitted a heathen, who had been turned down by Hillel's contemporary, Shammai, for wanting a fast conversion. Instead, Hillel told him, "What is hateful to you, do not do to your fellow. This is the entire Torah, all of it. The rest is commentary. Go and learn it" (BT Shab. 31a). And, even though rabbinic texts record some derogatory statements about the *ger*, others are positive, such as, "proselyte are beloved, for in each and every passage, the Torah likens them to Israel" (Num. R. 8:2).

## The Process

Though the process of conversion may vary from place to place, there are three basic steps that most rabbis require of prospective converts: In case of a male, a) the candidate must study the basic principles of Judaism; b) then, he immerses in water (*tevilah*) as a symbol of renewal, and, c) if he is not circumcised, he undergoes an adult circumcision. All American Reform Rabbis require study of Judaism prior to conversion, and many use their discretion regarding the last two steps. In case of a female, the candidate is expected to study Judaism and then immerses in water. In Orthodox and Conservative Judaism, immersion is a requirement. Many Reform Rabbis in America today strongly encourage *tevilah* for all their converts.

Rabbinic law requires that when a circumcised adult converts to Judaism, he must undergo a procedure called *hatafat dam berit* ("drawing a drop of blood for the covenant") from his penis, with certain prescribed blessings. This procedure can be done by a physician or by a Mohel. Some Reform Rabbis do not require this procedure.

After these rituals, the convert receives a Hebrew name of his/her choice, and is then called "*(Chosen Name), the son/daughter of Abraham and Sarah,*" implying that Jewishness goes all the way back to the beginnings of Jewish history.

Jewish tradition not only welcomes converts into the household of Israel but also encourages other born-Jews to integrate these *gerim* ("converts") into the fabric of the Jewish community and to accept them as equal members.[4]

# ISRAEL: THE LAND

## Terminology

In the Hebrew Bible, the term "Israel" refers to the "people of Israel" but also to the "Land of Israel," as for example, "The territory of Israel" (2 K 10:32) or, "I will plant it in Israel's lofty highlands" (Ez. 17:23). The context often helps determine the correct meaning. The word "Zion" stands for "Jerusalem" and, by extension, to the whole land of Israel.

## THE LAND

Modern Israel is long and narrow, about 290 miles in length, from north to south, and about 85 miles wide at the widest point between the Dead Sea and the Mediterranean. It is bordered by Lebanon in the north, Syria in the northeast, Jordan in the east, Egypt in the southeast, and the Mediterranean Sea in the west.

In "Facts about Israel," the Israel Ministry of Foreign Affairs (Dec. 07) pointed out that, although small in size, Israel encompasses the varied topographical features and climates of a continent. In the north, the forested highlands of Galilee merge with fertile green valleys; sand dunes and farmland mark the coastal plain bordering the Mediterranean shoreline; the rocky peaks of the Samarian and Judean mountain ranges in the center of the country descend sharply to the semi-tropical Jordan Valley and the Dead Sea, the lowest place on earth. Mountainous deserts, stretching southward through the Negev and Arava, end at the Gulf of Eilat, the northernmost tip of the Red Sea.

Here is a map of the land of Israel:

## CLIMATE

The country's temperate climate is characterized by abundant sunshine, with a rainy season from November to April. Total annual precipitation ranges from about 20 to 30 inches (50 to 75 cm.) in the north to just over an inch (about 3 cm.) in the far south. Regional climatic conditions vary considerably: hot, humid summers and mild, wet winters in the coastal plain; dry, comfortably warm summers and moderately cold winters, with rain and occasional light snow in the hill regions; hot, dry summers and pleasant winters in the Jordan Valley; and year-round, semi-arid conditions, with warm to hot days and cool nights in the south.

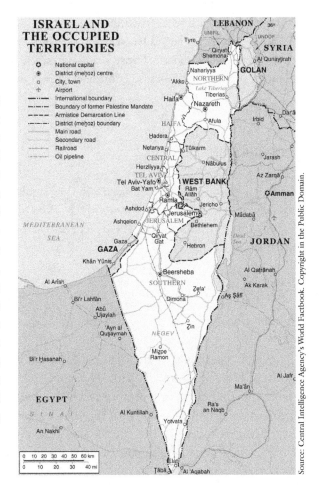

Source: Central Intelligence Agency's World Factbook. Copyright in the Public Domain.

# Water

Since water is scarce in the region, intense efforts are made to maximize the use of what is available and to seek prospective sources. In the 1960's, the country's fresh water sources were joined in an integrated national grid, whose main artery, the National Water Carrier, brings water from the north and center of the country to the semi-arid south through a network of giant pipes, aqueducts, open canals, reservoirs, tunnels, dams, and pumping stations. Ongoing projects for the utilization of new sources include cloud seeding, recycling of sewage water, and the desalination of seawater.

# Flora And Fauna

The rich variety of Israel's plant and animal life reflects its geographical location as well as its varied topography and climate. Over 500 kinds of birds, some 100 mammal and 90 reptile species, and nearly 3,000 plant types (150 of which are endemic to Israel) are found within its borders. Over 150 nature reserves and 65 national parks, encompassing nearly 400 square miles (almost 1,000 sq. km.), have been established throughout the country, with several hundred additional sites in the planning stages.

# Population

Israel is a country of immigrants. Since the establishment of the State, Jews have flocked to the country from all over the world. On the eve of 2012, the population had grown to 7,836,000, with 75.3% Jewish (= 5,978,600), 20.5% Arab, and 4.2% Christian and other groups.

# Main Cities

Jerusalem, the capital of the State, is located on the ridge of the Judean Mountains, north of Hebron. A very old city, its name already appears in the Canaanite texts of the nineteenth and eighteenth century BCE. Other important cities: a) Tel-Aviv, founded in 1909, is the commercial center of the country. b) Haifa sits on the slopes of Mt. Carmel by the Mediterranean Sea. Its history goes back to biblical times. c) Beer-Sheva is a desert city located in the southern part of Israel. Its name frequently appears in the story of the biblical patriarchs.

## System Of Government

Israel is a parliamentary democracy with legislative, executive, and judicial branches. The head of the State is the president, whose office is mostly ceremonial. The official languages of the State of Israel are Hebrew and Arabic.

## Historical Background

The Land of Israel is the spiritual home of all Jews today. From the earliest times, the Israelites believed that this land was promised to them by God (Gen. 12:1, 7; Deut. 34:4). The patriarchs traversed the land (Gen. 13:17), erected places of worship (Gen. 12:7; 26:25; 35:7), purchased a burial site (Gen. 23), and were buried there in the cave of Makhpelah, near Mamre (Abraham in Gen. 25:9; Sarah in Gen. 23:19; Isaac in Gen. 35:27-29; 49:31; Rebekah in Gen. 49:31; Jacob in Gen. 49:29-33; Leah in Gen. 49:31; even Joseph in Gen. 50:13). Only Rachel, Jacob's wife, was buried in Bethlehem (Gen. 35:19). For many centuries, the people of Israel settled, worked the land, and established in this area a state that lasted until the Romans destroyed the Second Temple in 70 CE.

Long after this tragic event, Jews, who were exiled to other parts of the Mediterranean basin, never forgot the land of their ancestors, and daily prayed, "O bring us in peace to our land from the four corners of the earth, and make up go upright to our land." Many Rabbis taught that it is a *Mitzvah* to make *a'liyah* to Israel. (The Hebrew word *a'liyah* means "going up," for as once approaches the hills of Jerusalem one "goes up," both physically and spiritually.) In fact, they believed that "Dwelling in Eretz [land of] Yisrael is equated to all the Torah precepts put together" (Sifre, Reeh, Piska #80). According to one Rabbi, the land of Israel is considered to be so holy that anyone who walks even a few steps on it is assured a place in the world-to-come (BT. Ket, 111a). In medieval times, Judah Halevi (1085–1141), a Jewish poet from Spain bewailed the fact that, "My heart is in the East [namely, Israel], even though I am at the end of the West [namely, Spain]." In the 16th century, Joseph Caro, the author of the authoritative Jewish code of Law, Shulhan Arukh, (Orah Hayyim #560), mandated that a bridegroom should put ashes on his head "in order to remember Jerusalem."

## Modern Zionism

This passive yearning continued until the late 19th century, when a group of young Jews, who called themselves *Hoveve Tziyon* ("The lovers of Zion"), began to talk about restoring a national life in Palestine. Some of them even immigrated there, using the slogan *BILU*, an acronym of the biblical Hebrew expression, "O House of Jacob, let us go up" (Isa. 2:5). However, the movement did not become politically viable until Theodore Herzl (1860–1904) attended the Dreyfus trial in Paris (see chapter on history) and published his book, *The Jewish State* in 1896, thereby establishing the modern Zionist movement. In this book, Herzl suggested that in order to solve the problem of anti-Semitism in Europe, sovereignty should be given to Jews "over a portion of the globe adequate to meet our rightful national requirements." Initially, Herzl did not insist on the land of Israel but other leaders of the new Zionist movement stated that national aspirations could be realized only in the land of Israel where the Jewish people was born. In a series of Congresses, the Zionists appealed to international powers for help. At the time, Palestine, as it was called then, was in the hands of the Ottoman Empire, and this "Sick Man of Europe," was getting weaker by the day. Consequently, many nations, including the Germans and the British, vied for influence and hegemony in this part of the world.

## REACTION TO ZIONISM

Some European Jews supported the idea of political Zionism; others viewed it as a utopian ideal. Even among those who believed in the goals of Zionism, there was a division of opinions as to how to realize this dream. Many ultra-Orthodox Jews, for example, maintained that the State of Israel should be established only when the Messiah comes at the end of time, and therefore, to engage in political activity now is to "press the end-times"—an arrogant approach unworthy of Judaism. Other Jews, such as the writer Asher Ginzberg (1856–1927), who called himself Ahad Haam ("one of the people"), argued that the goal should not only be political independence but also spiritual renewal, namely, to set up in Palestine a spiritual center for the whole Jewish people. Jewish Socialists maintained that the Jewish problem would be solved only when the world becomes one utopian classless society.

Reform Jews in the States confronted the issue of Zionism with discomfort. In the 19th century, these liberal Jews were trying to establish themselves as a religious group who were loyal citizens and without any foreign national aspirations. So in the 1885 Pittsburgh Platform, American Reform Jews declared, "We consider ourselves no longer a nation but a religious community and expect neither a return to Palestine...nor the restoration of the laws concerning the Jewish State." By 1937, however, sentiments started to change, and American Jews, in response to the rise of Hitler, began to adopt a more positive posture toward Zionism. In the Columbus Platform, they stated, "We affirm the obligation of all Jewry to aid in its (Palestine's) upbuilding as a Jewish homeland." After the 1967 War, when the Israeli army emerged victorious over the Arabs and Jerusalem was liberated and reunited, the Reform Jewish attitude became clearly pro-Zionist. In the 1976 Centenary Perspective, the CCAR unequivocally said, "We have both a stake and a responsibility in building the State of Israel...We encourage *a'liyah* for those who wish...." In 1978, to demonstrate solidarity with Israel, American Reform Jews established the Association of Reform Zionists of America (ARZA), an affiliate of the Union for Reform Judaism (then known as the Union of American Hebrew Congregation), with Rabbi Roland Gittlesohn of Boston, a staunch Zionist, as its first president. The latest Reform pronouncement, The Statement of Principles for Reform Judaism (1999) stands strongly behind Israel: "We are committed to *medinat Yisrael* [State of Israel]."

## The Establishment Of The State Of Israel

In 1917, the British Government issued a famous declaration indicating that "His Majesty's Government view with favour the establishment in Palestine of a national home for the Jewish people, and will use their best endeavours to facilitate the achievement of this object, it being clearly understood that nothing shall be done which may prejudice the civil and religious rights of existing non-Jewish communities in Palestine, or the rights and political status enjoyed by Jews in any other country." This statement that came during World War I from the British Foreign Secretary Arthur James Balfour to Lord Rothschild, a former member of the British parliament and one of the most renowned representatives of European Jewry at the time, was intended to secure world Jewish support in the war against Germany. For Jewish leaders, this promise was historical. Finally, they were able to obtain some international support from a world power. After World War I, the League of Nations gave Palestine to the British through a special mandate.

In the 1930's, Jewish immigration to Palestine increased, which greatly displeased the Arabs. The British, trying to appease both sides, arranged the St. James Conference in 1939, but the Arabs refused to meet with Jews face to face. So the British government issued the 1939 White Paper on its own, proposing the establishment of an Independent Palestinian country within ten years, jointly run by Arabs and Jews in proportion of their numbers. They also limited Jewish immigration to 75,000 over a period of five years, with any subsequent increase requiring Arab acquiescence. For all practical purposes this represented the British repudiation of the Balfour Declaration. To be expected, Jews in Palestine were outraged by this decision. Arabs, for their part, rejected the White Paper because, they claimed, it did not go far enough. Even though the League of Nations did not withdraw the legal mandate from the British, the White Paper remained the basis of British policy until the end of the mandate in 1948.

After the Second World War, the League of Nations affirmed the British mandate for Palestine. The British continued to favor the Arabs because of their sheer number and vast countries. They also made Jewish immigration to Palestine difficult if not impossible. In response, Jews, at times, had to resort to violence or subterfuge in order to bring Jews from the four corners of the world, especially those who had escaped the Holocaust in Europe. The Jewish population grew slowly, and Jews managed to organize themselves in the country, setting up the infrastructure needed to run their own affairs.

On Nov. 29, 1947, when the United Nations' General Assembly voted for the partition of Palestine, Jews accepted it, even though they were left with a very small territory. The Arabs, on the other hand rejected it, claiming all of Palestine for themselves. On May 15, 1948, the British mandate came to an end. But the night before, on Friday May 14, David ben Gurion, the Zionist leader, supported by his fellow Zionists, proclaimed the State of Israel. He declared, "We, members of the People's Council, representatives of the Jewish Community of Eretz-Israel and of the Zionist movement, are here assembled on the Day of the termination of the British mandate over Eretz-Israel and, by virtue of our natural and historic right and on the strength of the resolution of the United Nations General Assembly, hereby declare the establishment of a Jewish State in Eretz-Israel, to be known as the State of Israel." He added, "The State of Israel will be open for Jewish immigration and for the Ingathering of the Exiles; it will foster the development of the country for the benefit of all its inhabitants; it will be based on freedom, justice and peace as envisaged by the prophets of Israel; it will ensure complete equality of social and political rights to all its inhabitants irrespective of religion, race or sex; it will guarantee freedom of religion, conscience, language, education and culture; it will safeguard the Holy Places of all religions; and it will be faithful to the principles of the Charter of the United Nations." (For the complete text, see below.)

The new state was immediately recognized by the USA and by the (former) Soviet Union, and soon by many other nations. Though Jews were euphoric around the world, Arab countries did not take the establishment of Israel well. The day after the state was established, Arab armies attacked Israel from all sides, and the Israelis had to defend themselves with meager power. This War of Independence lasted until 1949 with the signing of an armistice agreement. Finally, Israel was victorious and sovereign within its own borders, and the millennial dream was fulfilled.

The surrounding Arab countries had no wish to recognize the reality of Israel, and therefore various wars ensued in the following years: 1956, the Sinai War against Egypt; 1967, the Six Day War, against surrounding Arabs countries (during which the old city of Jerusalem was liberated); and 1973, Yom Kippur

*David Ben Gurion (1886–1973)*

War (when Egypt attacked Israel by surprise). Israel was the victor in every one of these conflicts and so the state survived.

In 1975, the United Nations, under the influence of many Arab nations, declared Zionism as "racism." This infuriated the Jews and many liberal-minded people around the world, for Israel had welcomed people of all races into the newly established country, and it still does. The ill-conceived resolution was revoked in December of 1991. In 1979, a peace agreement was signed between Israel and Anwar Sadat's Egypt. This established what was named "a cold peace" between the two former enemies.

In 1982, Israel invaded Lebanon in order to eliminate the constant attacks from the North, but the war ended inconclusively. The Palestinian Arabs in the meantime launched an Intifada, a popular revolt. The Oslo agreement signed in 1993 in Washington, DC, through the mediation of President Bill Clinton, between Prime Minister Yitzhak Rabin and Yasser Arafat, the leader of the Palestinian Liberation Movement, brought a limited lull in the fighting between the Palestinians and Israelis. In fact, in 1994, Rabin, Arafat, and Shimon Peres (the then-foreign minister) received the Nobel Prize for their efforts.

The same year, Israel and Jordan signed a peace treaty in Washington, DC, with the participation of Prime Minister Rabin, King Hussein, and President Bill Clinton. Regrettably, however, Rabin was assassinated on Nov. 4, 1995 by Yigal Amir (b. 1970), an extremist of Yemenite background and a student at Bar Ilan University.

Other momentous events followed: The Second Palestinian Intifada began in 2000. Israel retreated from Lebanon in May of the same year. In 2004, Arafat died, and was replaced by Mahmoud Abbas. Israel unilaterally disengaged from Gaza in 2005. In 2006 there was a war between Israel and Hezbollah in Lebanon. In 2007, a radical group called Hamas took over Gaza, and the Palestinians were consequently divided into two groups: Hamas, which is opposed to Israel's existence, in Gaza; and the Palestinian

*Yitzhak Rabin (1922–1995)*

Source: http://www.defenseimagery.mil/imagery.html#a=search&s=yitzhak%20rabin&guid=5c7 9528a5ec14a2144c39cdad4c295df47b5017c. Copyright in the Public Domain.

Authority, which recognizes Israel, in the West Bank. At the end of December 2008, the Israeli army entered Gaza in order to stop the incoming rockets launched by Hamas terrorists into some of the southern cities of Israel, and inflicted a great deal of damage to the city. About two weeks later, on Jan. 18, 2009, under pressure from the European communities and the United Nations, Israel and Hamas accepted a cease-fire engineered by France and Egypt. According to some Arab sources, 1,200 Palestinians and 13 Israelis died during the war. Across-border skirmishes still continue between Hamas-ruled Gaza and Israel. Iran has recently emerged as a threat to Israel, because its president, Mahmoud Ahmadinejad, continues to affirm that Israel must be destroyed. Furthermore, Iran is reportedly developing atomic energy that could destabilize the entire region. In 2012, the West put Iran on notice against developing an atomic bomb.

What the future will bring is not clear. Peace will be established only when the Palestinians and the Israelis accept the reality of each other, realize that they are bound to live together as neighbors, next to one another in two different countries, and are willing to make the painful compromises that this process would require.

## ZIONISM TODAY

Once the State of Israel was established the question was raised about the meaning of Zionism. If the purpose of Zionism was to set up a Jewish State in Israel, there was no reason to continue to pursue such an ideology after 1948. So in recent times the purpose of Zionism has been reinterpreted. In fact in 1966, the "Jerusalem Program," proposed the following aims for the new Zionism:

1. The unity of the Jewish people and the centrality of Israel in Jewish life;
2. The ingathering of the Jewish people in its historic homeland, Eretz Yisrael, through aliyah from all countries;
3. The strengthening of the State of Israel, which is based on the prophetic vision of justice and peace, and
4. The preservation of the identity of the Jewish people through the fostering of Jewish and Hebrew education and Jewish spiritual and cultural values;
5. The protection of Jewish rights everywhere.

These goals remain valid in the Jewish community around the world today. Israel is one of the few democracies in the Middle East. It is pro-West, wants peace with its neighbors based on security and mutual recognition, and plays a major role in the identity of Jews everywhere around the world.

# Declaration of Israel's Independence 1948

## Issued at Tel Aviv on May 14, 1948 (5th of Iyar, 5708)

The land of Israel was the birthplace of the Jewish people. Here their spiritual, religious and national identity was formed. Here they achieved independence and created a culture of national and universal significance. Here they wrote and gave the Bible to the world. Exiled from Palestine, the Jewish people remained faithful to it in all the countries of their dispersion, never ceasing to pray and hope for their return and the restoration of their national freedom.

Impelled by this historic association, Jews strove throughout the centuries to go back to the land of their fathers and regain their statehood. In recent decades they returned in masses. They reclaimed the wilderness, revived their language, built cities and villages and established a vigorous and ever-growing community with its own economic and cultural life. They sought peace yet were ever prepared to defend themselves. They brought the blessing of progress to all inhabitants of the country.

In the year 1897 the First Zionist Congress, inspired by Theodor Herzl's vision of the Jewish State, proclaimed the right of the Jewish people to national revival in their own country.

This right was acknowledged by the Balfour Declaration of November 2, 1917, and re-affirmed by the Mandate of the League of Nations, which gave explicit international recognition to the historic connection of the Jewish people with Palestine and their right to reconstitute their National Home.

The Nazi Holocaust, which engulfed millions of Jews in Europe, proved anew the urgency of the re-establishment of the Jewish state, which would solve the problem of Jewish homelessness by opening the gates to all Jews and lifting the Jewish people to equality in in the family of nations.

The survivors of the European catastrophe, as well as Jews from other lands, proclaiming their right to a life of dignity, freedom and labor, and undeterred by hazards, hardships and obstacles, have tried unceasingly to enter Palestine.

In the Second World War the Jewish people in Palestine made a full contribution in the struggle of the freedom-loving nations against the Nazi evil. The sacrifices of their soldiers and the efforts of their workers gained them title to rank with the peoples who founded the United Nations.

On November 29, 1947, the General Assembly of the United Nations adopted a Resolution for the establishment of an independent Jewish State in Palestine, and called upon the inhabitants of the country to take such steps as may be necessary on their part to put the plan into effect.

This recognition by the United Nations of the right of the Jewish people to establish their independent State may not be revoked. It is, moreover, the self-evident right of the Jewish people to be a nation, as all other nations, in its own sovereign State.

ACCORDINGLY, WE, the members of the National Council, representing the Jewish people in Palestine and the Zionist movement of the world, met together in solemn assembly today, the day of the termination of the British mandate for Palestine, by virtue of the natural and historic right of the Jewish and of the Resolution of the General Assembly of the United Nations, HEREBY PROCLAIM the establishment of the Jewish State in Palestine, to be called ISRAEL.

WE HEREBY DECLARE that as from the termination of the Mandate at midnight, this night of the 14th and 15th May, 1948, and until the setting up of the duly elected bodies of the State in accordance with a Constitution, to be drawn up by a Constituent Assembly not later than the first day of October, 1948, the present National Council shall act as the provisional administration, shall constitute the Provisional Government of the State of Israel.

THE STATE OF ISRAEL will be open to the immigration of Jews from all countries of their dispersion; will promote the development of the country for the benefit of all its inhabitants; will be based on the precepts of liberty, justice and peace taught by the Hebrew Prophets; will uphold the full social and political equality of all its citizens, without distinction of race, creed or sex; will guarantee full freedom of conscience, worship, education and culture; will safeguard the sanctity and inviolability of the shrines and Holy Places of all religions; and will dedicate itself to the principles of the Charter of the United Nations.

THE STATE OF ISRAEL will be ready to cooperate with the organs and representatives of the United Nations in the implementation of the Resolution of the Assembly of November 29, 1947, and will take steps to bring about the Economic Union over the whole of Palestine.

We appeal to the United Nations to assist the Jewish people in the building of its State and to admit Israel into the family of nations.

In the midst of wanton aggression, we yet call upon the Arab inhabitants of the State of Israel to return to the ways of peace and play their part in the development of the State, with full and equal citizenship and due representation in its bodies and institutions—provisional or permanent.

We offer peace and unity to all the neighboring states and their peoples, and invite them to cooperate with the independent Jewish nation for the common good of all.

Our call goes out the Jewish people all over the world to rally to our side in the task of immigration and development and to stand by us in the great struggle for the fulfillment of the dream of generations—the redemption of Israel.

With trust in Almighty God, we set our hand to this Declaration, at this Session of the Provisional State Council, in the city of Tel Aviv, on this Sabbath eve, the fifth of Iyar, 5708, the fourteenth day of May, 1948.

## ENDNOTES

1. The status of the priests continued to be patrilineal even in rabbinic times (See, M. Kid. 3:12).

2. For a discussion of this issue, read, "Patrilineal and Matrilineal Descent" (1983), in *Contemporary American Responsa* by Walter Jacobs, Central Conference of American Rabbis, 1987, 61–68.

3. *Gates of Mitzva*, ed. By Simeon J. Maslin, New York: Central Conference of American Rabbis, 1979, 23.0.

4. On more details about conversion, see, Joseph R. Rosenbloom, *Conversion to Judaism.* Cincinnati: Hebrew Union College, 1978. 8.

# CHAPTER THREE

# MODERN JEWISH RELIGIOUS MOVEMENTS

The Jewish people, spread around the world, includes all kinds of races. There are Caucasian Jews, black Jews, Asian Jews, and others. What they have in common is a history, sacred texts, festivals, and a list of Mitzvot that determine their Jewish discipline.

## JEWISH SECTS

Throughout history, Judaism gave rise to various sects with differing levels of attachment to mainstream Judaism. As we noted in Chapter One, the Jewish historian Josephus listed four different sects in the second century BCE: Sadducees, Pharisees, Essenes, and Fourth Philosophy. Philo of Alexandria also knew of a Jewish group called the Therapeutae. Then, at the end of the first century CE, the early Christians began to set up their own type of "Judaism." The following are listed among the major sects of Judaism today: Karaites, Samaritans, and the Dönme.

### *Karaites*

This group originated in Persia around the eighth century CE. The followers of this sect accept the authority of the Hebrew Bible but reject the Oral Law as well as the entire rabbinic tradition. They do not celebrate *Hanukah* or light Sabbath candles, for example. Having rejected the rabbinic calendar, which is based on the movements of both the sun and the moon, they follow only the lunar calendar. They also have different dietary rules.

Their attachment to the study of the Hebrew Bible gave rise to a rigid scholarship of biblical grammar and exposition, forcing rabbinic Jews to do the same.

Around 760, Anan ben David established a rival Jewish exilarchate, and founded a group called Ananites. In the ninth century, the Ananites began to call themselves Karaites. Marriages between Karaites and mainstream Jews are prohibited by both sides. Most of the Karaites today (~25,000) live in Israel.[1]

## Samaritans

There are many theories about the origin of the Samaritans. According to the dominant view, their origins stretch back to the eighth century BCE when the Assyrians destroyed the Northern Kingdom of Israel. Some went south to the Kingdom of Judah and others were deported to parts of Mesopotamia. The Assyrians subsequently introduced colonists who mixed with the local people. This mixture gave rise to the Samaritans. In 332 BCE, with the permission of King Alexander III of Macedon (Greece), often called "the Great," their temple was built on Mt. Gerizim, near Shechem (today Nablus). Throughout history, Samaritans and Jews have been largely at odds.

Samaritans are monotheists who accept Moses as the only legitimate prophet. They reject any other Biblical text outside the Pentateuch. They also have their version of the Five Books of Moses. They assume the sanctity of Mt. Gerizim, instead of Jerusalem; they believe in the arrival of a Messiah, the Taheb, who will be a restorer, and in the resurrection of the body at the end of time. It is estimated that there are about 1,000 Samaritans living in Israel today, mostly in the area of Holon.[2]

## Dönme

After Rabbi Sabbetai Zevi, the pretending Messiah of the Ottoman Empire, converted to Islam in 1666, his followers, numbering close to one million Jews, were terribly disappointed. The overwhelming majority of Jews subsequently abandoned him and returned to mainstream Judaism, but about 200 families remained loyal to his ideology. They lived as Jews at home but as Muslims in public life. Turks called them "Dönme," which (in Turkish) means "converts." There is no organized "Dönme" life today in Turkey, but there are a number of Dönmes around the world, including in the States, who still expect the return of Zevi as the redeeming Messiah.[3]

In addition to these sects, there are a number of religious groups that claim to be Jewish but are not accepted by the Jewish community worldwide. Among them, Jews-for-Jesus and other Messianic Jews are, from the perspective of mainstream Judaism, Christians and not Jews at all. They remain outside the pale of the Jewish community.

## SEPHARDIC AND ASHKENAZIC JEWS

The major division among Jews today is that between Sephardic Jews, who are of Spanish and Mediterranean background, and Ashkenazic Jews, who are of European and mostly east-European origin. Some Jews who are not of Spanish descent (such as those from Iran, Iraq, or Yemen), still claim to be Sephardic because they have adopted Sephardic religious practices. The overwhelming majority of Jews in the United States are of Ashkenazic background.

The differences between these two major groups are not always religious in nature but often cultural and regional. For both celebrate the same festivals and life-cycle events; both treasure the same sacred books, and share mostly the same religious philosophy; but each has its distinctive liturgical tradition, its own culinary preferences, and its intellectual tradition.

Some of these differences between these two groups are blatant. Among them, one can mention the pronunciation of Hebrew: Ashkenazic Jews pronounce the vowel *kamatz* as "O," (e.g., *Borukh Ato...*), whereas Sephardic Jews as "A," (e.g., *Barukh Atah...*). Sephardic Jews call their religious leaders "Hakham"; the customary title used by Ashkenazic Jews is "Rabbi." The pulpit from which the prayer leader reads the service is called by Sephardic Jews *Tevah*, whereas Ashkenazic Jews refer to it as *Bimah*. Sephardic Jews eat rice and legumes during Passover, Ashkenazic Jews do not. Sephardic Jews name their children after living relatives; Ashkenazic Jews do not. Sephardic Jews allow flowers at funerals, Ashkenazic Jews do not. Great differences exist between the two groups with regards to the form of service held in the house after death as well as customs observed during the mourning period.[4]

## RELIGIOUS MOVEMENTS IN CONTEMPORARY JUDAISM

The different religious movements in Judaism are found primarily in the Western world, whether Sephardic or Ashkenazic, even though most Sephardic Jews tend to be Orthodox, and Ashkenazic Jews are splintered into various religious denominations.

Though each of the synagogue-affiliated religious groups differs from the other in terms of theology and practice, there are common structural patterns that apply to all of them. They all have a national umbrella organization that brings together various synagogues belonging to the same denomination and each has its own rabbinic seminary as well as a professional association of their own clergy.

In the past, it was easier to differentiate between these religious movements based on their beliefs and practices. Today, by contrast, the line of demarcation is very thin, and Jews move easily from one to another, at times, based on convenience or sheer necessity.

A major separation still exists between Orthodox Judaism and all the others: Orthodox Jews, by definition, believe in divine verbal revelation that makes religious observance binding and obligatory; the other groups subscribe to the notion that God's will is still being discovered by inquisitive human beings even today, and our Sacred Texts are, at most, divinely inspired but not authored by God.

What follows are the major Jewish religious movements in the world today.

## Orthodox Judaism

Orthodox Jews believe that the Torah was divinely revealed on Mt. Sinai, and is therefore authoritative and binding on all Jews. They are committed to the performance of Mitzvot. They are non-egalitarian, teaching that women and men have not equal but different roles in society and in the synagogue. There are no women Orthodox Rabbis or Cantors today. During worship, men and women sit separately, often divided by a partition called "Mehitzah." Most of the Orthodox Jews are Zionists, but there are some who are not (such as the Hasidic group, Neturei Karta, in Israel). They are subdivided in many groups, some Hasidic, others modern Orthodox.

There are Orthodox Jewish congregations in almost every part of the world. In Israel they play a major political role as potential coalition partners, and, therefore, exert a great deal of influence in Israeli society, especially in the area of family life, which is their prerogative. This leaves many non-Orthodox at the mercy of their religious rules and their own Halakhic interpretation. The attempt to get recognition for the non-Orthodox religious movements is often met by strong opposition by the various Orthodox groups in Israel. At the present time, no other Jewish religious leader belonging to a non-Orthodox movement in Israel can officiate at a Jewish marriage or divorce. This prerogative is solely in the hands of the Orthodox rabbinate. Thus, many Reform or Conservative Jews are compelled to get a civil marriage outside of Israel, often in Cyprus, in order to get a non-Orthodox marriage.

Orthodox Jews have many organizations in America. The following are the most representative: The Union of Orthodox Jewish Congregations of America (OU) was established in 1898. The Rabbinical Council of America (RCA), set up in 1935, is part of this organization. A more traditionalist group, the Union of Orthodox Rabbis of the United States and Canada (UOR), also called Agudat Harabanim, goes back to 1901. Orthodox Jews train their Rabbis either at Rabbi Isaac Elchanan Theological Seminary, New York (established in 1896), of Yeshiva University, or at the Hebrew Theological College in Chicago (established in 1922), or in other smaller seminaries. In addition, there are numerous Orthodox rabbinic seminaries and Yeshivot around the world, many in Israel, that ordain Orthodox Rabbis.[5]

# REFORM JUDAISM ✗

Since its inception, Reform Jews have supported the idea that the Torah has been progressively revealed from ancient times to the present days, and has been recorded by human beings eager to understand their own existential situation. Reform Jewish positions have been delineated in successive platforms published since its early days (see Excursus at the end of this book). Fully committed to biblical criticism, Reform Jews assert that the teachings of the sages of our time are as valid as of those who lived in the past. Reform Judaism supports gender equality, and grants the same duties and responsibilities to men and women, irrespective of their sex and sexual orientations. It has promoted the lineal descent for the identification of "Who is a Jew," thus allowing one to be called a Jew whether the mother or the father is Jewish, provided the child goes through certain prescribed life-cycle events and Torah study (see above, Chapter Two). It also supports the rights and privileges of gays, lesbians, and transgenders, including their right to marry and adopt children. Today there are many women as well as gay and lesbian Rabbis and Cantors serving Reform congregations around the world. Reform Jewish liturgies are inclusive and gender-sensitive. Reform Judaism stresses the importance of the study of the Torah and the observance of the Mitzvot based on individual autonomy and informed choice. Not observing any Mitzvah is not a choice but an abuse of this prerogative. Committed to *tikkun o'lam* (the perfection of the world), Reform Jews give high priority to social action. Reform Jews today strongly support the State of Israel's right to exist, and even recommends *a'liyah* ("immigration") to those who can.

Reform congregations in America are now united under the umbrella of the Union for Reform Judaism (formerly the Union of American Hebrew Congregations organized in 1873). Rabbinic students are ordained at the Hebrew Union College-Jewish Institute of Religion (HUC-JIR), in one of its three campuses in the States (New York, Cincinnati, Los Angeles), and one in Jerusalem, Israel. The Hebrew Union College (HUC) was established by Rabbi Isaac Meyer Wise in 1875 in Cincinnati, OH. The Jewish Institute of Religion (JIR) is the product of the efforts of Rabbi Stephen S. Wise of New York in 1922. The two merged in 1950. Reform Rabbis belong to the Central Conference of American Rabbis (CCAR), which was established in 1889. It is estimated that there are over a million and half Reform Jews in the USA and Canada.

Reform congregations are found in almost every part of the world. In England they go by either Liberal or Reform Jews. Europe has now two rabbinic seminaries: Leo Baeck College in London, England (opened in 1956) and Abraham Geiger College in Potsdam, Germany (opened in 1999).

All Reform congregations around the world belong to the World Union for Progressive Judaism (WUPJ), set up in London in 1926. It now represents the Reconstructionist movement as well. Since 1973, its headquarters is in Jerusalem. The WUPJ's Zionists youth movement, Netzer Olami (an acronym for *Noa'r Tziyoni Reformi*, "Reform Zionist

Youth") has about 18,000 members world-wide. (More on Reform Judaism, see Chapter One[6]; for the Reform Platforms, see Excursus.)

## CONSERVATIVE JUDAISM

*Rabbi Zacharias Frankel*

Conservative Judaism emerged in Germany out of Reform Judaism as a result of an internal debate about the role of Hebrew. Zacharias Frankel of Prague (1801–1875), head of a rabbinic seminary in Breslau, disagreed with his colleagues who were active in the nascent Reform movement, and founded "Historical Judaism," the precursor to Conservative Judaism in America. Once transplanted to the United States, it developed as an independent group with its own theological approach and religious institutions.

Conservative Jews follow the middle road between Orthodoxy and Reform. They affirm the idea of progressive revelation and accept the teachings of biblical criticism. On the other hand they observe Shabbat and the laws of Kashrut more strictly than many Reform Jews. They are egalitarian, and have ordained women Rabbis and Cantors. They are strongly Zionist.

Conservative Jews train their Rabbis at the Jewish Theological Seminary (JTS) in NY (established by Sabato Morais and Marcus Jastrow in 1886), and at the Ziegler School of Rabbinic Studies of the American Jewish University (AJULA) (formerly, the University of Judaism) in Los Angeles. The Rabbinical Assembly of America (RA), the professional association of the Conservative Rabbis was founded in 1900. Conservative congregations function under the umbrella of the United Synagogue of Conservative Judaism (USCJ) (since 1913). There are Conservative Congregations in many parts of the world. In Israel they are known as "Masorti" ("Traditional").

In addition, there is a rabbinic seminary in Buenos Aires, Argentina called "El Seminario Rabinico" that was established in 1952 under Conservative auspices, and a number of congregations affiliated with this movement exist in many parts of South America.[7] (For the basic beliefs of Conservative Judaism, see Excursus.)

## RECONSTRUCTIONIST JUDAISM

Founded in the 1920's by Rabbi Mordecai Kaplan (1881–1963), the dean of the Teachers' Institute of the JTS, Reconstructionist Judaism, though relatively small, has had a great influence on modern Jewish thought. It considers Judaism more of a culture ("Civilization" in Kaplan's term) than a religion, thus moving the center of gravity in Judaism from religion to peoplehood. Kaplan rejected supernaturalism and divine law, and considered God as "The Power that makes for salvation," "salvation" meaning "self-realization." Put differently, in Kaplan's naturalism, God is "the totality of those forces in life that render human life worthwhile." In Reconstructionism, ceremonial laws are "folkways," but no less important. Equality of sexes is affirmed, and consequently many women Rabbis and Cantors have been ordained by the leaders of the movement. It was Kaplan who created the first Bat Mitzvah in America in 1922. Reconstructionist Jews are strongly Zionists. After Kaplan's death, the movement veered away from his naturalism and now includes more mystical tendencies.

Source: Menorah Journal. Copyright in the Public Domain.

*Rabbi Mordecai Kaplan*

The Jewish Reconstructionist Federation (JRF) that includes all the Reconstructionist congregations in the country was established in 1955 but goes back to Kaplan's Society for the Advancement of Judaism that he founded in 1922. The Reconstructionist Rabbinical Seminary (RRC) in Philadelphia has been in existence since 1968, and their graduates belong to the Reconstructionist Rabbinical Association (RRA) (since 1974).[8] (For more details, see Excursus.)

## HUMANISTIC JUDAISM

This movement owes its origin to Rabbi Sherwin Wine (1928–2007) of Detroit, MI, a Reform Rabbi who was ordained by the Hebrew Union College in Cincinnati. He was the Rabbi of the Birmingham Temple, which he established in 1963. Humanistic Judaism is one of the smallest movements in Judaism, but has a wide appeal. It is non-theistic; in fact, afraid that the word "God" would immediately conjure a theistic image, many Humanistic Jews refuse to use it even in their liturgy. Humanists stress human values; they are egalitarian and Zionists.

The Association of Humanistic Rabbis (AHR) was established in 1967, two years before the Society for Humanistic Judaism in 1969. Their Rabbis receive ordination from the International Institute for Secular Humanistic Judaism in North America, or from

T'murah, the Institute's seminary in Israel. Religious humanists have a few congregations outside of the United States.[9] (For other details, see Excursus.)

## The Jewish Renewal Movement

The origin of this group goes back to the late 60's and early 70's in Boston, MA, where Havurat Shalom was organized by Arthur Waskow, Arthur Green, Everett Gendler, Michael Strassfeld, and others. Later on, it received a greater impetus from Rabbi Zalman Schachter-Shalomi (born in Poland and raised in Vienna) who came to America and graduated from Yeshiva University in 1947. He had a strong Hasidic background, but soon broke away from Orthodoxy over the rigidity of the movement. Schachter-Shalomi taught philosophy at the University of Manitoba and then at Temple University. In 1962, he founded the B'nai Or Religious fellowship, which in 1978 changed its name to P'nai Or, and later to ALEPH: Alliance for Jewish Renewal. It is the most recent but rapidly growing religious movement in Judaism.

The members of Jewish Renewal are dedicated to the Jewish people's sacred purpose of partnership with the Divine in the inseparable tasks of healing the world and healing the hearts. They are neo-Hasidic, and are grounded in prophetic and mystical traditions of Judaism. They are egalitarian, strong Zionists, many of them pacifists and environmentalists, and committed to the religious experiences on a personal level, including meditation, eco-kashrut, and intense worship.

The Aleph Rabbinic Program was set up in the early 1980's and in the 1990's the Network of Jewish Renewal Communities was established.[10]

## What Do Jews Have In Common?

The contemporary religious movements listed above represent only a part of the organized Jewish world. There are many Jews who, though active in Jewish life, are not part of the synagogue community. And there are a number of Jews who are nominally Jewish with very limited participation (or none at all) in any type of Jewish activities. This raises the question about the unity of the Jewish people.

Diversity has always been the hallmark of Jewish life. There has never been a time when Jews were not divided along religious or secular lines. Yet, somehow, Jews see themselves, and the world considers them, as one people. What *do* they have in common?

The major religious divide today is between Orthodox and non-Orthodox Jews. The first group, by definition, maintains that the Torah, both written and oral, comes from

Sinai, is divine (namely, is God's word), and consequently, authoritative and binding. Throughout the centuries, Rabbis, using hermeneutic rules that they devised, adapted old norms to contemporary situations, and, in rare cases, did not hesitate to abrogate some rules because of necessity. Non-Orthodox Jews, on the other hand, accept that the Torah is, at most, divinely inspired, but written by fallible human beings. Therefore, it can be reinterpreted, adapted, and even ignored when it strongly clashes with present values. In spite of this major difference, the overwhelming majority of Jews share the following characteristics:

a. A feeling of belonging to the same people—an almost tribe-like sentiment—sharing the glories and fate of all the other Jews.
b. A great regard for Jewish tradition, cultural or otherwise, with some people placing a higher value on religious values.
c. A strong attachment to the existence and security of the State of Israel as a unique state for the Jews in the world.
d. A strong commitment to social action and *tikkun o'lam* ("the repair of the world") as a way to preserve and perfect the world in which we live.
e. A firm belief in the sacredness of human life and the free will of every individual. Unless confronted with "radical evil" (like the Nazis, or others who wish to destroy the Jewish people), Jewish sages have urged negotiation rather than violence, dialogue rather than war.

In addition, non-Orthodox Jews are said to support these values:

a. Progressive revelation: The Torah is still being discovered by teachers and sages of our time; their instruction is as valid as those in the past.
b. Sexual equality: All men and women, irrespective of their sexual orientation, have the same duties and responsibilities. Liturgies must be inclusive and gender-sensitive. God must be conceived not as a male figure, but beyond gender.
c. Religious pluralism: This is the basis of democracy, and must be defended around the world, including Israel for all Jews.
d. Informed choice: Every Jew has the right and privilege to choose the religious venue that fits him/her. However, choosing religious observances should be based on knowledge, commitment, and sensitivity toward other Jews. Not observing Mitzvot is not a choice, but an abuse of this prerogative.
e. Valuing the scientific method: Religious texts (such as the Bible) and historical and literary documents should be read through the eyes and methodology of the critics, considering them in flux, changing and adjusting to new conditions, both past and present. Judaism has always reformed itself, and this is likely to continue and is a key to its survival.

The Hebrew Bible orders all Israelites: *lo titgodedu* (from the Hebrew root *gdd*, meaning "to cut oneself"), "you shall not gash yourselves" (Deut. 14:1). However, the ancient Rabbis, aware of internal Jewish divisions, urged people to come together. Deriving the biblical verb from the Hebrew word *agudah* "cluster," they taught, "Do not form many clusters, but all of you should stay as one cluster" (Sif. Deut. #96). The same idea was formulated centuries ago by the biblical prophet Jeremiah who hoped that in the future all tribes will get together: "In those days, the House of Judah, shall go with House of Israel, they shall come together from the land of the north to the land I gave your fathers as a possession" (Jer. 3:18).

There is no doubt that in greater unity, there is more strength. When Jews are confronted with an outside enemy, they tend to come closer together. When things are quiet, they assert their individuality and their God-given rights. That too spells strength.

## ENDNOTES

1. On the Karaites, see the article in the EJ, 2007, Vol. 11, 785–802.
2. On the Samaritans, see, op.cit., Vol 17, 718–740.
3. On the Donme, see, "Doenme," op.cit., Vol 5, 730–733.
4. For further details, see H. J. Zimmels, *Ashkenazim and Sephardim*. London: Marla Publications, 1976, and Herbert C. Dobrinsky, *A Treasury of Sepharadic Laws and Customs*. NY; Yeshiva University, 1986.
5. A web page on Jewish Orthodoxy: http://www.ou.org/
6. A Web page on Reform Judaism: http://urj.org/
7. A Web Page on Conservative Judaism: http://www.uscj.org/
8. A Web Page on Reconstructionism: http://www.jrf.org/
9. A Web Page on Jewish Humanism: http://www.shj.org/
10. A Web Page on the Jewish Renewal Movement: https://www.aleph.org/

# CHAPTER FOUR

# THE JEWISH FESTIVALS

## THE JEWISH CALENDAR

Because Judaism has its own calendar, one can talk of "Jewish time." In fact, Rabbi Samson R. Hirsch (1808–1888), an Orthodox Rabbi from Hamburg, Germany, said, "The catechism of the Jew consists of his calendar."[1]

The Jewish week of seven days is marked at the end by a day of rest, the Sabbath. The passage of each season is linked to the sequence of holidays: *Rosh Hashanah, Yom Kippur, Sukkot, Hanukkah, Purim, Pesah, Shavuo't*. Each holiday season has a special flavor, each marks the passage of time, each is an indicator of Jewish values and traditions, each is the repository of Jewish experience, each has a relevance to the human condition. Each has its own foods, its own music, its own special message that reinforces the Judaism of the present and links it to an ancient heritage.

The sacred occasions of Jewish religious life follow an ancient calendar, which is both solar (~365 days and a quarter) and lunar (~354 days). To harmonize the two systems, ancient Jewish sages added a thirteenth month in the calendar, seven times within each cycle of 19 years. The years are counted since the presumed creation of the world. To calculate the Hebrew year, one needs to add 3,760 to the secular date in the months before the Jewish New Year September/October, and 3,761 after that holy day.

In Jewish usage, the terms "Common Era" ("CE") and "Before the Common Era" ("BCE") are customary, rather than the Christian points of reference, "AD" ("Anno Domini," "the Year of the Lord") and "BC" ("Before Christ").

In the early biblical period, the year began in the fall. However, when Jews returned from Babylonia in the sixth century BCE, they brought with them the Babylonian calendar that started in the springtime.

# THE MONTHS

| | | | |
|---|---|---|---|
| Nisan | March/April | Tishri | September/October |
| Iyar | April/May | Heshvan | October/November |
| Sivan | May/June | Kislev | November/December |
| Tammuz | June/July | Tevet | December/January |
| Av | July/August | Shevat | January/February |
| Elul | August/September | Adar | February/March |
| | | Adar II | March (leap years) |

The Hebrew month begins with the new moon (*Rosh Hodesh*) and alternates between 29 and 30 days in length. Months carry names that reflect their ancient Babylonian background. They also contain a number of anomalies that reflect changes in the Jewish calendar system over the centuries. Thus, *Nisan* (March/April), the first month of the calendar, falls in the spring, while the New Year (*Rosh Hashanah*) begins on the first day of the seventh month.

The day starts at sundown. This is based on the Biblical text in Genesis 1:5: "There was evening and there was morning, the first day [or, day one]," where evening precedes the morning. In Hebrew usage, the days of the week do not have special names; they are simply known as "first day" or "second day." The seventh day, however, is special and thus has a special name, *Shabbat*, the Sabbath.

One of the greatest calendar changes the Rabbis made in the third century CE was the addition of the "Second Days for the Diaspora." At the time, it was customary for the rabbinic courts to identify the beginning of the month on the basis of witnesses who saw the new crest. Then, they would light a fire and notify all the surrounding communities. However, the Samaritans, a hostile Jewish sect, were confusing the Jewish people about the start of the month by lighting fires at the wrong time. Thus, the Rabbis decided to add an extra day, except for Yom Kippur, so that personal messengers would bring to communities outside of Israel the news about the festivals in time, and the holy days would be celebrated during one of the two days. Even though later calendars determined the exact date of the festivals, the custom remained. Thus today, Orthodox and Conservative synagogues follow the rabbinic calendar, whereas Reform congregations mostly follow the biblical calendar, without adding an extra day to the festivals.[2]

## SHABBAT: THE QUEEN OF DAYS

The Sabbath (Hebrew, Shabbat) is one of Judaism's greatest gifts to the world. People in the Ancient Near East, like those in the modern Far East, had nothing similar to the Jewish concept of a weekly sacred day of rest. The Bible provides two reasons for the observance of Shabbat in the two renditions of the Ten Commandments. According to Ex. 20:8-11, God created the world in six days and rested on the seventh. The implication is that just as God rested, so should all of God's creatures. Thus, Shabbat commemorates creation, an act of God. On the other hand, in Deut. 5:12-15, the observance of Shabbat is based on a humanitarian reason: "So that your male and female slave may rest as you do"—in other words, because Jews were slaves in Egypt and God ordained freedom.

Shabbat is intended to be a holy day set aside for sacred purposes. Ordinary work, therefore, should not be carried out. The Bible does not define the word "work" except to prohibit gathering wood (Num. 15:32), plowing and reaping (Ex. 34:21), and preparing a fire on Shabbat (Ex. 35:3). The Mishnah singled out thirty-nine activities as examples of labor (M Shab. 7:2; see text below), including most agricultural pursuits, as well as arduous labor like building or baking. Other rabbinic texts, like Codes, sought to elaborate further definitions of work.

In all Jewish literature, biblical and rabbinic, Shabbat stands for a number of basic values: a day of rest; a sign of the covenant between God and Israel (Ex. 31:17); a reminder of our commitment to freedom and justice, referred to historically as "a memorial of the Exodus from Egypt" (Deut. 5:15); a day of joy (*O'neg Shabbat*) set aside for personal growth and joy; a day of peace (*Shabbat Shalom*), "a foretaste of the Messianic times." According to Jewish law, funerals are not conducted on the Sabbath, and weddings cannot be held until after sundown on Saturday.

*Shabbat* extends from sundown to sundown. On Friday evening, it is customary to light candles (a symbol of divine light and creation), recite a blessing of sanctification (the *Kiddush*) over a cup of wine (a symbol of joy), and say the blessing (*ha-motzi*) over the bread (symbol of life). (For the text of these blessings, see end of this book.) The members of the household then share a festive meal. It is also appropriate to attend services in the synagogue on Friday evening and/or on Saturday morning. During the day of Shabbat, it is fitting to worship, study, and engage in good deeds and family recreation.

*Shabbat* ends with a special service of conclusion, *Havdalah*, marking the separation of the sacred from the secular, the *Shabbat* from the rest of the days of the week. For this ceremony, a glass of wine, various spices and a multi-wicked braided candle are used. A blessing is recited over each one.[3]

# Selected Texts About Shabbat From The Bible

Thus the heavens and the earth and all their array were completed. Since on the seventh day God was finished with the work he had been doing, he rested on the seventh day from all the work he had undertaken. So God blessed the seventh day and made it holy, because on it he rested from all the work he had done in creation (Gen. 2:1-3, NAB).

Remember to keep holy the sabbath day. Six days you may labor and do all your work, but the seventh day is the sabbath of the LORD, your God. No work may be done then either by you, or your son or daughter, or your male or female slave, or your beast, or by the alien who lives with you. In six days the LORD made the heavens and the earth, the sea and all that is in them; but on the seventh day he rested. That is why the LORD has blessed the sabbath day and made it holy (Ex. 20:8-11; cf. Deut. 5:12-15, NAB).

The LORD said to Moses, 'You must also tell the Israelites: Take care to keep my sabbaths, for that is to be the token between you and me throughout the generations, to show that it is I, the LORD, who make you holy. Therefore, you must keep the sabbath as something sacred. Whoever desecrates it shall be put to death. If anyone does work on that day, he must be rooted out of his people. Six days there are for doing work, but the seventh day is the sabbath of complete rest, sacred to the LORD. Anyone who does work on the sabbath day shall be put to death. So shall the Israelites observe the sabbath, keeping it throughout their generations as a perpetual covenant. Between me and the Israelites it is to be an everlasting token; for in six days the LORD made the heavens and the earth, but on the seventh day he rested at his ease" (Ex. 31:12-17, NAB).

# Rabbinic Prohibitions Regarding The Sabbath: "Thirty-Nine Categories of Forbidden Acts"

Sowing; Plowing; Reaping; Binding sheaves; Threshing; Winnowing; Selecting; Grinding; Sifting; Kneading; Baking; Shearing wool; Washing wool; Beating wool; Dyeing wool; Spinning; Weaving; Making two loops; Weaving two threads; Separating two threads; Tying; Untying; Sewing two stitches; Tearing; Trapping; Slaughtering; Flaying; Salting meat; Curing hide; Scraping hide; Cutting hide up; Writing two letters; Erasing two letters; Building; Tearing a building down; Extinguishing a fire; Kindling a fire; Hitting with a hammer; Taking an object from the private domain to the public, or transporting an object in the public domain (M Shab. 7:2).

# THE HIGH HOLY DAYS: ROSH HASHANAH AND YOM KIPPUR

The High Holy Days of Rosh Hashanah ("New Year") and Yom Kippur ("Day of Atonement") are synagogue-centered, spiritual holy days, when the synagogue is usually filled with worshipers who come to affirm their identity as Jews and to make amends for past errors. Introspection and self-analysis constitute the main thrust of the worship services.

During the month of Elul preceding Rosh Hashanah, Jews begin to prepare for the New Year. A service of penitence (*selihot*) is scheduled usually late in the evening the Saturday night prior to Rosh Hashanah, or every day before dawn, as is the custom among Jews of Sephardic origin.

## Rosh ha-Shanah

*Rosh ha-Shanah* falls on the first day of the month of Tishri (September/October), the seventh month of the Jewish calendar. Following the Biblical injunction (Lev. 23:24), most Reform Jews celebrate the New Year for one day only. In recent years, however, a number of Reform congregations have opted to celebrate a second day, as is the custom among Conservative and Orthodox Jews. A highlight of the *Rosh ha-Shanah* service is the dramatic sounding of the Shofar, an ancient musical instrument mentioned in the Bible.

Various traditions are associated with *Rosh ha-Shanah*. For example, according to one rabbinic teaching the universe was conceived this day; according to another, Rosh Ha-Shanah marks the day on which the first human being was formed. A third one claims that the binding of Isaac took place on this holy day.

The New Year festival has various names: *Rosh ha-Shanah* (literally "Head of the Year"), as we are reminded of the creative power in the universe and express gratitude for being part of it; *Yom ha-Zikaron* ("Day of Remembrance"), as individually and collectively we look back on our past and evaluate our actions; *Yom ha-Din* ("Day of Reckoning"), as we examine our past in light of our educated conscience and resolve to improve ourselves; and *Yom Terua'h* ("Day of Sounding the Ram's Horn"), as the shofar is sounded to awaken us from our moral lethargy.

On the first day of Rosh Hashanah in the afternoon, it is customary to do the *Tashlih* ("casting away") ceremony. The origin of this custom is uncertain. Some derive it from the words of the prophet Micah, "You will hurl (*vetashlih*) all our sins into the depths of the sea" (7:19). Usually people go to a body of water, like a river or a well, and as they shake out their pockets and throw away the crumbs of bread into the water, they symbolically cast away their accumulated sins and transgressions. Recently even some Reform synagogue in America, which had abandoned this custom long ago, are reviving it with a modern meaning of self-purification.

Rosh Hashanah initiates a ten-day period of more intense penitence until Yom Kippur. According to one rabbinic tradition, Moses was on Mt. Sinai from the first day of Elul until Yom Kippur writing the second set of the Decalogue. Another one describes how at Rosh Hashanah the fate of each individual is tentatively inscribed in either The Book of Life or The Book of Death. During the Ten Days of Penitence, the ancient Rabbis taught, the severity of the inscription may be altered through repentance, prayer, and good deeds. According to the legend, on Yom Kippur, The Book of Life is sealed.

The traditional greeting during the Rosh Hashanah season is *Le-Shanah Tovah Tikatevu* ("May you be inscribed for a good year"), or more simply *Le-Shanah Tovah* ("For a good year"). Sephardic Jews usually say, *tizku leshanim rabbot*, namely, "May you merit [to celebrate] many more years." It is also customary to eat apples and honey as symbols of a sweet year.

## Yom Kippur

Yom Kippur is the Sabbath of Sabbaths, the holiest day of the Jewish calendar. It is celebrated ten days after Rosh Hashanah, on the 10th day of Tishri. A twenty-four hour period of self-examination, repentance, and reconciliation, the Day of Atonement lasts from sundown to sundown. Yom Kippur is a day of purification of the soul, a time for self-analysis and prayer. Accordingly, all traditional Jews, including many in the Reform Jewish community, regard this as a fast day of total abstinence from food and drink.

On the eve of Yom Kippur, congregants listen to the haunting melody of the famous *Kol Nidre* ("All Vows") chant (Sephardic Jews pronounce it as *KAL NIDRE*; see text below). Once recited by medieval Jews who had been forcibly converted to Christianity, *Kol Nidre* calls for the cancellation of all rash promises made to God by the individual. They deal with religious vows, not with business commitments. The following day is often one of continual prayer in the synagogue.

At Yom Kippur a communal confession of sins is recited as the worshipers ask forgiveness from one another for their collective shortcomings as human beings, which are regarded as sins by them against their neighbors. In Reform Judaism a special memorial service (*Yizkor*) is included, usually in the afternoon service. Among Orthodox Jews this is recited in the morning.

At the end of the Day of Atonement, as the sun begins to set, the shofar is sounded as a last call to repentance. This is followed by *Havdalah*, because Yom Kippur is also considered a Sabbath Day.

The customary greeting at the end of this holiest of days is *Hatimah Tovah* ("Good inscription,") referring to the prayer that one may be inscribed in The Book of Life for a good year to come.

## Selected Texts About The High Holy Days From The Bible: Rosh Ha-Shanah

The LORD said to Moses, 'Tell the Israelites: On the first day of the seventh month you shall keep a sabbath rest, with a sacred assembly and with the trumpet blasts as a reminder; you shall then do no sort of work, and you shall offer an oblation to the LORD' (Lev. 23:23-25, NAB).

On the first day of the seventh month you shall hold a sacred assembly, and do no sort of work; it shall be a day on which you sound the trumpet (Num. 29:1, NAB).

Now when the seventh month came, the whole people gathered as one man in the open space before the Water Gate, and they called upon Ezra the scribe to bring forth the book of the Law of Moses which the LORD prescribed for Israel. On the first day of the seventh month, therefore, Ezra the priest brought the law before the assembly, which consisted of men, women, and those children old enough to understand. Standing at one end of the open place that was before the Water Gate, he read out of the book from day-break till midday, in the presence of the men, the women, and those children old enough to understand; and all the people listened attentively to the book of the law. Ezra the scribe stood on a wooden platform that had been made for the occasion; at his right side stood Mattithiah, Shema, Anaiah, Uriah, Hilkiah, and Maaseiah, and on his left Pedaiah, Mishael, Malchijah, Hashum, Hashbaddanah, Zechariah, Meshullam. Ezra opened the scroll so that all the people might see it (for he was standing higher up than any of the people); and, as he opened it, all the people rose. Ezra blessed the LORD, the great God, and all the people, their hands raised high, answered, 'Amen, amen!' Then they bowed down and prostrated themselves before the LORD, their faces to the ground. (The Levites Jeshua, Bani, Sherebiah, Jamin, Akkub, Shabbethai, Hodiah, Maaseiah, Kelita, Azariah, Jozabad, Hanan, and Pelaiah explained the law to the people, who remained in their places.) Ezra read plainly from the book of the law of God, interpreting it so that all could understand what was read. Then (Nehemiah, that is, His Excellency, and) Ezra the priest-scribe (and the Levites who were instructing the people) said to all the people: 'Today is holy to the LORD your God. Do not be sad, and do not weep'—for all the people were weeping as they heard the words of the law. He said further: 'Go, eat rich foods and drink sweet drinks, and allot portions to those who had nothing prepared; for today is holy to our LORD. Do not be saddened this day, for rejoicing in the LORD must be your strength!'(And the Levites quieted all the people, saying, 'Hush, for today is holy, and you must not be saddened.') Then all the people went to eat and drink, to distribute portions, and to celebrate with great joy, for they understood the words that had been expounded to them (Neh. 8:1-12, NAB).

## Yom Kippur

The LORD said to Moses, 'The tenth of this seventh month is the Day of Atonement, when you shall hold a sacred assembly and mortify yourselves and offer an oblation to the LORD. On this day you shall not do any work, because it is the Day of Atonement, when atonement is made for you before the LORD, your God. Anyone who does not mortify himself on this day shall be cut off from his people, and if anyone does any work on this day, I will remove him from the midst of his people. This is a perpetual statute for you and your descendants wherever you dwell: you shall do no work, but shall keep a sabbath of complete rest and mortify yourselves. Beginning on the evening of the ninth of the month, you shall keep this sabbath of yours from evening to evening" (Lev. 23:26-32, NAB; cf. Lev. 16:29-34; Num. 29:7-11).

## From The Rabbinic Literature

On Yom Kippur, eating, drinking, washing, anointing, putting on sandals, and marital intercourse are forbidden. However a king or a bride may wash their faces and a woman after childbirth may put on sandals (M Yoma 8:1).

Children may not fast on Yom Kippur but they should be trained one or two years before they are of age so that they may become versed in the commandments. If a pregnant woman smelled (food and craved it), they may give her food until she recovers. A sick person is given food at the direction of a skilled person; if no skilled person is present, he/she may be given food at his/her own wish, until he/she says, 'Enough' (M Yoma 8:4-5).

## Translation Of Kol Nidre

All vows, prohibitions, oaths, consecrations, konam-vows, konas-vows [i.e., these were types of vows made during the second Temple period], or equivalent terms that we may vow, swear, consecrate, or prohibit upon ourselves from the last Yom Kippur until this Yom Kippur, and from this Yom Kippur until the next Yom Kippur, may it come upon us for good—regarding them all, we regret them henceforth. They all will be permitted, abandoned, cancelled, null and void, without power and without standing. Our vows shall not be valid vows; our prohibitions shall not be valid prohibitions; and our oaths shall not be valid oaths.

## THE THREE PILGRIMAGE FESTIVALS

In biblical times the Israelites were expected to make a pilgrimage to Jerusalem three times a year for the celebration of three major agricultural festivals (Ex. 23; Lev. 23; Deut. 16). These were the spring festival of *Pesah* ("Passover"), the early summer festival of *Shavuo't* ("the Feast of Weeks"), and the fall festival of *Sukkot* ("Tabernacles" or "Booths"). Each of these festivals was subsequently related to historical events and given a major theological dimension.

### Pesah

The main theme of Passover is freedom, primarily from the physical bondage of slavery in Egypt, but also, by extension, liberty from spiritual bondage. As such, the Passover festival has become a paradigm for many who strive after freedom, whether political or psychological.

Passover falls in March or April, on the eve of the 14th day of the first month, Nisan. In Reform Jewish tradition, in keeping with biblical instruction (Ex. 12:15, 23:15; Deut. 16:3), the festival lasts seven days. Orthodox and Conservative Jews celebrate it for eight days.

In Passover we see a combination of two festivals: the earlier spring festival of *Hag ha-Pesah*, a pastoral feast characterized by the slaughter and consumption of the paschal lamb (Lev. 23:5); and *Hag ha-Matzot*, the Feast of Unleavened Bread (Ex. 23:15; 34:18; Deut. 16:16), an agricultural festival marking the beginning of the winter grain harvest. Subsequently combined, the double festival was given a historical significance and became associated with the Exodus from Egypt, while maintaining a strong identification with spring through reading of passages from the Song of Songs.

Passover is primarily a home-centered festival. Through an elaborate ritual meal, the Seder (literally, "order"), participants share in the historic experience of the Jewish people. The text read at the Seder, the *Haggadah* ("narration"), states the purpose succinctly: "In each generation, every individual Jew should consider him/herself as if he/she had come out of Egypt."

In addition to the Seder traditionally conducted in the home, in Reform Jewish practice, many congregations sponsor a second seder in the synagogue. In Reconstructionist, Conservative, and Orthodox Judaism, a second seder is held, but usually in the home.

The Seder is intended to be a teaching and learning experience. Parents attempt to arouse the curiosity of their children by using a number of symbols: bitter herbs (*maror*) and salt water symbolizing the conditions of slavery; the matzah or unleavened bread, symbolizing the hasty departure of the Israelites from Egypt; a roasted egg representing the Passover sacrifice during the Second Temple; green herbs for spring; and a shank bone alluding to the paschal lamb. In addition, people partake of the Haroset, a mixture of grated apples, chopped nuts, cinnamon, and wine, symbolizing the mortar the Israelites allegedly used in building the two Egyptian royal cities, Ramses and Pithom. The Seder table also contains a Cup of Elijah, symbolizing the Messianic Era as well as Miriam's Cup, which stands for the great contributions made by women throughout Jewish history, and an orange, symbol of inclusiveness. Children are prompted to ask the question "why?" "Why is this night different from all others?" The older participants in the Seder then relate to them the story of the liberation from Egyptian bondage and its implication for us to do what we can to free those who are still enslaved.

According to Jewish tradition, fermented grain products (*hametz*) are not eaten during the Passover week. Thus, no wheat, barley, oat, rye, or other grain products are consumed (M Pes. 2:5). Among Jews of Ashkenazic background, it is also customary to abstain from eating legumes (*kitniyot* in Hebrew), such as rice, corn, beans. This custom is based on mistaken assumptions dating back to medieval times. In 1988 Rabbi David Golinkin, a prominent Conservative Rabbi in Israel, has answered this question in the following responsum where he makes the following points:

1.  It is permitted (and perhaps even obligatory) to eliminate this custom. It is in direct contradiction to an explicit decision in the Babylonian Talmud (BT Pes. 114b) and is also in contradiction to the opinion of all the sages of the Mishnah and Talmud except one (R. Yochanan ben Nuri, Pes.35a and parallels).
2.  This custom is mentioned for the first time in France and Provence in the beginning of the thirteenth century from there it spread to various countries and the list of prohibited foods continued to expand. Nevertheless, the reason for the custom was unknown and as a result many sages invented at least eleven different explanations for the custom. As a result, R. Samuel of Falaise, one of the first to mention it, referred to it as a "mistaken custom" and R. Yerucham called it a "foolish custom."
3.  The main halakhic question in this case is whether it is permissible to do away with a mistaken or foolish custom. Many rabbinic authorities have ruled that it is permitted (and perhaps even obligatory) to do away with this type of "foolish custom."[4]

There is a similar Responsum by the Reform Rabbinate, permitting the use of legumes during Passover. (See sidebar below)

In spite of this responsum there is a strong resistance in the American Jewish community, especially among Ashkenazic Jews, to abandoning the ban on the use of legumes during Passover. Most Sephardic Jews do not abide by this rule.

In recent years the meaning of Passover has broadened to include freedom for Jews who still live in oppressed countries, peace in the State of Israel, universal human rights, and the ultimate redemption of all humanity.

## CCAR Responsum: Pesach Kashrut and Reform Judaism 5756.9 [1996]

She'elah: What should be the standards of Pesach kashrut for Reform Jews? What foods should be prohibited? What is our position regarding rice and legumes (kitniyot)? How do we deal with the requirement of bi'ur chametz? Do we destroy our chametz, sell it, or put it away? (Rabbi Lawrence Englander, Mississauga, Ontario)

Teshuvah

These questions are dealt with in brief in Gates of the Seasons, one of a series of volumes published in recent decades which testify to a renewed interest in ritual observance among Reform Jews in North America. For many years, questions of ritual observance were deemed to be matters of personal choice and did not rank high at all on the communal agenda of the Reform movement. That situation, of course, has changed. Today, we acknowledge that an authentically Jewish way of life requires ritual as well as ethical expression. Reform Judaism perceives ritual practice as a mitzvah, a matter of central religious importance. Much pioneering work has been done, particularly in the published works mentioned above, in describing and setting forth the principles and details of Reform observance. The task of this teshuvah, on Pesach observance, is therefore not so much to issue a ruling as it is to supply the background and discussion necessary for an understanding of the practice of Pesach kashrut in our movement.

1. Chametz, Rice and Legumes. "It is a mitzvah to abstain from eating leaven (Chametz) during the entire seven days of Pesach." By "chametz," the tradition means those grains from which matzah may be baked: wheat, barley, oats, rye, and spelt. No other foodstuffs are regarded as chametz. In this, the halakhah rejects the opinion of R. Yochanan ben Nuri, who forbids the eating of rice and millet during Pesach because they "resemble chametz." Talmudic law, rather, forbids the use of rice and legumes (kitniyot) as flour for the baking of matzah and therefore permits us to eat them during the festival.

According to long-standing Ashkenazic custom, however, rice and legumes are forbidden for Passover consumption. This prohibition is first mentioned in the thirteenth century by two French authorities, R. Yitzchak of Corbeil and R. Manoach of Narbonne. R. Yitzchak writes that "our teachers observe the custom" of not eating rice and legumes during the festival, though he adds that this custom is not universally accepted and that "great sages" disregard it. Among these was his own teacher and father-in-law, the great tosafist R. Yechiel of Paris, who argued that since the Talmud ruled that these foodstuffs are not chametz there is no reason to prohibit them today. R. Yitzchak, though, reluctant "to permit something that for so long has been widely regarded as forbidden," feels the need to justify the custom. He does so, not on the grounds that rice and legumes are chametz ("since not even a beginning Talmud student would make that mistake"), but because these foodstuffs resemble chametz in that they are cooked in the same fashion.

Since this resemblance can lead to confusion—people might mistake a chametz mixture for one of rice or legumes—the rabbis issued a decree forbidding the latter. R. Manoach, for his part, suggests that the prohibition originates in a widespread—but mistaken—belief that rice and legumes are forms of chametz. Unlike R. Yitzchak, however, R. Manoach does not attempt to defend this "errant" custom, and he suggests a talmudic basis for dismantling the prohibition altogether.

These sources tell us a great deal about both the history and the halakhic status of the custom to abstain from rice and legumes during Pesach. We learn that while the prohibition was well known in France by the thirteenth century, some leading rabbis of those communities rejected it on clear halakhic grounds. We know that the custom did not spread beyond Ashkenazic Jewry; rabbis in Spain and elsewhere did not hesitate to express their astonishment against it. And although the prohibition did gain wide acceptance among the Ashkenazim, some leading Ashkenazic authorities, including R. Ya`akov Emden, were still criticizing it as late as the eighteenth century.

The early reformers in Europe, convinced that this observance was both unnecessary and burdensome, abolished it altogether. The orthodox opponents of the new movement responded to this decision in much the same way as they responded to virtually all the innovations which the reformers introduced into Jewish religious life, namely by insisting upon the sanctity of the entire received tradition. They defended the prohibition of rice and legumes despite its halakhic weakness and despite all the criticisms that had been leveled against it over the centuries. Few of them, to be sure, attempted to justify the minhag (custom) on the grounds of its original purpose. They argued, rather, that the very existence of the minhag (custom) is proof that it must be retained. They noted, for example, that a rabbinic decree which prohibits something in order to establish a "fence around the Torah," has the full force of law; we are not permitted to rescind it. Some claimed that once a minhag is widely accepted by a community it acquires the status of a vow, which is valid under the law of the Torah. While this prohibition, as a minhag, does not enjoy the same status as that of chametz, under normal circumstances orthodox rabbis continue to insist upon its observance.

Reform practice, following the standard of the Talmud, permits the eating of rice and legumes during Pesach. We do not take this stand because we disparage custom and tradition. On the contrary: our "rediscovery" of the centrality of ritual observance to Jewish life, described at the outset of this teshuvah, demonstrates that we take the claims of tradition with the utmost seriousness. This Committee, in particular, in its approach to the answering of the she'elot submitted to it, has tended to uphold the standards of traditional practice except in those cases where good and sufficient cause exists to depart from them. And our movement has recognized for nearly two centuries that the prohibition of rice and legumes is just such a case. This observance, which presents a significant burden upon Jews during Pesach, has no halakhic justification: the Talmud clearly rejects the suggestion that rice and legumes are chametz, and the likelihood that our people will confuse legume dishes with chametz dishes is too remote to be taken into serious consideration.

We do not accept the orthodox argument that a customary observance, once widely adopted, can never be annulled. This notion is questionable, in general, as a matter of halakhah, especially when the observance is based upon a mistaken interpretation of the law. In our specific case, moreover, there is absolutely no evidence that this customary prohibition was ever ratified by rabbinic decree or accepted as binding in the form of a vow. Had a decree or a vow existed, after all, those authorities who criticized the practice down to the eighteenth century would never have spoken so bluntly against it. We think, rather, that some rabbis resort to these arguments in order to support practices and customs whose original purpose—if there ever was a legitimate original purpose—no longer holds. When a religious practice has outlived its purpose, when its retention is perceived by the community as unnecessary and burdensome, Reform Judaism affirms the right of the observant community to alter or annul that practice in favor of a new standard which better expresses our understanding of Torah and tradition and the religious sensibilities of our age.

Our position does not, of course, prevent Reform Jews from adopting the traditional prohibition as a matter of choice. On the contrary: Gates of the Seasons notes that "Ashkenazi custom" adds rice and legumes to the list of prohibited foods on Pesach, implying that observance of this custom is a valid option for Reform Jews. The mere fact that a traditional practice is not "obligatory" does not imply that we should not follow it or that we should discontinue it. Jewish religious practice draws its strength from many sources. Chief among these, to be sure, is the "logic of the law," the nature of our observances as these are defined in the classic sacred texts. Also important, and in many ways no less important than the texts, however, is the "living law" as it has developed in the life of the religious community. Minhag is the concrete expression of the religious consciousness of the people, their way of expanding upon and adding texture to the more abstract principles derived from the texts. For many people who take religious living with all seriousness, the abstention from rice and legumes is an integral feature of Pesach observance precisely because this is the way the holiday has been observed for many centuries within their religious community. We do not urge them to abandon that practice; indeed, a number of members of this Committee observe it as well. We say rather that, as a matter of Reform communal practice, our "standards of Pesach kashrut" allow the observant Reform Jew to eat rice and legumes during the festival.

2. The Removal of Chametz. "It is a mitzvah to remove leaven from one's home prior to the beginning of Pesach." This mitzvah is based on the biblical injunction in Exodus 12:15: "on the very first day, you shall remove (tashbitu) leaven from your house." The precise manner of this removal is the subject of a controversy that stretches back to talmudic times. Some early rabbinic authorities interpret the word tashbitu as "nullification," an act by which the householder mentally renounces all ownership of the chametz.

The Talmud, too, declares that "according to Torah law, a simple act of nullification suffices" to remove chametz. According to this view, the practices of bedikat chametz, the search for leaven conducted on the night before the Seder, and bi`ur chametz, the burning or other physical destruction of the leaven the next morning, are requirements of rabbinic law, instituted perhaps in order to prevent against the possibility that one might accidentally eat some of the chametz stored in one's home during the holiday. Other commentators disagree. In their opinion, the Torah requires bi`ur, the physical removal of chametz, as well as its nullification. Indeed, they hold, the requirement of tashbitu is fulfilled primarily through bi'ur. If, as the Talmud says, "nullification suffices," this may refer to chametz in one's possession which one does not know about and therefore cannot burn or scatter. A third interpretation is that the Torah itself permits the "removal" of chametz in either manner, through nullification or through physical destruction; the rabbis, however, instituted the requirement that both procedures be performed.

The traditional practice observes both bi'ur and bitul (nullification). The "search" for chametz takes place on the night before the Seder (or two nights before, on 13 Nisan, when Pesach begins on Sunday and when it is forbidden to burn the chametz on Shabbat). Following both the search and the destruction of the chametz, one recites the formula of bitul, found in traditional haggadot, which declares that "all chametz in my possession...shall be as though it does not exist and as the dust of the earth." Thus, even if chametz inadvertently remains in one's possession, the process of renunciation succeeds in "removing" it in accordance with the Torah's requirement.

To destroy one's chametz becomes impractical and burdensome if one owns a large amount of leaven. The custom therefore arose for a Jew to sell his chametz to a Gentile before Pesach and to buy it back from him at the holiday's conclusion. The roots of this practice extend back to tannaitic times. We learn in the Tosefta that "when a Jew and a Gentile are travelling on board ship, and the Jew has chametz in his possession, he may sell it to the Gentile and buy it back after Pesach, provided that the sale is a full and unencumbered transfer (matanah gemurah)." The development of this law, which apparently deals with a special case, into a regular and normal transaction is a long story that cannot be recounted here. We can simply point to the Shulchan Arukh and its commentaries, which accept as a matter of course that a Jew may sell chametz to a Gentile "even though the Jew knows the Gentile and knows that the latter will guard the chametz and return it to him after Pesach." This custom is now universally practiced in traditional communities. In its most common form, all the Jews in a particular locale or congregation consign their chametz to the rabbi or other notable, who then sells it all to a single Gentile.

This device of mekhirat (sale of) chametz is effective because it is "full and unencumbered." Although the leaven remains physically within the Jew's property, its ownership is legally transferred to the Gentile buyer in a transaction which meets all the formal halakhic requirements of an act of sale. As such, it allows the householder to fulfill the mitzvah of the "removal" of chametz, not necessarily under the terms of Exodus 12:15, which as we have seen may demand the physical removal of leaven, but under Exodus 13:7, which is understood to permit one to "see" chametz that belongs to a non-Jew even though it remains within one's property. Therefore, traditionally observant Jews hold that this form of sale is a perfectly valid means of discharging the Toraitic obligation to remove chametz.

Reform Jews, of course, might well object to the fictitious aspect of this device. The sale may be fully "legal," but it is not serious: neither the Jew nor the Gentile intend that the chametz be transferred to the latter's permanent ownership. We might also ask whether the "sale" of chametz is a better and more serious means of fulfilling the mitzvah than the process of bitul, nullification, described above. As is the case with sale, chametz which is "nullified" remains within one's physical—though not one's legal—possession. Many authorities hold that the renunciation of chametz fully meets the requirements of Exodus 12:15 and/or 13:7. The traditional halakhah, it is true, does draw a distinction: while a Jew may make full use of chametz "bought back" from a Gentile after Pesach, leaven which is "renounced" is forbidden for use. The logic of this distinction, however, escapes us. The objection to bitul, say the authorities, is that one might declare falsely that "I annulled my chametz before Pesach" when in fact one did not do so; therefore, although renouncing chametz fulfills the Toraitic requirement, the rabbis impose this penalty to forestall the possibility that one might evade the law. Yet what is bitul but a formal legal act that effects the legal—but not the physical—removal of chametz from our possession? Is the "sale" of chametz any different in its purpose and substance? It may be true that some Jews do not seriously intend to "renounce" their chametz; it is certainly true, however, that none of them seriously intend to "sell" it.

We might also object to the sale of chametz on the grounds that it requires the participation of a non-Jew in order that we can fulfill our own religious requirements. While Jews have for centuries relied upon Gentiles to serve in such a capacity (the institution of the "Shabbos goy" comes readily to mind), the practice is inelegant at best and demeaning at worst. We prefer to fulfill our mitzvot on our own, especially in this case, when most authorities agree that the method of bitul allows us to meet the Torah's demand that we remove our chametz without incurring severe financial loss.

Therefore, "Reform Jews rarely resort" to the sale of chametz; rather, they "make leaven inaccessible in their homes." This is our way of renouncing our possession of chametz, and we believe that we can do so with full seriousness and sincerity. While Reform Jews may wish to sell their chametz, perhaps, again, out of solidarity with traditional Jewish practice, the standards of Reform Jewish observance do not require that they do so.

In spite of this responsum there is a strong resistance in the American Jewish community, especially among Ashkenazic Jews, to abandoning the ban on the use of legumes during Passover. Most Sephardic Jews do not abide by this rule.

In recent years the meaning of Passover has broadened to include freedom for Jews who still live in oppressed countries, peace in the State of Israel, universal human rights, and the ultimate redemption of all humanity.

---

## Selected Texts About Passover From The Bible

The time the Israelites had stayed in Egypt was four hundred and thirty years. At the end of four hundred and thirty years, all the hosts of the LORD left the land of Egypt on this very date. This was a night of vigil for the LORD, as he led them out of the land of Egypt; so on this same night all the Israelites must keep a vigil for the LORD throughout their generations (Ex. 12:40-42, NAB).

The Passover of the LORD falls on the fourteenth day of the first month, at the evening twilight. The fifteenth day of this month is the LORD'S feast of Unleavened Bread. For seven days you shall eat unleavened bread. On the first of these days you shall hold a sacred assembly and do no sort of work. On each of the seven days you shall offer an oblation to the LORD. Then on the seventh day you shall again hold a sacred assembly and do no sort of work (Lev. 23:4-8, NAB).

You shall keep the feast of Unleavened Bread. For seven days at the prescribed time in the month of Abib you are to eat unleavened bread, as I commanded you; for in the month of Abib you came out of Egypt (Ex. 34:18, NAB; 23:14-15).

Observe the month of Abib by keeping the Passover of the LORD, your God, since it was in the month of Abib that he brought you by night out of Egypt. You shall offer the Passover sacrifice from your flock or your herd to the LORD, your God, in the place which he chooses as the dwelling place of his name. You shall not eat leavened bread with it. For seven days you shall eat with it only unleavened bread, the bread of affliction, that you may remember as long as you live the day of your departure from the land of Egypt; for in frightened haste you left the land of Egypt. Nothing leavened may be found in all your territory for seven days, and none of the meat which you sacrificed on the evening of the first day shall be kept overnight for the next day. 'You may not sacrifice the Passover in any of the communities which the LORD, your God, gives you; only at the place which he chooses as the dwelling place of his name, and in the evening at sunset, on the anniversary of your departure from Egypt, shall you sacrifice the Passover. You shall cook and eat it at the place the LORD, your God, chooses; then in the morning you may return to your tents. For six days you shall eat unleavened bread, and on the seventh there shall be a solemn meeting in honor of the LORD, your God; on that day you shall not do any sort of work' (Deut. 16:1-8, NAB).

The exiles kept the Passover on the fourteenth day of the first month. The Levites, every one of whom had purified himself for the occasion, sacrificed the Passover for the rest of the exiles, for their brethren the priests, and for themselves. The Israelites who had returned from the exile partook of it together with all those who had separated themselves from the uncleanness of the peoples of the land to join them in seeking the LORD, the God of Israel. They joyfully kept the feast of Unleavened Bread for seven days, for the LORD had filled them with joy by making the king of Assyria favorable to them, so that he gave them help in their work on the house of God, the God of Israel (Ezra 6:19-22, NAB).

### From The Rabbinic Literature

During the reading of the Haggadah, a rabbinic liturgical creation, the youngest child usually asks the following four questions: "1) On all other nights we eat either *hametz* (leavened food) or *matzah* (unleavened bread). Why, on this night, do we eat only *matzah*? 2) On all other nights we eat all kinds of vegetables. Why, on this night, do we eat bitter herbs? 3) On all other nights, we do not usually dip vegetables even once. Why, on this night, do we dip twice? 4) On all other nights we eat either sitting upright or reclining. Why, on this night, we do we eat reclining?"

This text, mostly based on the Mishnah, is used by adults as a starting point to retell the Story of the Exodus. The Mishnah continues: "According to the understanding of the child, the parent instructs him (in our days, "her" too). The parent starts with the disgrace (of slavery) and end with the glory (of freedom)" (M Pes. 9:4 end).

# SHAVUO'T

On *Shavuo't* ("the Feast of Weeks") Jews reaffirm the revelation at Sinai and God's covenant with Israel as they rejoice in the Torah as the foundation of Judaism.

There is a wide variety of interpretations among Jews with regard to the meaning of such basic concepts as "revelation" or "covenant." Unlike Orthodox Jews who believe that the Torah was verbally "revealed" by God to Moses on Mt. Sinai, most Reform Jews, along with many other biblical scholars of our time, maintain that the Torah was written over a long period of time by many people who were inspired by the divine, and that it incorporates a variety of points of view, all compatible with the concept of one

God. For Reform Judaism, the Torah is the repository of the religious wisdom of the Israelites during the biblical period and their understanding of their encounters with God in the realm of history and nature. As for the "covenant," this usually refers to the ethical imperatives deriving from the Ten Commandments and the rest of biblical instructions, which reinforce the belief in the Jews as a people chosen, in the words of the Bible, to be "a kingdom of priests" (Ex. 19:6) and "a light of/to the nations" (Isa. 49:6). For others, such as many Reconstructionist Jews, Jews are not the "chosen people" but a "choosing people," namely, they chose God to live according to a disciplined life. The rabbis of old taught that the entire Torah, both written and oral, was given on Mount Sinai to the Children of Israel, through Moses, on this memorable occasion. One commentary adds: "Even the words which the prophets were to utter in the future" (Ex. R. 28:6).

*Shavuo't* is celebrated in May or June, on the 6th day of Sivan. It was originally a midsummer holy day marking the end of the barley harvest and the beginning of the wheat harvest. It is celebrated for one day in most Reform congregations but two days in Orthodox and Conservative Judaism. Like most Jewish holy days, *Shavuo't* has been historicized, that is, anchored in Jewish history by being given an historical dimension connected with the giving of Torah on Mount Sinai.[5]

The Bible calls this festival by a number of names: *Hag Shavuo't* ("The Feast of Weeks"), referring to the seven weeks following Pesah and preceding Shavuot; *Yom ha-Bikkurim* ("The Day of the First Fruits"), referring to the first products of the harvest brought by the pilgrims to the Temple in Jerusalem; *Hag ha-Katzir* ("The Harvest Festival"), referring to the summer harvest; and *Zeman Matan Toratenu* ("The season of the Giving of our Torah"), a term applied in the literature of the early rabbis as a reference to the revelation at Sinai.

It is customary in many Reform congregations to hold Confirmation ceremonies on this day for religious school students who complete their formal religious education at the end of 9th, 10th, or even 11th grade (age 15–16). It is also customary to hold a *Tikun Lel Shavuo't*, an all-night study session, on the first night of *Shavuo't*. Originating in Safed of the 16th century, and later on, in many parts of the Jewish world, many Jews spend the night reading different parts of the Torah as well as sections of the Mishnah and kabbalistic material.

*Shavuo't* has few rituals. In the synagogue the Book of Ruth is read for two reasons. First, the events in Ruth take place during the spring harvest. Second, according to tradition, Ruth, an ancestor of King David, died on *Shavuo't*. The characteristic of loyalty exemplified by Ruth is considered to be emblematic of Israel's loyalty to the Torah. Often dairy products are eaten on *Shavuo't*, following a rabbinic interpretation of the Song of Songs (4:11) that compares the Torah to milk, as well as the observation that the law of the first fruits is placed in juxtaposition to a law about milk (Ex. 23:19).

## Selected Texts About Shavuo't From The Bible

On the day of first fruits, on your feast of Weeks, when you present to the LORD the new cereal offering, you shall hold a sacred assembly, and do no sort of work (Num. 28:26, NAB; cf. Ex. 23:14-17; Lev. 23:9-22).

You shall count off seven weeks, computing them from the day when the sickle is first put to the standing grain. You shall then keep the feast of Weeks in honor of the LORD, your God, and the measure of your own freewill offering shall be in proportion to the blessing the LORD, your God, has bestowed on you. In the place which the LORD, your God, chooses as the dwelling place of his name, you shall make merry in his presence together with your son and daughter, your male and female slave, and the Levite who belongs to your community, as well as the alien, the orphan and the widow among you (Deut. 16:9-11, NAB).

## From The Rabbinic Literature

There are a number of Midrashim regarding the Revelation of Torah on Mt. Sinai. Here below are a few examples:

God offered the Torah to each of the nations of the world so that none of them could say: 'Had we been asked, we might have accepted.' God went to the first nation and said to them: 'Will you accept the Torah?' They asked: 'What is written in it?' God replied: 'Do not murder.' They said: 'No, thank you.' Then God went to the next nation and said to them: 'Will you accept the Torah?' They asked: 'What is written in it?' God replied: 'Do not commit adultery.' They said: 'No, thank you.' Then God went to a third nation and said to them: 'Will you accept the Torah?' They asked: 'What is written in it?' God replied: 'Do not steal.' They said: 'No, thank you.' Finally God went to the families of Israel and said to them: 'Will you accept the Torah?' Without asking any questions, they said: '*Na'aseh venishma*' 'We will do and we will listen' (Mekhilta, Bahodesh, Yitro 5).

The Torah says: 'Moses brought the people out of the camp to meet with God' (Exodus 19:17). From these words we learn the following: God lifted up Mount Sinai and held it over the heads of the families of Israel, like an open casket. God said: 'If you accept the Torah, good! If not, this is your burial place' (BT Shab. 88a).

'For what mortal has heard the voice of the living God speak out of the fire, and lived?' (Deut. 5:23) Come and see how the voice went forth to all Israel! Each and every one according to his or her own capacity. The elders according to their power, and the youths according to theirs… Rabbi Yosi bar Hanina said: 'You may learn this by the example of the manna. Just as the manna had the flavor that each person desired and provided for the nutrition of each individual, so also the Divine Word divided into many portions for the sake of each individual.' 'And all the people perceived the thunderings' (Ex. 20:15). Since there was only one voice, why is 'thunderings' in the plural? Because God's voice mutated into seven voices and the seven voices into seventy languages so that all the nations might hear it' (Ex. R. 5:9).

Rabbi Isaac said: 'Israel were worthy of receiving the Torah immediately upon leaving Egypt.' But the Holy One said: 'Because of their servitude in clay and bricks, my children's look of good health has not yet come back and, therefore, they cannot receive the Torah at once.' God's delay in giving the Torah may be illustrated by the parable of a king's son who had just got up from his sickbed. His tutor said: 'Let your son go back to school.' The king replied: 'My son's look of good health has not yet come back yet you say, "Let him go back to school!" Let my son be indulged for two or three months with good food and drink so that he may fully recover. Then he can go back to school.' Likewise, the Holy One said: 'My children's look of good health has not yet come back. They have just been released from slaving with clay and bricks. Shall I now give them the Torah? Let my children be indulged for two or three months—with the manna, with the waters of the well, with the quail—then I will give them the Torah' (Eccl. R. 3:11).

Rabbi Joshua ben Levi said: 'With each and every word that issued from the mouth of the Holy One, the entire world, all of it, was filled with the fragrance of spices. But if the first word filled the world, where did the fragrance of the second word go? Out of God's treasuries the Holy One brought forth the wind, which carried each fragrance along in orderly succession' (BT Shab. 88b).

Rabbi Abahu said in the name of Rabbi Yohanan: 'When the Holy One gave the Torah, no bird chirped, no fowl flew, no ox lowed, not one of the *ofanim* [personified "wheels" depicting divine movement in Ez.1:16] stirred a wing, not one of the seraphim [the angelic being mentioned by Isa 6:2] said: "Holy holy, holy!"' The sea did not roar, creatures did not speak. The whole world was hushed into breathless silence. It was then that the voice went forth: 'I the Eternal am your God' (Ex. 20:2). (Ex. R. 29:9).

## SUKKOT

The festival of *Sukkot* begins in late September or early October on the 15th day of Tishri, five days after the Day of Atonement. According to the Bible it is to be celebrated for seven days (Lev. 23:41). Most Reform Jews follow this practice; others add one more day. In

Jewish tradition, the seventh day is called *Hoshanah Rabba* and the eighth day is known as *Shemini A'tzeret* ("the eighth day of convocation"). The following day is *Simhat Torah* ("The Celebration of the Torah"). In Reform Jewish practice *Shemini A'tzeret* and *Simhat Torah* are combined and celebrated immediately after the seven days of *Sukkot*.

*Etrog, Lulav, and Hadas*

On *Simhat Torah*, the annual cycle of reading the scrolls of the Five Books of Moses is concluded with the reading of the last passage of Deuteronomy (the Death of Moses) and immediately renewed with the reading of the opening passage of Genesis ("When God began to create..."). Thus the continuity of Torah study is expressed. Students entering the younger grades of the religious school are usually consecrated on this day.

In the early biblical period, *Sukkot* was the most important festival of the year as it celebrated the fall harvest. It also marked the beginning of the rainy season in Israel. The Festival of *Sukkot*, like all major Jewish holy days, carries a number of names: *Sukkot* ("Tabernacles" or "Booths"); *Hag ha-Asif* ("The Festival of the [Fall] Harvest"); and *He-Hag* ("The Festival").

This festival has two major symbols: the *sukkah* ("a booth") and the *lulav* ("palm branch") with the *etrog* ("citron"). The *sukkah* is built as a reminder of the wanderings of the Israelites in the Sinai wilderness, where they dwelt in huts or portable booths sometimes called tabernacles (Lev. 23:42; Neh. 8:14). It also recalls the primitive huts built in the field to watch over the harvest. Both rich and poor are welcomed into the *sukkah* for a meal. As a small, temporary structure, it teaches us equality among all human beings, it points to our human limitations, and it is a symbol of our ephemeral life.[6]

During *Sukkot* it is customary for some families to build a *sukkah* or, if that is not possible, to visit someone else's *sukkah* and partake of a meal in it. In some communities, it is customary to welcome historical guests, *ushpizin*, (such as the patriarchs and matriarchs) as spiritual companions into the *sukkah* during this meal. Most synagogues have a *sukkah* built on their property and decorated by volunteers. It is also customary to bring to the congregational *sukkah* offerings of food for distribution among the poor.

The origin of the *lulav*, unique to *Sukkot* observances, is obscure. Its use is based on a rabbinic interpretation of the Biblical teaching: "On the first day, you shall take the product of *hadar* (goodly?) trees, branches of palm trees, boughs of leafy trees, and willows of the brook and you shall rejoice before God" (Lev. 23:40). The practice is to combine four plants: the *lulav* (English, palm branch); the *etrog* (English, citron); the *hadas* (English,

*A sukkah*

myrtle); and the *a'ravah* (English, willow). The myrtle, willow, and palm are bound together and held with the *etrog* and waved upward and downward and in the four cardinal directions as an affirmation of God's omnipresence. Rabbinic literature offers various explanations about the use of the *lulav* and the *etrog*:

a. Nature: Just as the four species cannot exist without water, so the entire universe cannot exist without rain.

b. History: The four components of the *lulav* represent the three patriarchs (Abraham, Isaac, and Jacob) and Joseph; or, alternatively, the four matriarchs (Sarah, Rebecca, Rachel, and Leah).

c. Human Nature: The four species represent four types of Jews. The *etrog* has taste and aroma, referring to Jews who know Torah and carry out *mitzvot*. The palm branch has taste but no aroma, referring to Jews who know Torah but do not practice it. The myrtle has aroma but no taste, referring to Jews who do mitzvot without knowing Torah. The willow has neither taste nor aromas, referring to Jews who neither know Torah nor practice it. Yet the failings of one are compensated by the virtues of the other. God brings them together in one bond.

d. Human Physiology: The *etrog* stands for the heart, the palm branch for the spine, the myrtle for the eye, and the willow for the mouth. All of them must be submitted to the service of God.

As a biblical harvest festival, *Sukkot* was the Pilgrims' inspiration for the first Thanksgiving in America.

---

### Selected Texts About Sukkot From The Bible

Tell the Israelites: The fifteenth day of this seventh month is the LORD'S feast of Booths, which shall continue for seven days. On the first day there shall be a sacred assembly, and you shall do no sort of work. For seven days you shall offer an oblation to the LORD, and on the eighth day you shall again hold a sacred assembly and offer an oblation to the LORD. On that solemn closing you shall do no sort of work. 'These, therefore, are the festivals of the LORD on which you shall proclaim a sacred assembly, and offer as an oblation to the LORD holocausts and cereal offerings, sacrifices and libations, as prescribed for each day, in addition to those of the LORD'S sabbaths, your donations, your various votive offerings and the free-will offerings that you present to the LORD. On the fifteenth day, then, of the seventh month, when you have gathered in the produce of the land, you shall celebrate a pilgrim feast of the LORD for a whole week. The first and the eighth day shall be days of complete rest. On the first day you shall gather foliage from majestic trees, branches of palms and boughs of myrtles and of valley poplars, and then for a week you shall make merry before the LORD, your God. By perpetual statute for you and your descendants you shall keep this pilgrim feast of the LORD for one whole week in the seventh month of the year. During this week every native Israelite among you shall dwell in booths, that your descendants may realize that, when I led the Israelites out of the land of Egypt, I made them dwell in booths. I, the LORD, am your God' (Lev. 23:33-36, NAB).

You shall celebrate the feast of Booths for seven days, when you have gathered in the produce from your threshing floor and wine press. You shall make merry at your feast, together with your son and daughter, your male and female slave, and also the Levite, the alien, the orphan and the widow who belong to your community. For seven days you shall celebrate this pilgrim feast in honor of the LORD, your God, in the place which he chooses; since the LORD, your God, has blessed you in all your crops and in all your undertakings, you shall do nought but make merry. 'Three times a year, then, every male among you shall appear before the LORD, your God, in the place which he chooses: at the feast of Unleavened Bread, at the feast of Weeks, and at the feast of Booths. No one shall appear before the LORD empty-handed, but each of you with as much as he can give, in proportion to the blessings which the LORD, your God, has bestowed on you' (Deut. 16:13-17, NAB).

At the order of Solomon, the elders of Israel and all the leaders of the tribes, the princes in the ancestral houses of the Israelites, came to King Solomon in Jerusalem, to bring up the ark of the LORD'S covenant from the city of David (which is Zion). All the men of Israel assembled before King Solomon during the festival [of Booths] in the month of Ethanim (the seventh month). When all the elders of Israel had arrived, the priests took up the ark; they carried the ark of the LORD and the meeting tent with all the sacred vessels that were in the tent. (The priests and Levites carried them.) King Solomon and the entire community of Israel present for the occasion sacrificed before the ark sheep and oxen too many to number or count (I K 8:1-5, NAB).

On the second day, the family heads of the whole people and also the priests and the Levites gathered around Ezra the scribe and examined the words of the law more closely. They found it written in the law prescribed by the LORD through Moses that the Israelites must dwell in booths during the feast of the seventh month; and that they should have this proclamation made throughout their cities and in Jerusalem: 'Go out into the hill country and bring in branches of olive trees, oleasters, myrtle, palm, and other leafy trees, to make booths, as the law prescribes.' The people went out and brought in branches with which they made booths for themselves, on the roof of their houses, in their courtyards, in the courts of the house of God, and in the open spaces of the Water Gate and the Gate of Ephraim. Thus the entire assembly of the returned exiles made booths and dwelt in them. Now the Israelites had done nothing of this sort from the days of Jeshua, son of Nun, until this occasion; therefore there was very great joy. Ezra read from the book of the law of God day after day, from the first day to the last. They kept the feast for seven days, and the solemn assembly on the eighth day, as was required (Neh. 8:13-18, NAB).

## From The Rabbinic Literature

Rabbi Eliezer said, 'A person is obligated to eat 14 meals in the Sukkah' (during the seven days of the festival). One on each day and one each night. The sages, however, teach, there is no fixed number except that on the first night of the festival (when one must eat a meal in the Sukkah). Rabbi Eliezer also said, 'If a person did not eat in the Sukkah on the first night of the festival, he may make up for it on the last night of the festival' (M Suk. 2:6).

MISHNA: If one constructs a Sukkah on the top of a wagon, or on board a vessel, it is valid, and he may ascend thereto on the festival. If he has constructed the Sukkah on the top of a tree, or on the back of a camel, it is valid; but he must not ascend thereto on the festival days. If two walls are formed by a tree, and one by human hands, or two by human hands and one by a tree, the Sukkah is valid, but one must not ascend thereto on the festival. This is the rule: Whenever the Sukkah can stand by itself, even should the tree be removed, the Sukkah is valid, and it is lawful to ascend thereto on the festival.

GEMARA: This Mishnah is in accordance with R. Akiba only, as we have learned in a Baraitha: If a Sukkah was made on a ship, Rabban Gamaliel makes it invalid, and R. Akiba makes it valid. It happened once that Rabban Gamaliel and R. Akiba were on a ship, and R. Akiba constructed a Sukkah on the ship. On the morrow a wind blew it off, and Rabban Gamaliel said to him: Akiba, where is thy Sukkah? Said Abaye: If the Sukkah cannot withstand an ordinary wind from land, all agree that it is not a Sukkah at all; if it can hold out a storm on land, all agree it must be regarded as a Sukkah; but if it can hold out an ordinary wind from land, but not an ordinary wind from the sea, there is the point of their difference: Rabban Gamaliel holds it must be a permanent dwelling, and as it cannot withstand an ordinary wind from the sea, it is not considered as anything; but R. Akiba holds that only a temporary dwelling is needed, and so soon as it is proof against an ordinary wind from land, it is called a temporary dwelling (BT Suk. 23a, Rodkinson).

# MINOR HOLY DAYS: HANUKAH

*Hanukah* (Hebrew for "dedication") celebrates the rededication of the Second Temple to the service of God during the successful revolt of the Maccabees against the foreign cultural and religious influences of the polytheistic Seleucid rulers of Syria (the Syrian Greeks) in the second century BCE. (See Chapter One for other historical details.)

Because of its present popularity in America, people are often surprised to learn that in Jewish tradition *Hanukah* is considered a minor holiday. It is not mentioned in the Hebrew Bible. Our basic knowledge of the festival comes primarily from the Books of Maccabees I and II, which are found in

*8-branch menorah, known as a Hanukah menorah*

the Apocrypha, a collection of books edited after the canon of the Hebrew Scriptures was closed. A number of references to *Hanukah* are also found in the writings of the first century Jewish historian Josephus and in the rabbinic literature.

The primary symbol of the festival is an eight-branched *menorah* appropriately called a *hanukiyah* (with a ninth candle, *shamash*, functioning as a helper). The custom is to light one candle for each of the eight nights of the festival, beginning on the 25th of *Kislev* (November/December) with one on the first night and concluding with eight on the final night.

It is not clear why the festival is celebrated for eight days. Some claim that *Hanukah* was intended to represent a second *Sukkot*. According to the Book of Maccabees, Judah Maccabeus proclaimed that the celebration should last eight days, "with rejoicing, in the

## Selected Texts About Hanukah From The Post-Biblical Literature

Now Maccabeus and his followers, the Lord leading them on, recovered the temple and the city; and they tore down the altars which had been built in the public square by the foreigners, and also destroyed the sacred precincts. They purified the sanctuary, and made another altar of sacrifice; then, striking fire out of flint, they offered sacrifices, after a lapse of two years, and they burned incense and lighted lamps and set out the bread of the Presence. And when they had done this, they fell prostrate and besought the Lord that they might never again fall into such misfortunes, but that, if they should ever sin, they might be disciplined by him with forbearance and not be handed over to blasphemous and barbarous nations. It happened that on the same day on which the sanctuary had been profaned by the foreigners, the purification of the sanctuary took place, that is, on the twenty-fifth day of the same month, which was Kislev. And they celebrated it for eight days with rejoicing, in the manner of the feast of booths, remembering how not long before, during the feast of booths, they had been wandering in the mountains and caves like wild animals. Therefore bearing ivy-wreathed wands and beautiful branches and also fronds of palm, they offered hymns of thanksgiving to him who had given success to the purifying of his own holy place. They decreed by public ordinance and vote that the whole nation of the Jews should observe these days every year (II Mac 10:1-8, RSV).

## From The Rabbinic Literature

What is [the reason of] Hanukkah? For our Rabbis taught: On the twenty-fifth of Kislev [commence] the days of Hanukkah, which are eight on which a lamentation for the dead and fasting are forbidden. For when the Greeks entered the Temple, they defiled all the oils therein, and when the Hasmonean dynasty prevailed against and defeated them, they made search and found only one cruse of oil which lay with the seal of the High Priest, but which contained sufficient for one day's lighting only; yet a miracle was wrought therein and they lit [the lamp] therewith for eight days. The following year these [days] were appointed a Festival with [the recital of] Hallel and thanksgiving (BT Shab. 21b, Soncino).

Our Rabbis taught: The precept of Hanukkah [demands] one light for a man and his household; the zealous [kindle] a light for each member [of the household]; and the extremely zealous (add a light for each person each night), — Beth Shammai maintain: On the first day eight lights are lit and thereafter they are gradually reduced; but Beth Hillel say: On the first day one is lit and thereafter they are progressively increased. 'Ulla said: In the West [Palestine] two amoraim, R. Jose b. Abin and R. Jose b. Zebida, differ therein: one maintains, The reason of Beth Shammai is that it shall correspond to the days still to come, and that of Beth Hillel is that it shall correspond to the days that are gone; but another maintains: Beth Shammai's reason is that it shall correspond to the bullocks of the Festival; whilst Beth Hillel's reason is that we promote in [matters of] sanctity but do not reduce' (TB Shab. 21 b, Soncino).

manner of the feast of *Sukkot*" (II Mac 10:6). According to a Talmudic legend, however, there is a different explanation. When the Maccabees purified the temple after it had been used for pagan purposes, they found a small flask of oil bearing the seal of the high priest. The flask contained enough oil to light the sacred candelabrum for one night only. But, as the text adds, this oil miraculously lasted for eight days (BT Shab. 21b). This is probably the most widespread explanation, but it is not the only one. Still another rabbinic source has it that when the Maccabees entered the Temple they found eight iron spears. They stuck candles on them and kindled them, thus poetically turning each spear into a lamp (Pesikta Rabbati 2:1). A symbol of warfare thereby became a symbol of hope. For this reason, too, *Hanukah* is also called the Festival of Lights.[7]

*Hanukah* has assumed a major importance in the American Jewish community, partly because of its message of religious freedom, partly because of the joy it holds for children, and partly because of its occurrence in the Christian holiday month of December. Many parents light the festival candles with songs and jubilation. In our time, it has become customary to exchange gifts. In the synagogue, a number of games are organized for students in the religious school. Children spin the four-sided dreydl or *sevivon* (Yiddish and Hebrew, respectively for "top") and enjoy eating latkes or *levivot* (Yiddish and Hebrew, respectively for "potato pancakes") or *sufganiot* (Hebrew for a doughnut-like pastry).

At the universal level, *Hanukah* proclaims the right to be different as a basic human right in any society. The Maccabees fought for the right to live according to their tradition. Theirs was the first battle fought in history for religious liberty.

# PURIM

The festival of *Purim* ("the Feast of Lots") celebrates the heroism of the beautiful Queen Esther and her cousin Mordecai as described in the biblical book that bears her name. The main motif of The Book of Esther is how a Jewish woman captured the heart of the king of Persia through her charm and encouraged and thereby saved her people from certain death on a day to be selected through the casting of lots (*purim* in Hebrew).[8]

Esther is not a historical text but a historical novel, reflecting Jewish life in ancient Persia. The story, however, became a paradigm for many other potential calamities in Jewish history. A number of Jewish communities have recorded their own *purims* for posterity, such as *Purim* of Cairo (1323), *Purim* of Tiberias (1743), *Purim* of Adrianople (Turkey), (1786), and the *Purim* of Sebastiano (1578).[9]

One of the most joyous festivals of the Jewish calendar, *Purim* takes place on the 14th day of *Adar* (in Jerusalem on the 15th), in March/April. It is celebrated for one day. The festival emphasizes the importance of Jewish peoplehood. Masquerades, balls, and dances are the fashion. Many congregations organize fairs and carnivals. People come to

## Selected Texts About Purim From The Bible

Then Esther the queen, the daughter of Abihail, and Mordecai the Jew, wrote down all the acts of power, to confirm this second letter of Purim. And he sent letters unto all the Jews, to the hundred twenty and seven provinces of the kingdom of Ahasuerus, with words of peace and truth, to confirm these days of Purim in their appointed times, according as Mordecai the Jew and Esther the queen had enjoined them, and as they had ordained for themselves and for their seed, the matters of the fastings and their cry. And the commandment of Esther confirmed these matters of Purim; and it was written in the book (Est. 9:29-32, JPS).

And the king Ahasuerus laid a tribute upon the land, and upon the isles of the sea. And all the acts of his power and of his might, and the full account of the greatness of Mordecai, how the king advanced him, are they not written in the book of the chronicles of the kings of Media and Persia? For Mordecai the Jew was next unto king Ahasuerus, and great among the Jews, and accepted of the multitude of his brethren; seeking the good of his people and speaking peace to all his seed( Est. 10:1-3, JPS).

## From The Legends Of The Jews (Ginzberg)

Both her names, Esther as well as Hadassah, are descriptive of her virtues. Hadassah, or Myrtle, she is called, because her good deeds spread her fame abroad, as the sweet fragrance of the myrtle pervades the air in which it grows. In general, the myrtle is symbolic of the pious, because, as the myrtle is ever green, summer and winter alike, so the saints never suffer dishonor, either in this world or in the world to come. In another way Esther resembled the myrtle, which, in spite of its pleasant scent, has a bitter taste. Esther was pleasant to the Jews, but bitterness itself to Haman and all who belonged to him.

The name Esther is equally significant. In Hebrew it means 'she who conceals,' a fitting name for the niece of Mordecai, the woman who well knew how to guard a secret, and long hid her descent and faith from the king and the court. She herself had been kept concealed for years in the house of her uncle, withdrawn from the searching eyes of the king's spies. Above all she was the hidden light that suddenly shone upon Israel in his rayless darkness.

In build, Esther was neither tall nor short, she was exactly of average height, another reason for calling her Myrtle, a plant which likewise is neither large nor small. In point of fact, Esther was not a beauty in the real sense of the word. The beholder was bewitched by her grace and her charm, and that in spite of her somewhat sallow, myrtle-like complexion. More than this, her enchanting grace was not the grace of youth, for she was seventy-five years old when she came to court, and captivated the hearts of all who saw her, from king to eunuch. This was in fulfilment of the prophecy which God made to Abraham when he was leaving the home of his father: 'Thou art leaving the house of thy father at the age of seventy-five. As thou livest, the deliverer of thy children in Media also shall be seventy-five years old.'

As a memorial of the wonderful deliverance from the hands of Haman, the Jews of Shushan celebrated the day their arch-enemy had appointed for their extermination, and their example was followed by the Jews of the other cities of the Persian empire, and by those of other countries. Yet the sages, when besought by Esther, refused at first to make it a festival for all times, lest the hatred of the heathen be excited against the Jews. They yielded only after Esther had pointed out to them that the events on which the holiday was based were perpetuated in the annals of the kings of Persia and Media, and thus the outside world would not be able to misinterpret the joy of the Jews.

Esther addressed another petition to the sages. She begged that the book containing her history should be incorporated in the Holy Scriptures. Because they shrank from adding anything to the triple Canon, consisting of the Torah, the Prophets, and the Hagiographa, they again refused, and again they had to yield to Esther's argument. She quoted the words from Exodus, 'Write this for a memorial in a book,' spoken by Moses to Joshua, after the battle of Rephidim with the Amalekites. They saw that it was the will of God to immortalize the warfare waged with the Amalekite Haman. Nor is the Book of Esther an ordinary history. Without aid of the holy spirit, it could not have been composed, and therefore its canonization resolved upon 'below' was endorsed 'above.' And as the Book of Esther became an integral and indestructible part of the Holy Scriptures, so the Feast of Purim will be celebrated forever, now and in the future world, and Esther herself by her pious deeds acquired a good name both in this world and in the world to come (Chapt. XII).

the Temple dressed in costumes representing the major characters of the Book of Esther and eat *hamantashen* (Yiddish for "Haman's pockets"), three-cornered pastries filled with poppy seeds or fruit preserves. *Purim* is also traditionally a time to exchange gifts of food and to give *tzedakah* (charitable giving) as a reminder of the strength that comes from material support.

One of the characteristics of the Book of Esther is that it does not contain any prayer or any religious ritual, not even the name of God. It only mentions fasting. This caused some discomfort among the rabbis who edited the final texts. The inclusion into the Canon was done through ingenious interpretation of some oblique references, such as, "If you (Esther) keep silent in this crisis, relief and deliverance will come to the Jews from another quarter" (Est. 4:14). This was taken to refer to God. The personalities listed in the Book of Esther are also literary and moral paradigms. Thus, Haman, the villain of the story, is not only a tyrant who tried to exterminate the Jewish community in the past, but also represents every enemy of the Jewish people who has endeavored to put an end to its existence.

## OTHER HOLY DAYS

a.   *Rosh Hodesh* (Hebrew for "New Month") begins when the new moon appears in the sky. Before the destruction of the Second Temple, there were special procedures to determine the beginning of the month. Today, most Jews simply follow the printed Jewish calendars for this purpose. According to an ancient tradition, *Rosh Hodesh* was considered a woman's holiday, a reward for their refusal to join the men who sinned in the Golden Calf incident (Ex. 32). Presently, many women create new liturgies to celebrate this special day. Otherwise, its observance is limited to some changes in the daily prayer service.

b.   *Yom Ha-Shoah* (Hebrew for "Holocaust Day") is usually observed on the 27th of *Nisan* (April/May) in commemoration of the destruction of European Jewry during the Nazi period. The observance has developed a powerful emotional impact in recent years. On this day it is also considered appropriate to commemorate the Warsaw Ghetto Uprising of 1943. During *Yom Hashoah*, the ideas of survival, peoplehood, hope, courage, resistance, inhumanity, mutual help, and the sacredness of human life are stressed.

c.   *Yom ha-Atzmaut* (Hebrew for "Independence Day"), observed on the 5th of *Iyar* (May/June), celebrates the establishment of the State of Israel on May 14, 1948 and reflects the resurgence of contemporary Jewish interest in the ancestral homeland and its modern development. During this celebration, one concentrates on the ideas of freedom, survival, the centrality of Israel, the gathering of the exiles and "love of Zion."

d.   *Lag Ba-O'mer* (Hebrew for "The Thirty-third Day of the *O'mer*") is a semi-holy day, 33 days after the beginning of Passover. Between the second day of Passover until *Shavuo't*, the *o'mer* is counted. The word *o'mer* refers to the unit of measure for dry goods in biblical times. An *o'mer* of barley was brought to the Temple of Jerusalem during this period as an offering. The origin of the festival is obscure. It is celebrated on the 18th of *Iyar* (May/June) with bonfires and by playing in the meadows with bows and arrows. According to one rabbinic explanation, a plague that had killed a number of Rabbi Akiba's students ceased on this particular day (Yev. 62b). According to another, the manna began to fall in the wilderness on Lag Ba-omer, thus sustaining the Israelites who had gone out of Egypt. Among those who are more traditionally inclined, it is customary to rejoice on this day and, in particular, to hold weddings.

e.  *Tisha Be-Av* (Hebrew for "The Ninth Day of *Av*") in July/August commemorates a number of calamities that have befallen the Jewish people, including the destruction of the First Temple in 586 BCE, the fall of the Second Temple in 70 CE, and the expulsion of the Jews from Spain in 1492. Many Jews fast on this day. Once abandoned by Reform Judaism precisely because of its emphasis on past tragedies, the day has assumed a new meaning in the summer camps for youth because of the Holocaust. On *Tisha Be-Av* it is traditional to read the book of Lamentations and to wrap the synagogue columns with black cloths as symbol of mourning. Some Jews sit on low benches for the same reason.

f.  *Tu Bi-Shvat* (Hebrew for "The Fifteenth Day of Shevat") is a minor festival that had its origins in an ancient midwinter nature celebration. The rabbis placed no historic interpretation on the day. The day is also known as the New Year for the trees, when it is customary to contribute to the Jewish National Fund (JNF) to plant trees in Israel. Some congregations hold a "Tu Bi-Shvat Seder," a ritual meal of nuts and fruits, largely for the benefit of the children enrolled in religious schools, but it is also becoming very popular among ecologically oriented adults.

# ENDNOTES

1.  *Judaism Eternal.* Trans. By I. Grunfeld. 1956, Vol. 1, 3
2.  On the Jewish calendar, see EJ, 2007, Vol. 4, 354–359.
3.  More on Shabbat observance, see Gates of Shabbat, New York: Central Conference of American Rabbis, 1991.
4.  For the full Responsum, see: (http://www.responsafortoday.com/engsums/engsums.htm).
5.  For the foundational myth of "What Happened at Mount Sinai?" see, Rifat Sonsino, *Did Moses Really Have Horns?*, 82–96.
6.  On the background of the Sukkah, see, Rifat Sonsino, op.cit., 165–176.
7.  On the so-called Hanukah miracle, see, Rifat Sonsino, op.cit. 155–164.
8.  According to Joseph H. Prouser, it comes from the Hebrew root *prr* meaning "to fail." Therefore, Purim is "The Feast of Fruitless Plots." (See, Conservative Judaism, Vol. 53/2, 2001).
9.  See, "Special Purims" by Larry Domnitch in "My Jewish Learning" (online); EJ, 2007, Vol. 16, 742–744.Me et excestestem fugiati umenem sit acculla tenitiat estrum voluptate omnis nia sit modipsam aut dolorru ptaepudam fugiaer ibustius vera volupta tessit ut unto dessequatem quatem doloruntest volore sant volum sitatur aut pro vererib usapitis re volo debitas essi berum am debit rem. Tem il molorum, odit re comninim nobis velenis doluptis etur? Veliquid que et id quae volorpo rioratia perum nimus auta nosam archili gnienese dolorunt aciliandit rem dolorem. Et quodi nus rernatem rerum rest, offici ulliquia dolorit erem ne

# CHAPTER FIVE

# JEWISH LIFE-CYCLE CEREMONIES

Judaism often plays an important role in the life of individual Jews, whether they are religiously observant or not. Bound by custom, every Jew goes through critical moments in life that are often sanctified through religious ceremonies. Beginning with birth and ending with death, ancient and modern teachers of Judaism have taught us how to act with all such transformational events that occur on the path of life.

## BIRTH

According to Jewish teaching, for those who are physically capable, it is a *mitzvah* to bring children into the world. This is based on the commandment to Adam and Eve, "be fruitful and multiply" (Gen. 1:28). What is the ideal size of a Jewish family? According to the Talmud, a person is required to "bring into the world a son and a daughter" (BT Yev. 61b; Shulhan Arukh, Even Ha-Ezer, 1:5). In our time, some Jewish teachers suggest three children: two to replace the parents and another one to make up for those who perished during the Holocaust.

Reform Judaism respects the rights of the parents to decide on the number of children they should have, and therefore approves of birth-control methods. Already Jewish law permits the use of contraceptive absorbents for young women, as well as pregnant and nursing women (Tos. Niddah, 2:6).[1]

Rabbis have taught that life is sacred but that conception does not necessarily mark the beginning of life. In fact, according to the Talmud (BT Yev. 69b), "the embryo is considered to be mere water until the fortieth day." According to Rashi (see his comments on BT San. 72b), as long as the fetus does not go forth "into the air of the world," it is not considered a *nefesh* (a human being). Therefore, if the life or health of the mother is in danger, or if cases of genetic disease or malformation, abortion of the fetus is permitted. In Reform Judaism, the emotional health of the mother is considered to be as important as her physical well-being.[2]

Though the Bible does not formally mention adoption, it is a Mitzvah to adopt a child in our time. This is considered equal to procreation. The Talmud states, "Whoever raises an orphan in his house is regarded by the Torah as the child's biological father" (BT San. 19b). Adopted children need to honor and respect their adoptive parents as if they were their own biological parents. In the same vein, an adoptive child should observe all the Jewish mourning rites ordained for his/her adoptive parents.

## Entering The Covenant

If the baby is a boy, he is circumcised, and receives a Hebrew name through ritual and prayer. If the baby is a girl, she receives a Hebrew name during a special naming ceremony.

## Berit Milah: The Covenant Of Circumcision

According to Jewish law, a boy is circumcised on the eighth day of his life (the day the child is born is counted as day one) with a special ritual and appropriate prayers. This is in accordance with the Biblical command directed to Abraham, "At the age of eight days every male among you throughout your generations shall be circumcised" (Gen. 17:12).

The origins of circumcision in the ancient Near East are unclear. It is known that Egyptians were circumcised, but it seems that this practice was limited to priests. We know that the Philistines were not circumcised (Judg. 14:3; I Sam. 17:26). There is no indication that circumcision played any role in the religious life of the Sumerians, Assyrians, or Babylonians. In the modern period, Muslim boys are circumcised at a young age, though not at birth.

We do not know how and when the Israelites adopted the custom of circumcising their sons. While a number of scholarly theories have been put forth to explain the adoption of this custom, none are convincing. The most reasonable explanation is that the procedure originally was done before marriage (Ex. 4:24-26; Gen. 34). It subsequently became required of all male children in the early days of their life. Circumcision, along with the Sabbath, seems to have played a key role in preserving the Jewish identity of the Exiles after the destruction of the First Temple in the sixth century BCE (e.g., Isa. 56:4).

It is important to note that circumcision does not represent the "covenant" made between God and the Jewish people. It is only "a sign of this covenant" (Gen. 17:11). In other words, circumcision does not make the child Jewish. He is Jewish from the moment of birth. The ritual of circumcision is an element of his identity. If a child is not circumcised for any reason, including medical, that child is still considered a Jew (BT Hul. 4b; cf. Shulhan Arukh, Yoreh Deah 264/1).

A *berit milah* is performed on the eighth day, even on the Sabbath or during a holy day. However, if for any medical reason, the ceremony is postponed, it cannot take place on the Sabbath (BT Shab. 137a). Some rabbinic authorities say that if a child is born as a result of a caesarian procedure, he should not be circumcised on the Sabbath but on the next day.

The responsibility of circumcising the son devolves upon the father. Usually, he delegates this role to a professional circumciser called a *mohel* (or, also in Reform Jewish practice, a *mohelet*, a woman circumciser). According to Jewish law, many people can act as *mohalim* (pl. of *mohel*), including women, slaves, children, even a non-Jewish physician (BT Avodah Zara 26b; Maimonides, Yad, Milah ii/1). In the United States, the B'rit Milah Board of Reform Judaism trains and certifies *mohalim*. Today, there are more than three hundred practicing Reform *mohalim*—men and women alike—throughout the United States, Canada, Argentina, and Spain who have completed the program and received their certification. These *mohalim* combine a medical expertise that puts parents at ease with a religious orientation and knowledge to make *berit milah* a meaningful and beautiful part of each Jewish family's life-cycle rituals.

*Berit milah* is not performed for health reasons, even though medical experts argue that there are health benefits to circumcision, such as reduced incidences of HIV, cervical cancer (in the circumcised males' female sexual partners), syphilis, and chlamydia. In Jewish practice it is done solely for religious reasons to affirm the covenant and to strengthen the Jewish identity of the baby boy.

The ceremony of circumcision can take place in the home, hospital, or in the synagogue. The *mohel* recites a special blessing, performs the circumcision, and the whole family and friends join in the recitation of a special prayer thanking God for the opportunity to witness this joyous occasion.

Various customs have emerged throughout the years about the ceremony of *berit milah*. Among them is the lighting of a candle in the room in which the circumcision takes place (symbolizing the new light that has shone upon the family), setting aside a chair for the prophet Elijah, who is known as "the angel of the covenant" (Mal. 3:1), the appointment of a *sandek* (a Greek word meaning the person who holds the baby during the procedure), and the presence of a *kvater* and a *kvaterin* (two German words referring to a godfather and godmother who present the baby to the *mohel* before the circumcision). It is also customary to give the baby boy some wine before the procedure, or apply anesthetics to alleviate the minor pain that the child may experience.

Once the medical procedure is completed, the boy is given a Hebrew name. This is usually done by the *Mohel* (or *Mohelet*). But if a Rabbi is present, he or she officiates at this particular ceremony. Linking the given name of the child to his parents, the child is called "...[given name] *ben* [meaning son of] [father's Hebrew name] and [mother's name]," such as, *Refael ben Avraham ve-Havvah*. This name may also be confirmed at a ceremony that takes place in the synagogue. The Hebrew name is used during many life-cycle events, such as Bar-Mitzvah, marriage, and death, as well as when the individual is called up to the Torah.

The responsibility of choosing a Hebrew name for the child falls on the parents. Among Sephardic Jews, it is a great honor to name a child after a living grandparent, whereas among Ashkenazic Jews this is rarely done, and the child is usually named after a deceased relative. It is customary to celebrate the *Berit Milah* with a festive meal after the ritual of circumcision and the naming of the child.

The baby boy of an interfaith married couple is circumcised on the eighth day follow-ing the Reform Movement's Patrilineal Descent Resolution of 1983, provided the parents commit themselves to raising the child solely in the Jewish faith. However, if the interfaith couple wishes to circumcise the baby and then baptize him as Christian, the Mohel/et should refuse to circumcise the boy, because circumcision of a Jewish boy is only the first step in the identity of the child, and needs to be followed by Jewish education and other Jewish life-cycle events.[3] The Mohel/et should also refuse to participate in a religious circumcision if it does not take place on the eighth day (unless there are valid medical reasons) or if it is done without appropriate blessings.

In the case of a baby girl, a new ceremony has evolved in our time called *simhat bat* ("celebration of a girl") or *zeved ha-bat* ("the gift of a girl" among Sephardic Jews) during which the baby receives a Hebrew name at a home ceremony followed by a party. This ceremony can also take place in the synagogue with appropriate readings and prayers.[4]

## PIDYON HABEN: THE REDEMPTION OF A SON

"The redemption of a son" is done by some traditional Jewish families on the thirtieth day of the child's life. The custom is based on the belief that God acquired the first-born children of the Israelites when the first-born Egyptian males died in the tenth plague of Egypt. During temple times, it was expected that all first-born males among the Israelites were to be consecrated to the temple: "Consecrate to Me every first born; man and beast, the issue of every womb among the Israelites is Mine" (Ex. 13:1). However, the family of a first-born could redeem the child by paying the temple five shekels at the end of the child's first thirty days of his life (Num. 18:16). According to Jewish law, this ritual has limited application: the child needs to be a "male," it must be "the first issue of the womb," and it cannot be a child of a Cohen or a Levi. Similarly, children born by a caesarian section are exempt from this ritual, because they do not "breach the womb."

Among Orthodox Jews today, the first-born are redeemed by the parents from another Jew bearing the last name of Cohen (or Levi), a descendant of the ancient priestly family, by paying him five shekels of silver, or, its equivalent, like five silver dollars, and with appropriate blessings. In Turkey it was customary to give the Cohen five silver spoons. First-born sons of priests (i.e., Cohen) or Levites are not required to undergo this ceremony, because these originally were given over to the ancient Temple to be trained as clergy. This custom is not usually practiced among Reform Jews today, because Reform Judaism does not recognize a hereditary priesthood and does not accept the difference between the ancient castes, namely the difference between Cohen, Levi, and Israel. In Reform Judaism, all Jews are all equal, and there is no expectation that a future Temple, with sacrifices and a priestly caste, will be built in the future.

## RELIGIOUS EDUCATION

Religious education is the foundation of Jewish identity. To know oneself, a person needs to study his/her background, and that includes Jewish subjects. It is a *mitzvah* to study Judaism. "Happy is the person," writes the Psalmist, in whom "the teaching of the Eternal is his delight, and he studies that teaching day and night" (1:2). Every one is expected to study Torah, irrespective of background or age, as the medieval Jewish philosopher Maimonides clearly states, "Every Jew, whether poor or rich, healthy or sick, young or old and feeble, is required to study Torah" (Mishneh Torah, 1:8).

In the past, the responsibility to teach Torah belonged to the priests (Lev. 10:11). In most cases, the topics covered issues dealing with the cult and temple ritual. In addition, prophets (Isa. 1:10) and wisdom teachers (Prov. 4:2) were involved in education. In most cases, however, the basic responsibility of teaching one's child devolves upon the parent, based on the teaching of the book of Deuteronomy, "Teach them to your children" (6:6). And if the parent does not carry out this obligation, the individual must do it on his/her own.

The study of Torah (*Talmud torah*, in Hebrew) is a priority among all the Jewish religious movements around the globe. Thus, for example, the "Statement of Principles of American Rabbis" of May 1999, approved by the Central Conference of American Rabbis (Reform) reads, "We are called by Torah to lifelong study in the home, in the synagogue and in every place where Jews gather to learn and teach."

What is the purpose of study? Ancient Rabbis discussed this issue and wanted to know which of the two was more important: study or practice? The majority of scholars maintained that it is not enough to know Judaism but that the ultimate goal is to practice

Judaism: "Your study should lead to practice" (M Av. 6:5). Ultimately, Jewish knowledge must be translated into ethical behavior.

The study of Judaism includes not only history, life-cycle events, festivals, and the elements of Jewish thought, but also the Hebrew language, which is a vital link between Jews and their past. In the Diaspora, every Jew needs to learn how to read the daily prayers in the original, follow the Torah and other sources of Judaism, and have a basic understanding of the meaning of the texts. Every Jew is encouraged to master some of the basic Hebrew vocabulary that pertains to Jewish life, and to have a minimum knowledge of conversational Hebrew as well.

In our time, some parents choose to give their children a Jewish education by sending them to an all-day private Jewish school, which covers both secular and Jewish subjects. However, outside of Israel, the normative way to impart Jewish education is through afternoon religious schools that are run by congregations of different denominations. In addition, a wonderful way to learn about Judaism is through informal education at Jewish summer camps, which, in addition to various sports, include Jewish topics in their programs. Some Jewish communities offer centralized supplementary education to students who excel in their Jewish knowledge. Jewish education does not end with childhood but continues through adult ages. Presently, almost all congregations offer programs in adult education for their own members, and communities have organized adult classes of great intensity.

## BAR/BAT MITZVAH

According to the Mishnah, "At thirteen years of age, one begins to fulfill the *mitzvot*" (Av. 5:21). When a boy reaches the age of thirteen, he is called a "Bar Mitzvah," namely, one who is responsible for the performance of Mitzvot (pl. of Mitzvah). Thus he is considered an adult member of the congregation with all the privileges and duties that come with it. In our time, girls too become a "Bat Mitzvah." Among some Orthodox and Conservative Jews, a Bat Mitzvah takes place at the age of 12, and often on Sunday mornings or Friday nights, without any Torah reading. Reform Judaism does not accept any differences between boys and girls with regard to Bar/Bat Mitzvah and both boys and girls observe the same ceremony. In reality, no specific ritual is required to mark this transition. Yet, in our time, this event has become a major cause for celebration.

The ceremony of Bar/Bat Mitzvah was practiced in medieval times, but the current iteration of the ceremony reflects a more modern approach. In the past, many Reform congregations paid little attention to Bar/Bat Mitzvah arguing that children were very young to assume adult responsibilities in the community. In fact, up until a few decades ago, only boys became Bar Mitzvah. Girls did not celebrate this particular life-cycle event.

The first Bat Mitzvah ceremony took place on March 18, 1922, when Judith Kaplan, the daughter of Rabbi Mordecai Kaplan, the founder of Reconstructionist Judaism, read from the Torah at the age of 12. The first Bat Mitzvah in a Reform synagogue was celebrated in 1931.

A Bar/Bat Mitzvah ceremony is not a private affair. It takes place during a regularly scheduled congregational service when the Torah is read. Among the privileges of this life-cycle event is having an Aliyah ("going up") to the Torah for the first time in the life of the young person. Often the Bar/t Mitzvah candidate reads or chants in Hebrew from the Torah portion of the week as well as from the Haftarah ("prophetic writings") assigned to that Shabbat, together with the blessings before and after both of them. This requires extensive preparation on the part of the young adult, which may last a number of months. Jewish law also states that after a child becomes a Bar Mitzvah, he can start to don *tefillin* ("phylacteries") during certain services. (See Chapter Eight).

In Jewish life the Torah is read on Shabbat mornings, Shabbat afternoons, Rosh Hodesh, and during the week on Monday and Thursday mornings. A Bar/Bat Mitzvah can be celebrated at any of these occasions. However, the overwhelming majority of the B'ne Mitzvah (pl. of Bar/Bat Mitzvah) in the Diaspora take place on Saturday mornings. This is a major family gathering. Relatives usually travel from different parts of the country and participate not only in the religious service but also in a festive meal that takes place at its conclusion.

In recent times, many adults who have never become Bar/Bat Mitzvah in their youth have been celebrating their "Adult Bar/Bat Mitzvah" with the reading or chanting of the Torah and Haftarah. This, too, is marked with a special family meal. As some families have the tendency to organize lavish celebrations, Rabbis urge that ostentatious displays should be avoided. A number of Jews prefer to celebrate the Bar/Bat Mitzvah of their children not only in their own communities but also in Israel, for example, in Jerusalem or Masada.[5]

## CONFIRMATION

Inspired by the Protestant churches, early Reform Jews established the ceremony of Confirmation, during which young men and women of ages fifteen and sixteen celebrated their understanding of the Mitzvot as more mature individuals. Today, even though, Bar/Bat Mitzvah has become normative in most Reform congregations, numerous Reform Temples hold Confirmation services.

The term "Confirmation" is not the most appropriate term for this celebratory occasion, because Jews do not need to "confirm" anything in their faith. At best, they must assume the obligation of Torah as more mature individuals. And that is what happens during Confirmation today.

There are some differences between Bar/Bat Mitzvah and Confirmation. In contrast to the Bar/Bat Mitzvah, which is celebrated by a single individual (or, at times, by two or three, in large congregations), Confirmation is done as a class activity. Furthermore, whereas a Bar/Bat Mitzvah takes place close to the young person's thirteenth birthday, Confirmation ceremonies are usually held for young men and women in the tenth grade (some do it in the ninth; others in the eleventh or twelfth). Furthermore, in contrast to a Bar/t Mitzvah, which usually takes place on Shabbat morning, Confirmation is usually held on the Eve of *Shavuo't*, which, among others, celebrates the giving of the Torah to the Israelites. The service of *Shavuo't*, which includes Confirmation, usually concludes with a festive meal for the candidates and the families and their guests. This is an appropriate occasion for the congregation and the candidates to mark the transition of their teenagers into adulthood when they are able to better appreciate the values of Torah. Confirmation does not mark the end of Jewish education; it is only a life-cycle event along the path of life-long Torah study.

## CONVERSION TO JUDAISM

(See Chapter Two)

## MARRIAGE

Even though Jewish custom puts a great deal of emphasis on marriage and home life, the Hebrew Bible does not contain a commandment to marry. The closest we have is that, "It is not good for a man to be alone; I shall make for him a fitting helper" (Gen. 2:18), and "Hence a man leaves his father and mother, and clings to his wife, so that they become one flesh" (Gen. 2:24). Most likely this is because the Bible takes marriage for granted, and deals only with issues that emerge after marriage, such as women's rights (Ex. 21:10; Deut. 21:15-17) or divorce (Deut. 24:1-4). In the rabbinic period, marriages were extensively discussed, and a number of rules set up for this most important life-cycle event.

The technical term for marriage among the Rabbis is *Kiddushin*, namely, being set aside for purposes of sanctification. Through marriage, husband and wife "set each other aside" exclusively for one another in order to create a home for themselves and their children, whether future of already born, biological or adopted. Among the basic Jewish values affirmed during marriage are equality between the bride and the groom, mutual respect and love for one another, and conjugal pleasure that may or may not lead to procreation.

Since biblical times, marriage between close relatives has been prohibited. The initial list in the Bible (Lev.18) has been extended by the Talmudic sages (BT Yev. 21a). Rabbinic law also sets aside a few days or periods during which marriages are not celebrated. Among them, the most prominent are the Sabbath and major festivals. In addition, in Orthodox and Conservative Judaism, weddings are not held during the intermediate days of Passover and *Sukkot*, and during the counting of the *o'mer* (between Passover and *Shavuo't*) and the three weeks before *Tisha Be-Av*. These prohibitions do not usually apply to Reform Jewish practice. However, even most Reform Rabbis would abstain from performing a wedding on *Tisha Beav* or on *Yom Hashoah*, because of their tragic associations in Jewish history.

A Jewish wedding can take place in a variety of places, including a synagogue, a hotel, or even under an open sky. In the United States the officiating clergy marries the couple in accordance with secular law (and signs the marriage license) as well as Jewish custom. In other parts of the world, the bride and groom need to go through a civil marriage before their religious wedding.

## Wedding Symbols

A number of symbols are used during a Jewish wedding:

a. A *huppah* is a marriage canopy, usually built with four poles and a piece of cloth or a *tallit* on top of it. It stands for the Jewish home, and more specifically, the marriage chamber where the couple will share intimate moments, as well as God's protection. The immediate family, standing in the structure's corners, supports the couple with their good wishes and blessings.

b. The *ketubah* is the marriage contract, which is signed by the witnesses, and today often by the clergy and the couple. Originally, the *ketubah*, written in Aramaic, was designed to identify the financial obligations of the groom (*hatan* in Hebrew) to the bride (*kallah* in Hebrew) in case of divorce, and also includes the dowry that the bride brings into the marriage for which the future husband is responsible, and many Orthodox-style marriage documents still contain such clauses. Conservative Jews usually include the so-called Lieberman clause compelling the couple to appear before a rabbinic court in case of divorce. Among Reform Jews, the *Ketubah*, usually written in Hebrew, is egalitarian, and contains only the values and hopes of the couple for a blessed married life.

c. Wine is used during the ceremony as a symbol of joy.

d. The rings, which in Reform Jewish practice are exchanged by the bride and the groom, are a symbol of the couple's enduring loyalty to one another.

e.  Wrapping the couple with a *tallit*: This custom is prevalent especially among Sephardic Jews. Toward the end of the wedding ceremony, the bride and the groom are wrapped by a *tallit* ("prayer shawl") and the fringes are held by the parents of the couple, thus symbolizing the loving unity of the family.

f.  The Breaking of the Glass: At the very end of the ceremony it is customary for the groom to break a glass (or a light bulb). The origin of this custom is unclear, so a number of explanations have been offered. For some, this signifies that even at the happiest moment of their lives, the bride and groom should remember the destruction of the First and the Second Temples of Jerusalem. Others say that the marriage should last as long as it would take to put together the broken pieces of shattered glass, that is, forever. Yet, for others still, the breaking represents future challenges the couple is sure to overcome through love, courage, and determination.

Some Rabbis add other symbols, such as a unity candle, which is lit by the bride and the groom during the ceremony. Local custom very often determines the number and significance of other objects used during the wedding celebration.

## The Wedding Ceremony

In some Jewish communities, it is customary to call up the groom to the Torah for a special blessing on the Sabbath before the wedding. This is called "Aufruf" (Yiddish, for "to call up") in congregations of Ashkenazic origin. In Reform congregations both the groom and the bride receive this honor. When the couple comes down from the pulpit, they are usually showered with candy. In some Sephardic congregations, the bride and groom participate in a celebratory ceremony called "henna" during which the hands (or even feet) of the bride are painted with special paint.

Among many Orthodox Jews of Ashkenazic background, the wedding usually begins with the groom's *tish* ("table"), the groom's reception, at which the *ketubah* is signed and the groom generally offers a *devar Torah,* a presentation on a Torah text. At times, even the bride can hold her own *tish*.

Just before the ceremony, some couples go through *bedeken*, (Yiddish for "covering up" or, perhaps, "investigation"), during which the groom places a veil over the bride's face. The origin of this custom is unknown. According to one explanation, it goes back to the biblical story of Jacob who ended up marrying Leah when, in fact, he wanted to marry her sister, Rachel. In order to make sure the groom is marrying "the right bride," he himself places the veil over her. In a Reform setting, to make it egalitarian, the groom covers his bride, and then the bride may give her groom a "kippah," a head covering.

In some Jewish communities, at the start of the ceremony, the bride walks around the groom a few times. The circle is an ancient sign of protection and, by walking this circle, the bride expresses her love and care for the groom. At times, even the groom goes around the bride. The numbers of circuits vary from three to seven.

There are two parts to the wedding ceremony: The first is called *Erusin* ("Formal Betrothal"; also called *Kiddushin*, "Sanctification") and the second, *Nissuin* ("Nuptials"). During the first half of the ceremony (which, in rabbinic literature is understood as a *kinyan*, "an acquisition"), the groom gives his wife a ring, and states, *Hare at mekudeshet li be-tabaat zo kedat moshe ve-Yisrael* (that is, "Behold, by means of this ring, you are consecrated to me [as my wife] according to the laws of Moses and the custom of Israel"). In Reform Judaism, which stresses equality between sexes, the bride and the groom exchange rings, and the bride says to her groom, *hare ata mekudash li be-tabaat zo kedat Moshe ve-Yisrael* ("By means of this ring, you are consecrated to me [as my husband] according to the laws of Moses and the custom of Israel"). A blessing over the wine precedes the exchange, and the couple sips from the same cup. Following the rings, the *ketubah* is usually read before the congregation, and, at times, even signed there by the witnesses.

The second part of the ceremony, the Nuptials, includes the reading or chanting of the Seven Blessings. These blessings mention family love and link the couple to future joys in Jerusalem. Often, the couple is wrapped by a *tallit* at this point. After sipping from a second cup of wine, the groom breaks the glass, and the whole congregation joyfully shouts, *Mazal Tov*, Congratulations. It is customary to allow the couple a few moments of privacy after the wedding. This is called *yihud*, ("seclusion"), which is reminiscent of the ancient custom of consummating the marriage after the ceremony. A festive meal often follows the religious ceremony.

## Religious issues in marriage ceremonies

### Gay and Lesbian marriages

Orthodox Judaism is opposed to gay and lesbian marriages. The Bible is against homosexual relations (Lev. 18:23; 20:13). Jewish texts say almost nothing about lesbianism, in particular. The Reform movement is on record for supporting the civil rights of gays and lesbians but is divided with regard to their right for religious unions. Some Rabbis oppose it on the basis that "none of the elements of *Kiddushin* (sanctification) normally associated with marriage can be invoked for this relationship."[6] Other Rabbis, using the argument that every human being is created in the image of God, allow such marriages, but call them "Commitment Ceremonies."[7] In the United States, some states (for example, Massachusetts) recognize the validity of gay and lesbian marriages, and Rabbis who officiate at them perform regular marriage ceremonies, not commitment ceremonies.

## Interfaith Marriages

Interfaith marriages in Western societies between Jews and non-Jews have risen considerably in recent times, in some places reaching as high as 52%. This has alarmed Jewish religious leaders of all denominations. Orthodox and Conservative Rabbis strongly oppose these marriages, and participate in marriages only between two Jews in the hope that the couple will transmit their Judaism to future generations. In the Reform movement in America (not in Europe or elsewhere), while some Rabbis oppose such marriages, others are more lenient, and do, in fact, officiate at these marriages, so as not to reject the Jewish partner, and in the hope that the children would be reared as Jews. The official position of the Reform Rabbinate is that "mixed marriages are contrary to the tradition of the Jewish religion and should therefore be discouraged" (CCAR, 1909, and reiterated in 1947 and 1973). Some Reform Rabbis who do officiate at interfaith marriages in the United States purposely omit the formula, *hare at mekudeshet li … kedat Moshe ve-Yisrael* ("you are sanctified to me … according to the laws of Moses and the custom of Israel"). It should be noted that a marriage between a Jew and a person who has converted to Judaism is a Jewish marriage, and is not to be viewed as an interfaith marriage.[8]

# DIVORCE

Since biblical times, Judaism has accepted divorce, at times, on liberal grounds. The Rabbis regarded divorce as a sad occurrence and taught that "when a man divorces his wife, even the altar sheds tears" (BT Git. 90b).

According to rabbinic law, only a husband can divorce his wife. During the medieval period, following the ruling of Rabenu Gershom (tenth century Germany), the husband cannot divorce his wife against her will. However, the wife can sue her husband and recoup the monetary value written in the *ketubah*. In rabbinic law, a divorcing husband is expected to give his wife, in the presence of two adult witnesses, a divorce document called *Get*. In our days, this ceremony often takes place before a rabbinic court (Bet Din). There are very strict rules about the wording of the *Get*. Without a *Get* a Jewish women cannot remarry, and if she does, she becomes an adulteress.

Reform Judaism in America does not require a religious *Get*, and a civil divorce is accepted as valid. However, in our time, some Reform Jews are asking for a *Get*, just in case they wish to marry again someone who is of Orthodox or Conservative background, or simply because they prefer to be divorced religiously just as they were married religiously. The Reform movement has issued such an egalitarian document, and has created a special divorce ceremony called *seder peredah* ("ritual of release"). It must be noted, however, that such a document and ceremony are not recognized by more traditional Jews around the world. Reform congregations outside of the United States do require a *Get* for remarriage.[9] From a traditional perspective, the child of a woman who has remarried without a *Get* is considered a *mamzer* ("illegitimate"). Reform Judaism has abandoned this concept because it finds it unacceptable to blame the child for what the parents have or have not done.

Jewish law also considers a woman whose husband has disappeared or is missing as an *a'gunah* ("chained"), and can never remarry without obtaining a *Get*. Reform Judaism has discarded this discriminatory practice. A civil divorce will do.


# DEATH AND MOURNING


## The Mystery of Death

Death is beyond human comprehension. Because of our limited abilities, a genuine understanding of death will always elude us. According to Jewish teachings, death is part of life. Mortality, as one writer pointed out, is the price we pay for the privilege of life, love, thought, and creative work. Even though human beings have longed for immortality for many centuries, no one lives forever. We accept death, albeit grudgingly. Traditional Jewish customs on this subject vary from place to place and from time to time; but, overall, they stress moderation in grief, recognition of the reality of death, respect for the dead, and equality in death between rich and poor.


## The Mitzvah of Writing an Ethical Will

It is considered a Mitzvah in Jewish life for individuals to write not only a will identifying financial issues for their descendants but also an ethical will for the edification of their children and the ethical values by which they ought to live.[10]


## The Mitzvah of Bikkur Holim ("Visiting the Sick")

It is meritorious to visit a person who is in pain, provided, the Rabbis add, this visit does not weary the sick individual. In spending time with the suffering, one must conduct him/herself properly, paying attention to the needs of the patient. In case of terminal illness, one should not give the sick person false hopes. Simply spending time with the sick brings comfort, because the patient knows that someone cares for him/her. In the past, friends visited the sick in the hospital. Today, with shorter stays at hospitals, the Mitzvah of *bikur holim* is often taking place in the house of the recuperating patient.

## Euthanasia

Jewish teachers prohibit active euthanasia, as one must abstain from hastening the death of a patient. This is murder, and the Decalogue prohibits it (Ex. 20:14; Deut. 5:17). However, many Jewish teachers accept that, at times, it is better to resort to passive euthanasia by eliminating all heroic measures, such as artificial means of life support, and allow death to come naturally. In this case, pain-killing drugs should be administered in order to ease the remaining time of the patient.[11]

## As Death Gets Closer

With the approach of death, it is a Mitzvah for the critically ill to recite a confession of sins (*viddui*), including the *Shema'*. If a person is not able to do so, someone else can do it on his/her behalf.

## When Death Comes

When death comes, the immediate family recites the formula of *Tzidduk Hadin*, ("Justification of the decree"), which is *Baruh Atah, Adonai Elohenu, Melekh Ha-O'lam, Dayyan Ha-Emet* ("Blessed is the Eternal our God, Sovereign of the Universe, the Righteous Judge"). Through this prayer, one affirms God and the fact that death is inevitable.

## Determination of Death

The question as to when exactly death occurs is a matter of controversy among Rabbis. According to the traditional view, when breathing is stopped and the pulse has ceased, the person is declared dead. However, many liberal Jews, including a large number of Reform Rabbis, accept brain death, i.e., they proclaim that death has occurred with the secession of neurological activities.[12]

## Definition of a "Mourner" (in Hebrew, avel)

Although many people are affected by the death of a loved one, Jewish law requires that only the following seven individuals are responsible to observe the rites of mourning. They are father, mother, son, daughter, brother, sister, and a spouse.

## Time of Burial

In Jewish practice, funeral services take place as soon as possible, namely, within a day or two after death. Burying the dead is the responsibility of the spouse and the children. In their absence, other family members can carry out this Mitzvah. According to Jewish law, funerals cannot be held on Saturdays or major holy days.

## The Officiants; The Location of the Funeral Service

According to Jewish law, any knowledgeable Jewish adult can conduct a funeral service. In most cases, however, this is done either by a Rabbi or a Cantor, or by both of them sharing the pulpit. The service usually takes place in a funeral chapel, but it can also take place in the Temple's sanctuary or at graveside. Rabbinic law reserves the honor of Temple funeral to "important people," but presently more services are being held in synagogues because of the members' wish to have a memorial service in a familiar setting.

The funeral service is divided into two parts: a) In the Chapel or Sanctuary: Here the liturgy includes a number of psalms, individual prayers, and a eulogy; and b) Interment at the Cemetery: The body is brought to the grave and often placed on top of a mechanical lift. After an introductory prayer, the officiant recites the *Kaddish*, a doxology praising God. The coffin is then lowered. Before the grave is filled, it is customary for members of the family to throw some earth on the casket, as a sign of their acceptance of the reality of death. When the family returns to the house of mourning, it is customary to light a seven-day candle as a memorial to the dead.

## The Mourning Periods

In Jewish custom, there are four consecutive periods of mourning following death:

a. *Aninut* (Hebrew for "grief"): this refers to the period between death and burial during which funeral arrangements are made. Although burial takes place as soon as possible, it is permissible to postpone the funeral service "for the honor of the dead," especially in order to allow the immediate family to come together.

b. *Shiva'h* (Hebrew for "seven"): this is the official mourning that begins with burial, and lasts, according to rabbinic law, seven full days. Among Reform Jews, the first three days are considered the minimum mourning period.

The first meal that the mourners eat after they return from the cemetery is called *seudat havraah* ("Meal of Consolation"), and is prepared for them by the friends of the family. In keeping with the solemnity of the occasion, lavish display of food is discouraged.

A memorial service is usually held daily, preferably at the home of the departed, to which relatives and friends come to comfort the mourners. Rabbinic law requires the presence of ten men for this service (*minyan*). Reform Jews count women in the *minyan*. Many would conduct the service even with fewer than ten individuals.

At the time of mourning, it is considered a *mitzvah* to make a contribution to a charity in memory of the deceased.

During the *shiva'h* period, it is customary to avoid any public entertainment. It is, however, a *mitzvah* to attend religious services in the synagogue on Shabbat, when *shiva'h* is suspended.

c. *Sheloshim* (Hebrew for "thirty"): This refers to the first 30 days of mourning, including *shiva'h*. During this period it is customary to avoid festivities. The tombstone or grave marker can be dedicated, if desired, any time after the completion of this period.

d. *Yahrzeit* (Yiddish for "annual time"): In order to mark the yearly commemoration of death, mourners (whether they choose the Hebrew or the English date of death) light a memorial candle, recite the mourner's Kaddish, and are encouraged to attend services in the synagogues as well as give money to charity. Among Sephardic Jews of Spanish origin, this is called *meldado* ("reading").

According to Jewish practice, the observance of *Shivah* is "suspended" during Shabbat and festivals. Jewish law requires that *Shivah* be "terminated" when a festival intervenes, such as when death occurs during the intermediate days of Passover or Sukkot. In Reform Jewish practice, *Shivah* is "suspended" during Shabbat and mourning is suspended only on the holy day itself.

## Other Mourning Customs: Preparation of the Body

Rabbinic law requires that the body be ritually cleaned (*taharah*) and covered with a shroud (*takhrikhim*). Similarly, Jewish law frowns upon embalming of the body, for it stresses that it be returned to the dust from which it came. In Reform Jewish practice, these are options and not requirements.

## The Casket

According to Rabbinic law the coffin should be a simple affair, preferably made of pinewood.

## Closing the Coffin

The coffin is kept closed during memorial services. The family may view the body privately before the service. During the memorial service the casket is kept closed and brought into the sanctuary or left outside in an atrium.

## Shemirah ("Keeping watch")

In order not to leave the body unattended, a reader is often engaged to read Psalms up until the time of the funeral service. This, too, is an option and not a requirement for Reform Jews.

## Keria'h ("Tearing apart")

This is the symbolic rending of one's garment, and is usually done just prior to the funeral service by cutting a black ribbon placed on the lapel. In other communities, mourners actually tear a part of their coats or garments.

## Tallit, Pouch of Earth from Israel

At times, families bury the deceased with his prayer shawl or with a pouch of earth brought from the land of Israel.

## Flowers

Among Jews of Ashkenazic background the use of flowers is not permitted. Such is not the case for Jews of Sephardic origin, however, who often put flowers either on the casket or use them in the procession to the cemetery (as in the case of Turkish Jews).

## Cremation

In Jewish practice, the deceased are buried in a grave, in the earth. Rabbinic law does not allow cremation, or entombment in mausoleums. Early Reform Jews had no qualms about allowing cremation. After the Holocaust, however, even some liberal Rabbis became uncomfortable with images associated with the burning of bodies. Yet they permitted them for those who asked for it, with the understanding that ashes of cremation would be treated with respect as human remains and that ashes would not be preserved in the house.[13]

## Recitation of the Mourners' Kaddish

The Kaddish is a prayer for the living. It praises God as a source of life. As such, it is an appropriate prayer to recite at a time of mourning when there is a need to affirm life's worth in spite of loss. The Kaddish should be recited by the children, spouse, siblings, and parents of the deceased.

## Autopsy and Organ Donation

Although rabbinic law prohibits autopsies, based on the rationale that the integrity and the wholeness of the body must be preserved, Rabbis have permitted them in special situations where the saving of life (in Hebrew, *pikuah nefesh*) is at stake. Reform Jews have no objection to autopsies as long as they are performed for the clear purpose of increasing medical knowledge.

Most Jews today permit donating one's body or specific organs to science or to save someone else's life. The CCAR's Responsa Committee has specifically stated (#5763.3) that "Organ retrieval is permissible when, but not before, the patient is declared to be brain dead."

## Non-Jews at Jewish Cemeteries

Many Jewish cemeteries do not allow burial of non-Jews in Jewish cemeteries. According to Reform Jewish practice, a non-Jew can be buried in a Jewish cemetery, provided that non-Jewish services are not recited and non-Jewish symbols are not displayed.[14]

## Dedication of the Tombstone or the Grave Marker

Jewish law does not require a dedication of the tombstone. It is a question of local custom. If needed, a short service can be conducted, even by the immediate family, any time after the first 30 days of death, or as soon as the tombstone or the grave marker is in place. Most Sephardic Jews do not have a custom of tombstone dedication.

## Pebbles on the Tombstone

In many Jewish communities, usually of Ashkenazic origin, it is customary to place a small stone on the tombstone after visiting the grave. The origin of this custom is not known. For some, it is to show that the visitor was at the grave to pay respect to the deceased. For others, however, placing a pebble of stone or even some grass is reflective of the belief in resurrection, following a rabbinic interpretation of Ps. 72:16, "They shall spring up like the grass of the field."[15]

## Children at the Funeral

When there is a death in the family, children usually know about it; therefore, they should not be denied the opportunity to grieve. They, too, need to recognize that death is part of the natural course of life, even though we do not fully understand it. In particular, children (except for the very young ones) should not be excluded from attending the funeral service, if they so wish and are properly prepared for it.

## At Home

Reform Jews do not usually keep certain customs that are still prevalent among traditionally observant Jews. Among these are entering the home through a different door after the funeral, washing the hands when leaving the cemetery or when entering the home, covering mirrors, burning the shoes of the deceased, sitting on low stools, not shaving, not bathing, and not wearing a washed garment.[16]

# ENDNOTES

1. Why would a pregnant woman need to use a contraceptive absorbent? According to the same Mishnah, it is in order to avoid superfetation; i.e., if a pregnant woman, during her pregnancy, becomes pregnant again, the younger fetus could crush the first one.
2. On a Jewish view on Abortion, see CCAR Responsa, 1958 [CCAR Yearbook, Vol. 68]; S. B. Freehof, *Recent Reform Responsa*, Cincinnati, 1963; Walter Jacobs, *Contemporary American Reform Responsa*, CCAR, 1987, 23–27.
3. CCAR Responsa, #109, 1987.
4. On Birth, see, Lewis M. Barth, Ed., *Berit Mila in the Reform Context* (Berit Mila Board of Reform Judaism, 1990); Anita Diamant, *The New Jewish Baby Book* (Vermont: Jewish Lights, 1993); Simeon J. Maslin, *Gates of Mitzvah* (NY: CCAR, 1979, 7–22.
5. On Bar/t Mitzvah, see, Jeffrey K. Salkin, *Putting God on the Guest List: How to Reclaim the Spiritual Meaning of Your Child's Bar or Bat Mitzvah* (Woodstock, VT: Jewish Lights, 1996).
6. Walter Jacobs, *Contemporary American Reform Responsa* (NY: CCAR, 1987, # 201, Dated Oct. 1985, p. 298.
7. CCAR Responsa, "On Homosexual Marriages," #5756.8 (1995).
8. On Marriage, see Anita Diamant, *Jewish Wedding* (NY: Summit, 1985); Hanna and Philip Goodman, *The Jewish Marriage Anthology* (Philadelphia: JPS, 1977); Maslin, op.cit. 25–44; Nancy H. Wiener, *Beyond Breaking the Glass* (NY: CCAR, 2001)
9. On Divorce, see, Netter, Perry. *Divorce Is a Mitzvah* (Woodstock, VT: Jewish Lights, 2002).
10. On Ethical Wills, see, Judah Goldin, *Hebrew Ethical Wills* (Philadelphia: JPS, 1976) Jack Riemer and Nathaniel Stampfer. *Ethical Wills:A Modern Jewish Treasury.* (NY: Schocken 1986).
11. For a Reform Responsum on Euthanasia, see, Jacob, Walter, *American Reform Responsa.* (NY: CCAR, 1983, #78 [1950] and #79 [1980])
12. See, Rabbi Solomon B. Freehof, *Modern Reform Responsa.* HUC, 1971, #34; CCAR Responsa, #5763.3.
13. Walter, op.cit, #100 [1893 and 1980])
14. Walter. Idem. 1983, #99 [1963].
15. Solomon B. Freehof, *Reform Responsa for Our Time* (HUC, 1977, pp. 291–293).
16. On Death and Funerals, see, Ron H. Isaacs and Kerry M. Olitzky, *A Jewish Mourner's Handbook* (Hoboken: K'tav, 1991); Maslin, op.cit, 45-64; Maurice Lamm, *The Jewish Way in Death and Mourning.* (NY: Jonathan David Publishers, 2000).

# CHAPTER SIX

# JEWISH VIEWS ON LIFE AFTER DEATH

## BEYOND THE GRAVE

Some people are under the false impression that Judaism does not entertain a teaching about life after death or that it does not concern itself with what happens after we die. Thus, for example, one author stated, "What lies beyond death is not nearly so important as how we prepare to face it."[1] It is true that Judaism tends to be more this-life oriented, but that does not mean that Jewish sages have not meditated upon our fate beyond the grave. The following observations will show that Judaism has very much dealt with life beyond this earth by subscribing to various scenarios.

## DEATH: A MYSTERY

Death is beyond human comprehension. Because of our limited abilities, a genuine understanding of death will always elude us. According to Jewish teachings, death is part of life. Even though human beings have for centuries longed for immortality, no one lives forever. Therefore, we accept death as a reality, though grudgingly. As an ancient Jewish sage taught, "Those who are born are destined to die.... You were created against your will. Despite your wishes you live, and against your will you shall die" (M Avot 4:22). The overall Jewish view is that we come from dust and to dust we shall return (cf. Gen. 3:18).

Throughout the ancient Near East, people yearned for eternal life, only to realize that this is not possible. Gilgamesh, the great hero of the Babylonian deluge, learned the secret of how to defy death but, at the last moment, a serpent snuffed out the fragrance of the magical plant he was about it to eat, and, consequently, he was compelled to give up his quest for immortality (See, ANET, Tablet XI, 93-97). Similarly, Adapa, the caretaker of the city of Eridu, missed his chance to reach immortality when the gods tricked him (See, ANET, 101-103). He was bitterly disappointed but he became the wiser on account of his experience. In the Hebrew Bible, God banished Adam from the Garden of Eden, lest he partake of the tree of life and then live forever (Gen. 3:22-24).

This, however, does not mean that Jews deny the reality of life after death. Throughout the centuries, Jewish sages maintained that some kind of life does exist beyond the grave. The *Sefer ha-Hinukh*, a 13th-century Jewish book written in Spain, clearly states, "Every thinking individual in the world holds a belief in the afterlife" (Preface). However, these teachings are mostly speculative, because according to Jewish belief no one has ever returned from the other world to tell us what awaits us, and, according to some, this will happen only when the Messiah arrives. Accordingly, in traditional Jewish teachings, we find various approaches concerning life-after-death. In reality, how we imagine heaven tells us more about who we are and what our values are. Our ideas of the afterlife tell more about our concept of life than our views on death.

Here below are some of the most significant Jewish perspectives on life-after-death:

## SHEOL

According to biblical texts, when a person dies, he/she is "gathered to [one's] kin" (Gen. 25:8, 17) by going "down to *sheol*." The etymology of the word *sheol* is unknown, with some suggesting that it comes from the root "to call" (namely, that it is a place of inquiry), or that it is taken from another Hebrew root meaning, "hollow hand/place." The Bible refers to *sheol*, among others, as "the ditch," "the pit," "the realm of death," "perdition," and "the grave."

Whatever its original meaning, *sheol* seems to be located beneath the earth (Num. 16:30; Ezek. 31:14), or at the base of high mountains (Jon. 2:7), or perhaps under the waters (Job 26:5). This, it was believed, was a place of darkness (Ps. 88:13), and of silence (Ps. 115:17), enclosed by barred gates (Isa. 38:10).

For biblical Israelites, *sheol* was not a place of punishment. It is not the equivalent of "hell." Everyone who dies goes down to *sheol* (Ezek. 32:18-32; Eccl. 3:19ff). It is often a place of no return. As Job indicates, "As a cloud fades away, so whoever goes to *sheol* does not come up" (7:9).

However, the dead do not seem to disappear totally in *sheol*. They live a shadowy life of existence (Isa. 14:9-11; Ps. 88:4-7). They "chirp" (Isa. 29:4), though they are "without strength" (Ps. 88:5); they "are freed from the sickness of the flesh" (Job 3:17). God can hear their voices (Jon. 2:3). And, in some rare occasions, they can even be brought up back to earth, as in the case of King Saul who forced the woman of En-Dor to raise the prophet Samuel from his grave (I Sam. 28:8-15). God has power over *sheol* and can draw out those who are worthy (Ps. 30:4; 49:16).

## RESURRECTION; HELL AND PARADISE

The idea of the resurrection of the body (*tehiyyat ha-metim*), which is based on the belief that the body will be brought back to life after death with the former or new soul, appears in the Bible toward the end of the biblical period, first as a symbol of national renewal (Ezek. 37), and then as a hope for a limited few: "Many of those that sleep in the dust will awake, some to eternal life, others to reproaches, to everlasting abhorrence" (Dan. 12:2; cf. Isa. 25:8; 26:19). During the second commonwealth, the Pharisees promoted the belief in resurrection, whereas the Sadducees rejected it. It is not known when or from where this idea came into Judaism. However, we know that it became a foundational belief among many Jews about the second century BCE, perhaps as a hope for those who were suffering under the Greek and Roman oppression. The Rabbis refer to this event at the end of time as *tehiyyat ha-metim* ("resurrection of the dead"), and to the period when it will presumably take place as *o'lam ha-ba* ("the world to come"), *a'tid lavo* ("what is to come"), or *yemot ha-mashiah* ("the days of the Messiah").

The Rabbis proclaimed that, in principle, "All Israelites have a share in the world-to-come" (M San. 10:1). However, for some ancient Rabbis, there are a few exceptions: For example, he who says that resurrection of the dead is not prescribed by the Torah, or those who say that the Torah is not divine, as well as an Epicurean[2] (idem)—these will not be resurrected. Some individuals, like the evil kings, Jeroboam, Ahab, and Manasseh, will not be resurrected (M San. 11:2). On the other hand, many Gentiles will benefit from this blessed event: "Righteous gentiles have a place in the world to come," said Rabbi Joshua ben Hananiah (Tos. Sanh. 13:2).

Even though the idea of bodily resurrection in the world-to-come was accepted by most Jews after the destruction of the Second Temple in 70 CE, the Rabbis remained divided regarding the timetable of this occurrence. The majority seems to prefer the following order: First the Messiah will come; then there will be a Final Judgment, during which the righteous will be rewarded (by going to Paradise) and the wicked punished (by going to Hell); finally, resurrection will take place. There is also a great deal of rabbinic speculation on how exactly this process of resurrection will take place at the end of time, with some being more fanciful than the others.

The ancient Rabbis, aware of the fact that resurrection is not clearly stated in the Torah until the later periods, tried to prove, through forced interpretation of the texts, that the concept is implied even in some earlier material. The following teachings represent an attempt, albeit a grammatically incorrect one:

It has been taught: Rabbi Meir said: From where do we know that [the belief of] resurrection comes from the Torah? [Answer:] From the verse, "Then shall Moses and the children of Israel sing [*yashir*] his song unto the Lord" [Ex. 15:1]: not *sang* but *shall sing* [namely, in the future] is written: thus resurrection is taught in the Torah. Likewise thou read, "Then shall Joshua build [*yivneh*] an altar unto the Lord God of Israel" [Josh. 8:30]: not *built*, but *shall build* [namely, in the future] is written: thus resurrection is intimated in the Torah. Again, Rabbi Joshua ben Levi said: From where is [the belief of] resurrection derived from the Torah? [Answer:] From the verse, "Blessed are they that dwell in thy house: they shall ever praise you" (Ps. 84:5). Not *they have praised you* but *they shall praise you* [namely, in the future] is stated: thus resurrection is taught in the Torah. (BT Sanh. 91b)[3]

## Hell and Paradise

The concept of Garden of Eden (*Gan E'den* in Hebrew) has its origins in the ancient Near Eastern literature. The Sumerians spoke of an idyllic island called Dilmun, the Babylonians of a garden of jewels. In the Hebrew Bible it refers to the garden planted by God for Adam and Eve (Gen. 2-3). During the rabbinic period this garden was identified with the final abode of the righteous after death. Some Rabbis provided different images of what *Gan E'den* would look like. For example, Rav, a Babylonian Talmudic scholar, opined that "In the world-to-come there is neither eating nor drinking; no procreation of children or business transaction, no envy or hatred or rivalry but the righteous sit enthroned, their crowns on their heads, and enjoy the luster of God's Presence" ("*Shekhinah*") (BT Ber. 17a).

Immanuel ben Solomon of Rome, a medieval Jewish writer and a contemporary (perhaps even a student) of Dante, was even more dramatic. In his book *Hell and Paradise*, he describes a section of Paradise as a place where, "Tables and candlesticks, thrones and crowns were there to be seen; they were for the souls that were pure and clean; there was a throne of ivory, great in size, overlaid with gold in wealth, giving life unto those who reached it, and unto their flesh giving health."[4]

On the other hand, "Hell" (*ge-hinnom*, "Gehenna" in the Bible) originally referred to a valley south of Jerusalem where a heathen cult practiced unspeakable acts, including burning of children (e.g., II K 23:10; Jer. 7:31). During the rabbinic period, Hell was conceived as a place of torment for the wicked after death. During medieval times, the same Immanuel of Rome described one scene in it in vivid terms: "there were pits full of serpents, poisonous and flying, hundreds and thousands of lions and leopards were dying, and round about angels of death with their swords were plying."[5] These terrifying descriptions of Hell were most likely used to frighten people about the consequences of wicked acts on this earth, just as the soothing terms of "Paradise" gave longing for those who were righteous or even suffering unjustly here.

The belief in resurrection has remained constant among many Jews for centuries, and is maintained today primarily by "traditional" Jews but also by some liberal Jews. The concepts of "Hell" and "Paradise" have influenced Christianity and Islam in their own ideologies about life after death.

Orthodox Judaism, and some non-Orthodox Jews, still maintain the belief in resurrection, and include prayers in their standard prayer books clearly referring to *tehiyyat ha-metim* ("resurrection of the dead"). Reform Judaism, in the Pittsburgh Platform, rejected this belief in 1885, but some Reform Jews today have returned to this assumption as a possibility. Thus, for example, the most recent Reform prayerbook, *Mishkan T'Filah* (2007) provides two options for the worshipers: in the same prayer, one can say either *mehayye ha-kol* ("[God] who gives life to all") or *mehayye ha-metim* ("[God] who revives the dead").

## IMMORTALITY OF THE SOUL

The belief in the immortality of the soul has its origin in Greek thought as reflected in the early Pharisaic writings, which combine it with the resurrection of the body. According to the Jewish-Greek philosopher, Philo of Alexandria (20 BCE–50 CE), after death, the body disintegrates and the soul returns to heaven where it rejoins other souls. The same idea was advanced by another Hellenistic Jew, the author of *The Wisdom of Solomon*, a book found in the Apocrypha (see 3:1-3), and in a disguised form by the great Jewish philosopher Maimonides (1135–1204), who spoke of the immortality of the "rational soul." The Talmud states that, "For a full twelve months [after death], the body is in existence, and the soul ascends and descends. After twelve months, the body ceases to exist, and the soul ascends but does not descend anymore" (BT Shab. 152b). It should be noted that most medieval Jewish philosophers spoke of "the survival of the soul" (*hisharut ha-nefesh*) and not of "the eternality of the soul" (*nitzhut ha-nefesh*), because they believed that God, being omnipotent, could destroy the soul at will.

In the modern period, the first Jewish thinker who openly embraced the idea of the immortality of the soul was Moses Mendelssohn (1729–1786), a pre-Kantian philosopher of the German Enlightenment, who stressed that the human soul is imperishable and possesses self-awareness. Reform Judaism has made this idea a cornerstone of its ideology.

Ever since the Philadelphia Conference of 1869, until recent times, Reform Jews praised God as the one "Who planted within us immortal life." Rabbi Kaufmann Kohler, one of the conveners of the Pittsburgh Conference of 1885, based this belief on "the God-likeness of the human soul, which is the mirror of Divinity."

Today, the concept of "soul" is debatable. Is the "soul" equivalent to "spirit," "mind," or "self"? At our time when we think of energy turning into matter (and vice versa), can we still speak of the ancient division between body and mind? Many people doubt it.

## Reincarnation

The Hebrew term for this idea is *gilgul neshamot*, literally, the "rolling of souls." It is not clear when it became part of the Jewish belief system, but it appears to be very old. It is said that Anan ben David, the 8th-century leader of Karaism, a Jewish sect, believed in the transmigration of souls. It is definitely part of the mystical literature, primarily the Zohar, the 13th-century classic text of Kabbalah.

Those who embrace reincarnation hold that the soul has an independent life, existing before and after death. Once the soul is separated from the body at the point of death, it returns to its source for its next "assignment." This movement can be repeated various times, the primary purpose of which seems to be the purification of the soul of its impurities. It is important to note that in Jewish thought, reincarnation is not a substitute for resurrection.

According to the mystics, there are three types of reincarnation: a) *Gilgul*—this is when the soul penetrates the body at pregnancy. b) *I'bbur*—this is when an "old" soul enters the body sometime during the body's lifetime, and finally c) *Dibbuk*—this is when an "evil" soul unites with the body of an adult; this, however, requires an exorcism.

The idea of reincarnation was both defended and attacked by many Jewish thinkers. Kabbalists usually supported it and non-mystical theologians were critical of it. Today, this belief is not widespread among Jews, even though it still has a strong appeal among a vocal minority.

## After Death: Perhaps Nothing

There are many prominent Jewish thinkers who maintain that we have no verifiable evidence that there is life-after-death. Sigmund Freud (1856–1939), for example, thought the whole idea is a "wish fulfillment."[6] Once death arrives, he said, there is a return to inorganic lifelessness. Similarly, Rabbi Richard L. Rubenstein (b. 1924) wrote, "I was convinced that I had arisen out of nothingness and was destined to return to nothingness."[7] Rabbi Alvin Reines (1926–2004) expressed a similar idea; "I do not believe there is a personal afterlife. When I die, my individual identity will be annihilated, and both my psyche and body will perish."[8] Rabbi Louis Jacobs (1920–2006), a British scholar, maintained an agnostic position: "we simply can have no idea of what pure spiritual bliss in the Hereafter is like."[9]

## LIVING THROUGH OTHERS

There are a number of Jews who believe that after we die, we shall live through what we have accomplished on this earth, for as Philip James Bailey (1816–1902), an English poet, once wrote, "We live in deeds; not years." This can take various forms:

### Biological Immortality:

We can achieve immortality through our children and their descendants: they carry our name, our genes, often bear our physical resemblance, and hold memories about us. In the Apocrypha, Ben Sira (second century BCE) wrote, "The father may die, and yet he is not dead, for he has left behind him one like himself" (30: 4). Obviously, this does not apply to those who do not have children of their own, but it does apply to those who have adopted children, or to step-parents.

### Immortality Through Our People:

As we are part of the Jewish people, we all feel the pain of its suffering and take pride in its accomplishments. Though we expect to pass away one day, we still maintain, *a'm Yisrael hai*, "The people of Israel lives." In that spirit, Rabbi Bernard Raskas (1924–2010) stated, "I was with my people when they were part of the exodus from Egypt. I stood with them at Mount Sinai to receive the Ten Commandments ... Every time I touch down at the airport in Israel, I think of Theodore Herzl, David Ben-Gurion, and Golda Meir."[10] By extension, some individuals can celebrate their immortality through humanity as a whole. Thus, Rabbi Joshua L. Liebman (1907–1948) spoke of the "immortality of the human race."[11]

## Immortality Through Our Influence and Deeds:

Just as we have been influenced by others, such as parents, teachers, or friends, we, too, have the capacity to shape and mold others with our words or deeds, at times even without being aware of it. When we carry out laudable acts, our beneficiaries praise and bless us for many years to come. For as the poet Hugh Robert Orr (1887–1967) wrote, "They are not dead who live in hearts they leave behind." Thus, Rabbi Alexander Schindler (1925–2000), the former head of the Union of American Hebrew Congregations (now, Union for Reform Judaism), talked about "the immortality of the human deed."[12] Furthermore, through our influence, we can also become the transmitters of Jewish values as Rabbi Harold M. Schulweis (b. 1925), affirmed, "My Jewishness is validated not only by the origins of my past, but by the continuities resonating in my grandchildren. I am not only descendant but ancestor of my tradition."[13]

Influence, however, is a two-way street. Our good deeds are hopefully recognized and, at times, even praised, but our evil actions often remain as a black mark on our reputation. Thus, for example, Alexander Fleming, a British bacteriologist who discovered penicillin in 1928 will be immortal for all the good things he did for humanity, but Hitler, the chancellor of Nazi Germany, will always remain accursed.

The diversity of opinion on life after death within Judaism comes from the recognition that death is a mystery, but also from the hope that our life has a meaning and that something of us will remain forever, even though, we fully understand, that it is impossible for us to conceive of "eternal life." I personally tend toward the belief that, after I die, I will remain in the memory of those I have influenced through my words and actions, but I also assume that the energy I now have will eventually join the sources of nature after I am gone. But all this is speculation. True, it would be comforting to find out what would happen to us after we die. But that knowledge is not vouchsafed us. We simply do not know. We can only hope, and therefore must try to live every day fully, creatively, and nobly. [14]

## ENDNOTES

1. Samuel Rosenbaum, *To Live as a Jew*. (New York: KTAV, 1969), 193.
2. Term is not clear. Perhaps it applies to gentiles and Jews who are opposed to rabbinic instructions.
3. In reality, in Biblical Hebrew, the imperfect tense (what the Rabbis spoke of as the "future") simply refers to an act that is not completed. Therefore, their interpretation is forceful and tenuous.
4. Immanuel ben Solomon of Rome, *Tofet and Eden*. Translated by H. Gollancz (London: University of London, 1921) 6.

5. Op.cit., 46.

6. Sigmund Freud, *The Future of an Illusion.* (New York: Anchor Books, 1964), 54.

7. Richard I. Rubenstein, "The Making of a Rabbi," ed. I Eisenstein, Varieties of Jewish Belief (New York: Reconstructionist Press, 1966), 179.

8. Alvin Reines, "Death and Afterexistence: A Polydox View," in Rifat Sonsino and Daniel B. Syme, *What Happens After I Die?* (New York: UAHC Press [today, URJ], 1990), 136.

9. Louis Jacobs, *A Jewish Theology.* (New York: Behrman House, 1973), 321.

10. Bernard S. Raskas, "A Jewish View of Immortality," *The American Rabbi*, 19/1, Aug. 1986, 59, 58.

11. Joshua L. Liebman, *Peace of Mind.* (New York: Benta, 1961), 109.

12. Alexander M Schindler, "Here and Hereafter," *What Happens After I Die?* Op.cit., 75.

13. Harold M. Schulweis, "Immortality Through Goodness and Activism," *What Happens After I Die?* Op. cit., 105.

14. FOR FURTHER STUDY: Neil Gillman, *The Death of Death: Resurrection and Immortality in Jewish Thought.* (Vermont: Jewish Lights, 1997); Rifat Sonsino and Daniel B. Syme, *What Happens After I Die? Jewish Views of Life After Death* (NY: URJ, 1990).

# CHAPTER SEVEN

# JEWISH COMMUNITY ORGANIZATIONS

## THE SYNAGOGUE

### *From Temple to Synagogue*

The word "synagogue" comes from Greek, and means "place of meeting." During early biblical times, the Israelites went to the local temples to worship God by offering different kind of sacrifices. Thus, for example, Elkanah, the father of Samuel, the prophet and seer, "used to go up year by year from his town to worship and to sacrifice to the Eternal at Shiloh" (I Sam. 1:3). After the Deuteronomic Reformation in the seventh century BCE, when all the local temples were destroyed by the royal decree of King Josiah of Judah, the Israelites came in from other parts of the country as pilgrims to worship God solely in a central sanctuary in Jerusalem. The Temple became the main religious institution of the country. It is here that priests imparted their teachings, the Levites sang their songs, and the high courts passed judgment. The Temple also became the economic center of the kingdom. Some of the rules and regulations about the cult in the book of Leviticus most likely go back to the practices of this First Temple. This pattern continued for centuries, even after the Exile when the returning Jews built themselves a Second Temple in the city of Jerusalem (sixth century BCE).

The synagogue developed during the Hellenistic period, but its origins are obscure. Some scholars trace it back to the Exilic period when Jews lived in Babylonia after the First Temple was destroyed in 586 BCE. It is most likely that even before the destruction of the Second Temple (how far back is unclear), some Jews began to gather outside of the temple compound for a variety of reasons, including worship. The earliest mention of a synagogue comes from Egypt in the third century BCE. During the first century CE, the synagogue was already an established institution, and a number of them co-existed with the Temple of Jerusalem. The Jewish historian Josephus (first century CE) is very much aware of the central role that the synagogue played in the study of Torah during the Second Temple period (Against Apion 2:175).

*The Second Temple of Jerusalem*

The New Testament mentions that on several occasions Jesus and Paul attended synagogues (e.g., Luke 4:14:16-22; Acts 13:13-16).

Things changed dramatically after 70 CE when the Romans destroyed the Second Temple. After that tragedy, there was no longer a special place to worship God through offerings. The altar and the priests were gone. Most of the Jewish population was forcefully removed from the capital. Rather, Jews congregated by necessity in certain meeting places, often in the Galilee, where they could express the longings of their heart.

The Synagogue became the primary place of worship after 70 CE by combining various functions unknown before in the Temple of Jerusalem: It was a *bet tefilah*, "a house of worship," a *bet keneset*, "a house of meeting," as well as a *bet midrash*, "a house of study." As these terms indicate, it was to this new gathering place that local Jews flocked to engage in daily study, to worship three times a day, and to discuss community matters. As a result, hundreds of such new community centers emerged to meet the needs of the communities around the country. In large cities, the synagogues were larger and luxurious; in other places they were no bigger than a modern living room. In the last few decades archaeological digs undertaken in Israel have uncovered many synagogues around the country in places such as Bar'am, Capernaum, Jericho, Gamla, and Masada.

Today, some Jewish houses of worship are called "synagogues," whereas others are called "temples". However, both terms refer to the same institution. The first word comes from Greek, and the second from Latin. Both refer to the same sanctuary.

## Synagogue Traditions

There is no required structure to a synagogue, even though historically speaking, among Sephardic Jews, the pulpit is usually placed in the center and the congregation sits around it, whereas among Ashkenazic Jews, the pulpit is at one end of the building, usually in front of the Ark, and the congregation is seated auditorium style facing the Ark. According to the Jewish tradition, in the Western World, the congregation worships facing east toward Jerusalem, in remembrance of the Holy of Holies that used to be in the Temple of old.

Following the second commandment in the Decalogue, synagogues do not contain any images, paintings, or sculptures of human beings. This is done in order to allow for undistracted devotion, even though certain animal designs or abstracts are permissible. In the past, however, especially in the early Roman period, some synagogues, such as the one in Dura-Europus (third century CE), did contain paintings of human beings.

Jewish tradition requires that the synagogue be treated with reverence. Thus, for example, it must be kept clean, it should not be used for purposes of taking shelter from the heat or rain, or to take a shortcut in the street, and, unless it is for religious purposes, one is forbidden to eat, drink, or sleep in places of worship. Jewish law specifies that members of the community may compel one another to build a synagogue and to buy books for study purposes. (See Shulhan Arukh 12).

## Religious Objects in the Synagogues

1. *Sefer Torah* ("Scroll of Torah")

Each synagogue usually has one (or more) Torah Scroll, containing "The Five Books of [attributed to] Moses." Though the writing of some scrolls may be larger than others, they all the have the same number of columns: 248 columns written on 80 pieces of parchment.

These scrolls are professionally inscribed by a *sofer* ("scribe") on a parchment, using a special ink and pen. Tradition dictates that the scribe should not write by memory but using a correctly written text in front of him. In the past, all scribes were male. Reform Judaism does not object to a woman acting as a scribe (*soferet* in Hebrew), however, and there are quite a few today.

*A Sefer Torah*

The Torah Scroll is adorned with a *keter* ("a crown") on *rimonim* ("pomegranates") that are placed over the wooden rollers of the scroll. Most often these scrolls are covered with decorated mantles. A *hoshen* ("breastplate") is usually placed on these mantles. Many congregations have colored mantles for the weekdays, Sabbaths, and Festivals, and white ones for the High Holy Days. It is also customary not to touch the parchment itself during the Torah reading; instead a *yad* ("hand") is used as a pointer to help the reader follow the text without losing his place. In Reform Judaism, women are allowed to read from the Torah as well.

*Holy Ark*

The Torah is considered a holy object, and needs to be treated with reverence by the congregation. Every few years, a Torah scroll should be checked by a competent scribe to make sure it does not contain mistakes or unreadable words or letters. When the Torah can no longer be used because of old age or because it has suffered decay, it cannot be thrown away but must be either stored at a *Genizah* (a storage place for religious books and scrolls containing the name of God) or buried in a cemetery through a special service.

### 2. *Aron ha-Kodesh* ("Holy Ark")

Each synagogue contains a Holy Ark in order to house the Torah scroll/s. This could be an upstanding simple box or an ornate container. Often arks are covered with a *parokhet*, (a "curtain-covering") of different colors.

### 3. A *Bimah* ("Pulpit")

In modern synagogues in the West, the pulpit usually stands in front of the Ark. It is from here that the service is conducted. Sephardic Jews call the pulpit a *tevah* ("box"); it is usually placed in the middle or toward the opposite end of the sanctuary. In Orthodox and some Conservative synagogues, the officiant faces the Ark during worship, whereas in Reform congregation, he/she faces the congregation, and may turn toward the Ark during some parts of the service.

*Pulpit, Synagogue of Turin*

### 4. A Seven-Branch *Menorah* ("Candelabrum")

On the side of the pulpit, most synagogues have a seven-branch *menorah*. The seven-branch *menorah*, surrounded by two olive branches and the word "Israel" underneath, is now the official symbol of the State of Israel. It is for this reason that in front of the Israeli Knesset today stands a giant Menorah. The Star of David is a more recent symbol in Jewish life (see Chapter Eight).

*Menorah in front of the Israeli Knesset*

The *Menorah* is first mentioned in connection with the Tabernacle in the wilderness period (Ex. 25:31-40; cf. 37: 17- 24). The Temple built by King Solomon had ten lampstands (I K 7:49). When the Romans captured Jerusalem and destroyed the Second Temple, they carried away the *menorah* to Rome as a trophy. A depiction of it is now visible in the Arch of Titus, which is located between the Coliseum and the Roman Forum.

This seven-branch *menorah* should not be confused with the *Hanukah menorah*, which has eight branches plus a helper light. (See Chapter Eight).

### 5. A *Ner Tamid* ("Perpetual Light")

In front of the Ark, synagogues place a "perpetual light" lit either with electricity or with cotton wicks in oil. This perpetual light is traced back to the tabernacle (Ex. 27:20; Lev. 24:2), where a perpetual light was to be kept "regularly." In the rabbinic period "regularly" was interpreted as "permanently."

The Perpetual Light stands either for the Presence of God (BT Shab. 22b) or as the Symbol of Torah (Ex. R. 36:2).

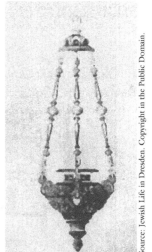

Source: Jewish Life in Dresden. Copyright in the Public Domain.

*Perpetual Light*

### 6. *E'zrat Nashim* (Women's Gallery)

In the Temple of Jerusalem, women remained in the "Women's Court." In Orthodox synagogues today, and in some Conservative synagogues too, women sit separately from the men in an area called "Women's Gallery," which is separated by a *mehitzah* ("partition"). The rationale is to allow each sex to concentrate on prayer rather than on

*Women's Gallery in the Synagogue of Lyon*

*View from the Women's Gallery in the
Synagogue of Saluzzo*

each other. In Reform synagogues,
and in many other denominational synagogues, men and women sit next to one another
without such a concern.

### 7. Prayerbooks

Prayerbooks, a creation of the ancient Rabbis, are used during worship services in the
synagogue or at home. There were no standard prayerbooks during the temple period.
Sacrifices were offered by the priests, while the worshipers, with few exceptions where they
were required to recite a personal prayer (e.g., during the offering of the first ripe fruit,
Deut. 26:5-10; 12-15), watched mostly in silence.

Temple worship centered on offerings brought to the altar of certain animals, liquids,
grains, or fruits. Some animals were burned totally; others were partly burned and the
rest eaten by the priests. During the second temple, we find references to the levitical
priests singing during services (e.g., I Chr 15:17-24). On occasion, prayer services were
conducted at the temple in addition to sacrifices. When the Temple of Jerusalem was
destroyed by the Romans in 70 CE, prayer totally replaced sacrifice, and rabbinic sages
started to formulate prayers for various occasions.

The ancient Rabbis created the prayerbook based on the temple worship schedule, which required offerings in the mornings and late afternoons, but added a third one for the evening (BT Ber. 26b). The morning service is called *shaharit*, the afternoon, *minhah*, and the evening, *ma'ariv* (Sephardic Jews call it *a'rvit*). Usually, *minhah* is immediately followed by *ma'ariv*.

The Jewish prayerbook is built on three basic components: 1. The recitation of the *Shema'* (Deut. 6: 4ff ) and its blessings; 2. The *tefillah*, the nineteen prayers of petition; and 3. The concluding prayers with a doxology (*kaddish*) at the very end. The prayerbook contains three different types of prayers: petition, gratitude, and praise. (For the theological issues involved with prayers, see Chapter Two). In Jewish practice, any knowledgeable adult can lead this service. (In Orthodoxy, only males.) A quorum (*minyan*) of ten individuals (in Orthodoxy, only males) is usually needed for any formal service.

The language of prayer is Hebrew, with some prayers read in Aramaic. However, Jewish law allows the recitation of all prayers in the vernacular as well. Orthodox Jews and Conservative Jews pray primarily in Hebrew. Others include some prayers in the language of their country.

The first compilation of prayers was edited by Rav Amram Gaon of Sura, Babylonia, in the 9th century, in response to a question from the Jewish community of Barcelona, Spain. In 1486, Joshua Solomon Soncino printed the first Hebrew prayerbook, *Mahzor Minhag Roma* ("A Prayer Book of the Roman Rite"), in the city of Soncino, Italy, following the Ashkenazi tradition. Since then, many prayerbooks have been published by different religious groups all over the world to meet individual and community needs. The prayerbook for daily services, festivals, and Sabbaths is called *siddur*, whereas the prayerbook for the High Holy Days is referred to as *mahzor*.

Today, for daily, Sabbath and festival services, most Orthodox Jews use *The Complete ArtScroll Siddur* (2003); Conservative Jews have their *Siddur Sim Shalom* (2003); the Reconstructionist Jews, *Kol Haneshamah* (1998) and Reform Jews, *Mishkan T'filah* (2007).[1]

## SYNAGOGUE PERSONNEL

In today's synagogue the work is done cooperatively between the professionals and lay volunteers. Among the professionals:

## The Rabbi

The Rabbi (meaning, "teacher," "master") is the religious leader of the congregation. In the past only men were ordained Rabbis. The first woman to become a Rabbi in the United States is Sally Priesand, who received her ordination in the Reform movement in 1972. Other Jewish denominations followed suit, beginning with Sandy Eisenberg-Sasso by the Reconstructionists (cf. Chapter Three) in 1974 and Amy Eilberg by the Conservatives (cf. Chapter Three) in 1985. However, the Orthodox (cf. Chapter Three) still refuse to ordain women Rabbis, mostly based on traditional teachings and a rabbinic principle that considers *kol ishah* ("the voice of a woman") to be sexually provocative and, therefore, an impediment to prayer and meditation (see, BT 24a; Kid. 70a).[2] Today, there are more than six hundred women Reform Rabbis in America, almost a third of all the Reform Rabbis in the United States and Canada.

Rabbis are usually ordained by reputable seminaries sponsored by different religious Jewish denominations. For example, as we noted in Chapter Three, the Reform movement has its Hebrew Union College-Jewish Institute of Religion (HUC-JIR), with its four campuses in New York, Cincinnati, Los Angeles, and Jerusalem. The Conservative movement trains its rabbis at the Jewish Theological Seminary in New York or at the American Jewish University in Los Angeles. On the other hand, Hebrew College of Boston is a non-denominational rabbinic school that prepares rabbis for various Jewish denominations in the United States.

After completing college, rabbinic students master a number of Judaica subjects, such as Hebrew, the Bible, rabbinic literature, Jewish philosophy, Jewish education, etc., and receive their ordination upon completion of all the academic requirements. This program ordinarily lasts five years, including a year of study in Israel. Even though, in recent times, a few individuals who have a good Judaica background have been privately ordained by a group of Rabbis, this is not normal in Jewish life.

The Rabbi is in charge of the overall religious philosophy of the institution, and presides over life-cycle events and congregational worship. The difference between a Rabbi and a layperson in the synagogue lies in the extensive training the Rabbi has received in matters of Jewish law and lore. Religiously speaking, however, there is nothing that a Rabbi does that another layperson cannot do, including leading prayers and officiating at life-cycle events. In the United States, secular laws require that only an ordained clergy member perform a wedding.

The relationship between a Rabbi and a congregation is contractual. If both parties are happy with one another, this contact is renewed many times. In large congregations, many Rabbis begin their career as Assistant Rabbis. If they remain in their position, they are promoted to Associate Rabbis and eventually become Senior Rabbis.

---

## On The Title "Rabbi"

The Hebrew word "Rabbi" means "my master," and comes from the word *rav*, which means "big" or "great." As a title, it appears in the Bible in construct with other nouns, such as, *rav hovel* ("chief of sailors" Jon. 1:6), or *rav tabbahim* ("chief of guards", II K 25:8). In time, it assumed the meaning equivalent to "Sir." In the rabbinic period, before 70 CE, no rabbinic sage was ever called "Rabbi." Even in the New Testament, the title appears to be more honorific and is applied to teachers in general (cf. Math. 23:7-8). Slowly, however, the title Rabbi was given to recognized religious leaders of the community. Thus, for example, even though Hillel (c. 110 BCE–10 CE) was not referred to by any title, toward the end of the first century CE, Simeon ben Gamaliel I, and Johanan ben Zakkai are called "Rabban," as a sign of respect for the president of the Sanhedrin. By the second century, the title "Rabbi" was applied to major rabbinic sages. Thus, for instance, Akiba, was always called "Rabbi Akiba" (c. 40–137 CE), and the editor of the Mishnah, Judah ha-Nasi (c. 135–220 CE), carried the title "Rabbi" (or, simply "Rabbi" without a name). During the Talmudic period, sages in Israel were called "Rabbi," but those in Palestine, "Rav." Today, Ashkenazic Jews use the title "Rabbi," whereas Sephardic Jews prefer the term "Ribbi." In the modern times, some people have suggested the title of *Rabbah* for women Rabbis, but this not been popularly accepted by the Jewish community. In the non-Orthodox communities today, women Rabbis are still called "Rabbis."[3]

---

## The Hazzan/Cantor

To enhance the beauty of the service, many congregations hire an invested Cantor, who specializes in the musical traditions of Judaism. There are many cantorial schools around the USA. Some Cantors, though not invested by a specialized school, still function as "cantorial soloists."

Except in the Orthodox movement where only male cantors are allowed to sing the musical parts of the service, including chanting of the Torah, other Jewish movements are free to retain the services of either male or female cantors. The relationship between the Cantor and the congregation is also contractual.

## Religious Education

Many synagogues have afternoon religious schools for children ages 6 to 16 where they learn the basics of Judaism. The person who runs this program is a Religious School Principal (or Director) who has been Judaically trained in a specialized school for this purpose. However, in some cases, these directors come from the secular school system. In the overwhelming majority of the religious schools in America, classes are run by professional teachers who get paid for their services. Many congregations also hire Youth Advisors, Children Center ("Nursery School") directors, and Adult Education specialists to meet the needs of families.

## The Office Staff

The daily operation of the synagogue is usually in the hands of a Temple administrator and his/her staff, which includes office assistants, secretaries and often a bookkeeper.

## The Board of Directors

Many lay volunteers and the Board of Trustees (or Directors) are elected by Temple members. The Board works cooperatively with the professional staff. Usually, a smaller group, an Executive Committee, composed of a president and a few trustees, deal with the day-to-day operations of the synagogue, in conjunction with the Rabbi and the Temple Administrator.

## Service Organizations

To better serve the members of the congregation as well as the community, many congregations have volunteers running different types of programs, including, for example, Brotherhood, Sisterhood, Family Education, Adult Education, Youth Groups, Caring Committee, and Garden Club.[4]

# Jewish Community Organizations

In addition to synagogues, many Jews in the USA and elsewhere belong to Jewish community organizations, which aim to improve the well-being of Jews (and often non-Jews) everywhere. Among them the following are the most important:

a. Fund Raising: UJA (United Jewish Appeal) and in Boston, CJP (Combined Jewish Philanthropies); in other places it is usually called the Jewish Federation.
b. Educational: Almost every major city has a BJE (Bureau of Jewish Education) or something similar.
c. Charitable: JCA (Jewish Charities of America); MAZON (a Jewish response to hunger); Hadassah (medical help); the Hebrew Rehabilitation Center for the Aged (in Boston).
d. Defense and Information: For example, JCRC (The Jewish Community Relations Council); ADL (B'nai B'rith's Anti-Defamation League); JDC (Jewish Joint Distribution Committee); HIAS (Hebrew Immigrant Aid Society); AJC (American Jewish Committee and Congress).
e. Zionist Organizations: ZOA (Zionist Organization of America); JNH (Jewish National Fund), AIPAC (American Israel Public Affairs Committee); ARZA (Association of Religious Zionists of America).
f. Recreation: JCC (Jewish Community Center).

# Endnotes

1. On worship services and prayerbooks, see Hayim Halevy Donin, *To Pray as a Jew*. (Basic Books, 1980); the set of books, beginning with *The Sh'ma and Its Blessings: My People's Prayerbook*, edited by Rabbi Lawrence A. Hoffman (Woodstock, VT: Jewish Lights 1997.
2. On recent attempts by the Orthodox, see Darren Kleinberg, "Orthodox Women (Non-) Rabbis," *The Reform Jewish Quarterly*, Spring, 2012, 80–99.
3. On the title "Rabbi," see *Encyclopaedia Judaica*, 2nd ed. Vol. 17, 11–19; *Anchor Bible Dictionary*, Vol. 5, 1992, 600–602.
4. For further study on the synagogue, see Lee I. Levine, *The Ancient Synagogue: The First Thousand Years*. (Yale University, 2005); Korros, Alexandra Shecket and Sarna, Jonathan D. *American Synagogue History: A Bibliography and State-of-the-Field Survey* (HUC-JIR, 1988).

# CHAPTER EIGHT

# THE JEWISH HOME AND JEWISH SYMBOLS

## SYMBOL

A symbol is an item that represents something else, either by association or convention. Thus, for example, an object may stand for an idea or a concept or an abstraction. At times, the significance of a symbol remains for a long period of time, and can easily be recognized by everyone through the centuries (e.g., a flag stands for nationalism; a red octagon means "stop"). In some cases, a symbol loses its original meaning and is invested with new significance (e.g., a swastika, a very old sign representing life, the sun, or strength, became the official emblem of the Nazi party), or new symbols are created to meet the needs of the present times (e.g., icons used in computers). Some symbols have religious significance, while others are secular in nature. Furthermore, the same symbol (e.g., Sabbath lights) may be used for both religious and non-religious purposes (e.g., birthday candles).

Jewish life is rich in symbolism. Some of these symbols were used in the Temple of Jerusalem, others were incorporated in the synagogue, and many of them made it into the Jewish home today.

## THE JEWISH HOME

Throughout history, Jews have given a high profile to their home life, and have considered their home a "small sanctuary" (cf. Ez. 11:16). Even though in the original text of Ezekiel, it is God who becomes an everlasting presence in many countries to which God has scattered the Israelites, early commentators applied this verse to the synagogues (See Targum Jonathan), and eventually to any Jewish home.

According to rabbinic teaching, one of the most important attributes of a Jewish home is that is should have *shalom bayit* ("peace at home") where people are respectful of one another, and each one looks for the well-being of the other. The Psalmist said, "Peace be within your walls" (122:7). A harmonious family life benefits everyone, and enables each member to flourish in a safe and loving environment. Similarly, a Jewish home ought to be a place where *haknasat orehim* ("hospitality") is practiced with openness and generosity. We are told by the ancient Rabbis that Abraham, our patriarch, used to keep his tent open on all four sides (cf. Gen. 18:1-5) in order to give shelter to people who wandered in his direction. Similarly, Rebekah, Isaac's future wife, invites Abraham's servant to the family house by saying, "There is plenty of straw and feed at home, and room to spend the night" (Gen. 24:23-24). Jewish homes should also be imbued with the spirit of *kedushah* ("holiness"); it should be a place where children practice *kibbud av va-em* ("honoring parents"), where education is encouraged, where Jewish symbols are displayed with beauty and pride, and where Shabbat and festivals are given their due.

The following represent the most important Jewish symbols that are usually found in a Jewish home. (The blessings to be recited over many of these symbols have been placed at the end of this book.)

### 1. Mezuzah

*Israel Safed Beit Hameiri Mezuzah*

A Mezuzah is a small cylinder-like container that is affixed to the doorpost of one's house, based on the biblical command that "you shall write them [meaning, the instructions of the Torah] on the doorpost of your house and on your gates" (Deut. 6:9). Inside the container, one places a parchment written by a scribe containing the words of Deut. 6:4-9, and 11:13-21. On the outside of the little box, the word *shaddai* (one of God's names in the Bible) is added. Frequently, a Mezuzah is a medium for elegant artistic expression.

The Mezuzah identifies the house as a Jewish home. It is a constant reminder of the Mitzvot. It is also a remembrance of God's providential care of the Israelites in Egypt when, according to legend, the blood of the paschal sacrifice was smeared over their doorposts so that, upon seeing it, God passed over the homes of the Israelites and protected them, even though this event sadly occurred at the expense of the death of the first-born Egyptians (See, Ex. 11-13).

According to accepted Jewish tradition, the Mezuzah is placed in the upper third part of the right doorpost, and is usually slanted toward the inside of the house. Except for the bathroom, other rooms may also contain a Mezuzah. A new house is "dedicated" by affixing a Mezuzah and by reciting an appropriate blessing that ends with the words "… *likboa' mezuzah*," "Praised be the Eternal, Sovereign of the Universe, who has sanctified us with divine commandments and has commanded us to affix a mezuzah." A Mezuzah must be "affixed"; if it is suspended, it is not valid.

Only permanent residences require a Mezuzah. If the residence is temporary, such as a Sukkah, it does not need a Mezuzah. When a house owned by a Jew is sold to another Jew, it is customary to leave the mezuzah for the incoming owner.

### 2. Shabbat Candles

Light is symbol of the divine. On Friday nights, two Sabbath candles are lit before sundown with an appropriate blessing. This is usually done by the lady of the house. In Reform Judaism, a man can also light the candle. In some Sephardic communities, it is customary to light seven wicks placed within a bowl of olive oil.

### 3. Kiddush Cup

In Jewish life, wine is considered a symbol of joy. We welcome Shabbat and the Festivals not only with light but also by reciting a special blessing over a cup of wine. A specially designed Kiddush cup, athough not required, enhances the performance of this Mitzvah.

### 4. Hallah Plate and Cover

After the blessings over candles and wine, we recite a blessing over two pieces of bread, or over hallah (i.e., a braided bread), in order to give gratitude to God for the food that we are about to eat. These Hallot (pl. of Hallah) are usually placed on a special plate and covered with a decorative piece of cloth. The reason two loaves of bread are used is that, according to tradition, after the Exodus and during the wilderness period, during Shabbat, Jews were given two portions of Manna (Ex. 16:22; BT Shab. 117b).

### 5. Havdalah Set

We conclude the Sabbath, as well as Yom Kippur (which is considered "a Sabbath of Sabbaths"), with the ceremony of Havdalah (see Chapter Four) for which we use three symbols: a) a twisted candle, b) a wine cup, and c) a spice box. Specials prayers accompany this ceremony.

## 6. Hanukiyah

Unlike a regular seven-branch Menorah found at most synagogues, a Menorah of nine branches called a "Hanukiyah" (with eight branches plus a helper branch) is used to light the candles during the eight nights of *Hanukah*, with appropriate blessings. According

to Jewish custom, on the first night of *Hanukah*, in addition to the helper candle, only one candle is lit: the one on the far right; on the second night, using the helper candle, one lights the second candle first and then the first, going backwards to the right; on the third night, one lights the third candle first, then the second and then the first, always going backwards to the right. And so on.

*Hanukiyah*

## 7. Tzedakah Box

In Jewish life, one is expected to give *tzedakah* to others. The expression *tzedakah* is more than "charity." Based on the Hebrew root, meaning "righteousness," it contains en element of obligation. According to Jewish law, even a poor Jew is expected to give *tzedakah* to others. Usually at every home, and every synagogue, there is such a box into which people deposit their own contributions for the needy.

## 8. Seder Plate

The Passover meal contains many symbols (see Chapter Four). The Seder plate is put before the person who leads the service. This plate tends to be larger than the others and more ornate, onto which some of the basic symbols of the Seder, such as an egg, a shank bone, harotzet, parsley, bitter herbs, or lettuce are placed.

*Seder Plate*

## 9. Tallit

A *tallit* is a prayer shawl that is usually worn over the shoulders in accordance with the biblical command, "The Eternal said to Moses as follows, 'Speak to the Israelite people and instruct them to make for themselves fringes (*Tzitzit*) on the corners of their garments throughout the ages'" (Num. 15:37). The stated purpose is, "That you may look upon it, and remember all the commandments of the Eternal" (Num.15:39). In Reform congregations women too are allowed to wear them, if they wish.

The *tallit* is worn (in Orthodox Judaism, by men only) mostly during morning services, but also during the whole day of *Yom Kippur* and during the afternoon service on *Tisha Be-Av*. The prayer leader wears it for all services, morning or evening. When a child becomes a Bar/t Mitzvah, he/she often wears a *tallit* for the first time, saying the appropriate blessings.

*The author wearing a tallit and head covering*

There are different styles of *tallitot* (pl. of *tallit*), some more ornate than others. However, what makes a *tallit* a ritually acceptable piece of clothing are the four fringes that are attached at the far end of the shawl (two on each side). These tassels are twisted in such a way as to spell the number 613, which is the number of commandments determined by the ancient Rabbis. In the past, fringes were viewed as part of one's personal identity, and, when given to others (such as a king), they implied loyalty. Thus, by wearing a *tallit* with its tassels, a Jew proclaims a commitment to observe the *Mitzvot*.

### 10. **Tefillin** ("Phylacteries")

*Tefillin* are two separate small square boxes that are connected to leather straps. During morning services, only from Sunday to Friday, worshipers (in Orthodox Judaism, men only) put them on in accordance with the rabbinic interpretation of the biblical text, "Bind them (i.e., the instructions) as a sign upon your hand and let them serve as a symbol on your forehead" (Deut. 6:8) and with appropriate blessings. *Tefillin* are put on after wearing a *tallit*. One of the boxes is placed on the head and the straps hang on the shoulders; the other is placed on the left arm, closer to the heart, and the leather straps are wrapped around the arm and left hand in a prescribed manner.

Inside the box for the head, one finds a parchment written by a scribe, containing biblical verses taken from Ex. 13:1-10, 11-16; Deut. 6:4-9; 11:13-21. The head box has four compartments, and a

different biblical text is inserted in each one. The hand box contains only one compartment, and all four texts are written on one scroll.

## 11. Shofar ("Ram's Horn")

During Rosh Hashanah as well as at the end of Yom Kippur, the *shofar* is sounded in the synagogue with appropriate blessings. In Sephardic custom it is also sounded during the month of Elul, which precedes the High Holy Days. Not every Jewish home has a Shofar but it can be found in most synagogues. The sounding of the Shofar is not easy and requires preparation and practice.

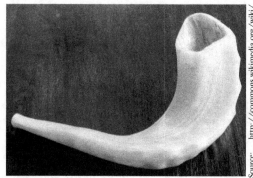

*Shofar*

In Jewish life, the shofar has been associated with various historic occasions: it reminds us of the ram that was brought to Abraham as he was about to sacrifice his son Isaac (Gen. 22); it was sounded at the start of a war, during a proclamation of the New Moon, at the revelation of the Torah on Mt. Sinai. For the Jewish philosopher, Maimonides, the shrill sound of the Shofar was a call to repentance during the High Holy Days.

## 12. Kippah ("Head covering," also called *Yarmulke* in Yiddish)

In Orthodox and Conservative synagogues, men are required to cover their heads during worship. This is seen as a sign of respect. Head covering is based on an ancient custom, the origin of which is obscure.[1] Reform Jews are free to cover or not to cover their heads during services. Today, even some women, in synagogues of all religious groups, are opting for the head covering.

## 13. Magen David ("Star of David")

The Star of David, a six-pointed star, made of two triangles superimposed on one another, is a very old symbol, often used for its magical powers. The legend is that the star was placed on the shield of King David's warriors and soldiers. In kabbalistic texts, the hexagram symbolizes the six directions of space, the divine union of male and female energy, and the four elements of the universe. In the 16th century, the Star of David was used in Prague, on the flag of the Jewish community. Later on, it appeared on the coat of arms of the famous Rothschild family in Vienna. During the Holocaust, it became a symbol of Jewishness. Since 1948 it has prominently appeared on the flag of the State of Israel.

### 14. Hai ("Eighteen")

A "hai" is a piece of jewelry that many Jews wear around their neck. It is not a religious symbol but it is often used for purposes of identity. In Hebrew every letter has a numerical value. Thus, for example, the first letter of the alphabet "Alef" stands for one; "Bet" stands for "two." The word "hai" is made of two letters: "Het" is eight; and "Yud" is ten. The two of them, eighteen, is "Hai," which in Hebrew means, "Life."[2]

### 15. Basic Jewish Library

Every Jewish home ought to have, at least, the following books of Jewish content.

a. A Hebrew Bible and, preferably, a Jewish translation in the vernacular, such as the one published by the Jewish Publication Society.

b. A Hebrew Prayerbook for daily services and the Sabbath; and another one for the High Holy Days.

c. A prayer book dealing with prayers and ceremonies at home, such as *On the Doorpost of Your House*, published by the CCAR.

d. A Haggadah for Passover.

e. A book on Jewish History, such as *The History of the Jews* (Mentor) by Solomon Grayzel or *A History of the Jews* (Harper&Row) by Paul Johnson.

f. A book on Israel, preferably one that has been recently published.

g. A basic book dealing with Jewish customs, such as *Jewish Living* (URJ), by Mark Washofsky, or *Jewish Home* (URJ) by Daniel B. Syme.

h. A book on the ideas and concepts of Judaism, such as *A Jewish Theology* (Behrman) by Louis Jacobs. In a Reform Jewish home, one should have also a book such as *Liberal Judaism* (URJ) by Eugene B. Borowitz, or *Response to Modernity* (Wayne State University) by Michael A. Meyer.

i. A book on Jewish Spirituality, such as *The Jewish Lights Spirituality Handbook* (Jewish Lights), edited by Stuart M. Matlins; or by Rifat Sonsino, *Six Jewish Spiritual Paths* (Jewish Lights).

j. A book on Jewish Ethics, such as *You Shall Be Holy* (Random), by Joseph Telushkin, or *The Jewish Moral Virtues* (JPS) by Eugene B. Borowitz and Frances W. Schwartz.

### 16. Other Objects

In addition, Jewish homes should have a Jewish Calendar; a Jewish cookbook; Jewish periodicals; Israeli products (such as wine, ritual objects, Israeli coins); and Jewish art.

# The Laws Of Kashrut

Jewish teachings cover almost all aspects of life, including the types of food that an observant Jew is allowed to eat. The term for that is *kosher*, meaning "fit to eat."(Among Sephardic Jews, this is pronounced *kasher*). The rules and regulations that deal with this matter are known as "the laws of *kashrut*" ("fitness"). These norms are found in the Bible and have been expanded by the Rabbis.

The rationale for these laws is not known. Keeping "kosher" was not done for purposes of health. Perhaps they were observed against a pagan background, and became an element of one's Jewish identity in time. In our time, many observant Jews follow the laws of kashrut in their home and outside of the house. Most supermarkets in America contain food items identified by the letter O (with a U inside), meaning that they have been approved by the Union of Orthodox Rabbinate. Some Jews, willing to invite other Jews to eat at their table, prefer to keep kosher at home, but will eat non-kosher food outside. And there are many Jews who do not keep kosher at all.

The following are the basic rules that determine if a certain food item is Kosher or not:

a.  All types of vegetables, fruits, grains, and nuts are kosher.
b.  The consumption of blood is prohibited (Lev. 19:26; cf. Gen. 9:4), However, the blood of fish is permitted.
c.  Kosher animals: According to Biblical law, one is allowed to eat the meat of an animal that "has true hoofs, with clefts through the hoofs and that chews the cud" (Lev. 11:3). Thus, for example, cattle and sheep are Kosher because they fulfill the requirement, but pigs, dogs, horses, and rabbits do not.

Furthermore, in order for meat to be considered kosher, it has to be slaughtered in a prescribed manner by a qualified *shohet* ("ritual slaughterer"). Following the rabbinic regulations, the blood of the animal is drained—Biblical law prohibits the consumption of blood (Gen. 9:4; Lev. 7:26; Deut. 12:23); meat is soaked in water, then in salt, in order to eliminate any remaining drops of blood, and then all excess fat is removed. Furthermore, according to Biblical law, the sciatic nerve is removed (Gen. 32:33).

Animals that die of natural causes (*nevelah*) or are "torn apart" by another animal (*terefah*) are not kosher (Lev. 22:8). (Today, the word *terefah*, or *tref* for short, refers to any food that is not kosher).

d.  Fowl: Domesticated birds like chicken, duck, turkey, and goose are considered kosher, provided they are slaughtered according to rabbinic rules. Eggs from kosher animals are kosher.

e. Fish: To be kosher, fish must have both fins and scales (Lev. 11:9). That is why sharks, whales, and all types of shellfish are considered not kosher. The case of the swordfish is disputed, because when it gets older, it loses its scales.

f. Insects: None of them are kosher (Lev. 11:20, 29). However, those animals with jointed legs above their feet, which enable them to jump (such as locusts, crickets, and grasshoppers), are permitted (Num. 11:22).

g. The laws of kashrut prohibit the mixing of meat and milk products, like a cheeseburger, based on a rabbinic interpretation of the biblical command, "You shall not boil a kid in its mother's milk" (Ex. 23:19; 34:26; Deut. 14:21). Though the original meaning of this text is unclear (Maimonides suggested a pagan background), the ancient Rabbis turned this prohibition into a major component of the laws of kashrut, for reasons that we still do not understand.

Customarily one waits six hours after eating meat before eating any dairy products. Some wait only two hours. One can eat dairy and then meat, some say immediately after; others, by waiting two or three hours. Very often, kosher homes keep two different sets of dishes: one set for meat and another for dairy. Glass may be used for meat or dairy.

h. Parve: Some food items are called *parve*, namely, they are neither dairy nor meat, and they can be eaten alone or with dairy or meat. Examples: fruits, vegetables, grains, fish, and eggs.

i. To be kosher, wine has to be certified by a reputable and observant Jew. The reason for this prohibition is most likely because in antiquity, wine was used for libations at pagan temples.

## Kashrut and Reform Judaism

Early Reform Jews did not follow the laws of Kashrut. In fact, the Pittsburgh Platform of 1885 clearly states that "Mosaic and Rabbinical laws as regulate diet ... originated in ages and under the influence of ideas altogether foreign to our present mental and spiritual state." Neither the Columbus Platform of 1937 nor the Centenary Perspective of 1976 mentions kashrut at all. The first reference to a sympathetic view of kashrut in the Reform movement appears in the *Gates of Mitzvah*, published by the CCAR in 1979, where it says that "the fact that kashrut was an essential feature of Jewish life for so many centuries should motivate the Jewish family to study it and to consider whether or not it may enhance the sanctity of their home." The latest Reform platform, "A Statement of Principles for Reform Judaism" (1999), does not have any clear reference to kashrut, but states that Reform Jews are "committed the ongoing study of the whole array of Mitzvot and to the fulfillment of those that address us as individuals and as a community." Kashrut is one of these issues, and more Reform Jews in recent times have opted to keep kosher in a significant way, either only at home or both at home and outside. Reform Judaism gives the individual the right to choose from among all the Mitzvot those that are meaningful and based on education and personal autonomy. [3]

## ENDNOTES

1. See the Responsum by Jacob Z. Lauterbach, "Worshiping with Covered Heads" (1928) in Walter Jacob, *American Reform Responsa* (NY: CCAR, 1983, 8–21).
2. On Jewish symbols, see also, Miriam Chaikin, *Menoras, Mezuzas, and Other Symbols* (NY: Houghton Mittlin, 1990); Kerry M. Olitzky and Ronald H. Isaacs, *The How To Handbook for Jewish Living* (NJ: KTAV, 1993).
3. For more details about Kashrut, see, *The Sacred Table*. Ed. By Mary L. Zamore, CCAR, 2011.

# CHAPTER NINE

# JUDAISM AND OTHER RELIGIONS

## JEWS AND NON-JEWS

For many centuries Jews lived with, and among, other people. They interacted with them in good times and bad. In the biblical period, they lived among the Canaanites, and were influenced by their neighbors, far and near. Later on, Jews had to deal with the impact of Zoroastrianism, early Christianity, and Islam. When times were good, Jews became more comfortable with the culture of their host society. When things turned ugly for them, they tended to withdraw. Thus, in studying any Jewish community around the world, it is important to understand the general culture of the host community.

## IN BIBLICAL TIMES

During most of the biblical period, the Israelites were surrounded by the Egyptians in the southwest, the Babylonians in the southeast, the Assyrians in the northeast, and the Arameans in the north. Within Judah and Israel, they often interacted with the various peoples who made up the Canaanites. At their immediate borders, they dealt with the Edomites, Moabites, and Ammonites, sometimes as friends, often as enemies. However, the Israelites also freely admitted foreigners into their midst (like Ruth, the Moabite), they believed that they could influence other societies (like Elijah or Jonah), and were particularly protective of the resident aliens (the *gerim*) who lived among them. Over and over again, the Bible commands, "You shall not oppress a stranger (*ger*), for you know the feelings of the stranger, having yourselves been strangers in the land of Egypt" (Ex. 23:9; cf. Lev. 19:33; Deut. 24:17).

After the destruction of the First Temple in 586 BCE, Jews in Exile lived among the Babylonians and later on in the large Persian Empire. In a letter (5974/3 BCE) that the prophet Jeremiah sent to those who had been sent to Babylonia, he, speaking in the name of God, wrote, "Build houses and live in them, plan gardens and eat their fruit. Take wives and beget sons and daughters; and take wives for your sons, and give your daughters to husband, that they may bear sons and daughters. Multiply there, do not decrease. And seek the welfare of the city to which I have exiled you and pray to the Lord in its behalf; for in its prosperity you shall prosper" (Jer. 29:4-7). The last part of this statement has rung true throughout Jewish history. In the first century CE, we already find Jews living even outside of Judea, in many parts of the Mediterranean basin. After 70 CE, when the Second Temple was destroyed, Jews spread throughout the Diaspora for the next 2,000 years. It is inevitable that Jews and non-Jews would learn from one another during their daily life.

Living in a cultural continuum with their neighbors, the Israelites of the biblical period absorbed from the gentiles a number of mythic stories and adopted many of their thinking patterns. Thus, for example, the stories and legends about Creation or Noah, once very popular among non-Israelites, were incorporated in the national history of Israel. However, this material was not literally copied word for word from their neighbors, but was very often transformed according to the Israelite understanding of religion and society. For example, the stories of the world's creation (Gen 1-2) or Noah and the Deluge (Gen. 6-9) were known in the entire Ancient Near East. They were not created by the Israelites, but were, in fact, already popular among the Sumerians long before the Israelites had emerged onto the historical scene.[1] But when they became part of the Hebrew Bible, the narrators/editors gave them an Israelite imprint. The Noah story, for instance, which is devoid of moral teachings in the ancient Near Eastern texts[2], was now given an ethical rationale: the flood came because of lawlessness in society. Similarly, in the Creation story, all references to mythologies were removed, and everything was subsumed to a single and unique God.

The Canaanites, in whose midst the Israelites lived a long time, had a tremendous influence on the religion and practices of the biblical Jews. Even though the Israelites strongly opposed the local people because of their polytheism and fertility cults, they appropriated from them many cultural trends, such as the agricultural calendar, the institution of kingship, the structure of the sanctuaries, and even their language. The ancient Egyptians had a tremendous influence in the development of the biblical wisdom literature and the Babylonians left their indelible imprint in all matters of law.

In biblical times, the greatest fear of the Israelites was that the pagan practices of their neighbors would lead them astray from the worship of *YHVH*. The book of Leviticus makes this clear: "You shall not copy the practices of the land of Egypt where you dwelt or of the land of Canaan to which I am taking you; nor shall you follow their laws" (Lev.

18:3). Therefore, the Bible urges the Israelites not to intermarry with the people around them, for fear that marriage with foreigners would open the door to idol worship: "You shall not intermarry with them [local Canaanites]: do not give your daughters to their sons or take their daughters for your sons. For they will turn your children away from Me to worship other gods" (Deut. 7:3-4). After the Israelites returned from the Exile, the Bible tells us, the number of interfaith marriages became so high that the returnees resorted to an extreme method, and were told to divorce their pagan wives (Ezra 10:1-17). Whether or not this actually took place is difficult to assert.

It is important to stress that the prohibition against intermarriage is not grounded on ethnic superiority but strictly on religious grounds. Moses asks his pagan father-in-law, Hobab, the Midianite, to join Israel, and promises him a share in the future among the Israelites (Num. 10:29 ff). Ruth becomes an Israelite by marrying Boaz. Female captives become wives quickly (Deut. 21:10), and the book of Deuteronomy makes it clear that "Children born to them (i.e., Edomites or Egyptians) may be admitted into the congregation of the Eternal in the third generation" (Deut. 23:9).

# Rabbinic Attitude Toward Non-Jews

The general rabbinic position vis-à-vis non Jews has been articulated by the principle that "The righteous of all nations have a place in the world to come" (Tos. Sanh. 13:2; Maimonides, Mishneh Torah, Repentance 3:5). In other words, one does not need to be a Jew in order to merit the blessings of the eternal life; all that is needed is to be a righteous individual. In contrast, medieval Christianity taught, *nulla salus extra ecclesiam*, ("there is no salvation outside of the Church").

Furthermore, ancient Rabbis argued that Jewish law is binding only on Jews. Non-Jews are not obligated to practice the teachings of the Torah. Yet, all human beings, added the Rabbis, must follow the universal laws of Noah, called the Seven Noahide Laws (See, BT Sanh. 56a), which include the following laws, six negative and one positive: 1) not to deny God (such as idolatry); 2) not to profane God's name; 3) not to engage in incest and adultery; 4) not to commit murder; 5) not to steal; 6) not to eat a limb from a living animal; 7) setting up courts of law. According to the Rabbis anyone who abides by these laws is called a "Righteous Gentile," and is assured a place in the world-to-come.

Ancient Rabbis set the principle that "for the sake of peace" (*mipene darkhe shalom*) one treats other people with equanimity. On the other hand, Rabbis set up certain rules and regulations to make sure that business transactions between Jews and non-Jews would not lead Jews to follow pagan customs (see M Avodah Zarah, for various examples). So, for example, they ruled that Jews were not allowed to purchase wine made by non-Jews, because of the fear that this wine could have been used by non-Jews for pagan libations.

Except for some Orthodox Jews today, most Jews ignore these rules, because the practice of idolatry in our time is almost non-existent.

During the Talmudic period, Rabbis assumed different positions regarding non-Jews, some positive, some negative, depending on the times and circumstances. On many occasions, the sages used certain derogatory expressions regarding gentiles, even though it is not totally clear to whom they specifically refer. Among them are the following: *A'kum*, (short for *O'vde Kokhavim u-Mazalot*, ("worshipers of stars and planets"); *O'vde Elilim* ("worshipers of gods"); *Nokhrim* ("foreigners"); *Goyyim* ("nations"); *Minim* ("heretics"—Judeo-Christians? Zoroastrians?); *Edom* (usually refers to Rome); *Kutim* ("Samaritans").

# Jews And Christians

## Background

Early Christians were Jews. Jesus and Paul, the two greatest figures in Christianity, were born Jewish and died as Jews. The beginnings of Christianity reflect the inner struggle of the Jewish community suffering under the Roman occupation. At the time, different groups within the Jewish community took different positions on this issue. Some of the Sadducees appeared to be more cooperative with the Romans, while the Essenes withdrew altogether to the Dead Sea area. The Pharisees were cautious, and the Zealots, violent. It was later on, especially after the Hadrianic wars in the second century CE, that Jews (now all Pharisees) and Christians parted company.

## Who Was Jesus?

Scholars know very little about the details of Jesus' life. There is no contemporary evidence of Jesus that refers to him or to his activities. It is presumed that he was a Galilean, born in Nazareth around 4 BCE, and killed by the Romans around 30 CE. The New Testament, which was edited about four decades after his death, at times tells contradictory stories about Jesus. From all we know, he was a Pharisee, and most likely belonged to a group of visionaries who predicted the end of the Roman Empire, causing the ire of the Roman authorities in Palestine. At the time, in addition to the Sadducees, the Essenes, the Pharisees, and the Zealots, the Jewish community in Palestine had a number of people who were messianists. Some of them were political messianists, who awaited the arrival of a human savior, a descendant of King David, to save them from Rome. Others, apocalyptic messianists, expected that a supernatural being would arrive who would destroy all evil forces in the universe, including Satan. There was also a small group of Jews who claimed that the Messiah had already come, that he had recently died, and had risen from his death. His name was Jesus. They became the early Christians. All of these groups hoped for the destruction of the Roman Empire and the redemption of the people of Israel from oppression.

In the 1st century, Rome did not differentiate between the messianists and the activists. Anyone who spoke about the fall of the Roman Empire was considered rebellious and was crucified. Jesus was not the first or the last to undergo this terrible death. However, his followers saw in him more than an ordinary teacher or a charismatic leader. Eventually they considered him not only as the long-awaited Messiah, but also as the son of God, and even part of the divinity. It was Paul who brought Jesus to the attention of the gentiles in Asia Minor, and Christianity grew, especially when he eliminated circumcision as a requirement for joining the emerging religion. Eventually, the Jewish-Christians, who insisted on circumcision, lost to those who advanced Christianity among gentiles without this religious mandate.

The New Testament claims that God came down and became a man in the person of Jesus. Consequently, God and Jesus are one and the same: "The Father and I are one" (John 10:30). Jews could not accept this assertion about Jesus, because according to Jewish teachings, a human being can never become God. As Maimonides taught, "We are to believe that He is incorporeal, that His unity is physical neither potentially, not actually" (Helek: Sanhedrin, 10). Furthermore, the arrival of the Messiah, Jews believed, should coincide with peace on earth and the redemption of the people of Israel. These had not happened yet. In response, early Christians argued that Jesus, who died at the cross, will come again.

Throughout Jewish history, Jews viewed Jesus differently. They never recognized him as the Messiah or as part of the triune-God, but perhaps as an influential teacher who had significant number of followers. Thus, for example, the Jewish historian Heinrich Graetz (1817–1891) considered him an Essene; the British thinker Claude Montefiore (1858–1938) described him as a prophet; Joseph Klausner (1874–1958), the literary critic, as a great teacher of morality and an artist in parables; Martin Buber (1878–1965), the Jewish philosopher, called him "my great brother." Many others argued he was a Galilean Rabbi (though the title appeared after Jesus). Even today, Jewish thinkers claim Jesus, as a person, to the Jewish community, but deny his messianic, divine, or religious role.

What is the status of the Jews-for-Jesus in the Jewish community? These individuals and all Messianic Jews who claim to be Jewish, consider themselves "fulfilled Jews," because they were born as Jews. However, they all accept Jesus as their savior. Jews around the world have refused to accept them as part of their own communities. The Jewish position is clearly articulated in a Reform Responsum, which states, "Anyone who claims that Jesus is their savior is no longer a Jew and is an apostate."[3]

Most Jews and Christians have a lot in common: a) both are monotheists; b) both share the same section of the Bible, namely what Christians call "the Old Testament"; c) both claim Jesus as one of their own; d) both share the concept of an eternal covenant with God, and assert that there is one covenant with the Jews and another parallel covenant with Christians. On the other hand, Christians and Jews differ in the following areas: a) Jews do not recognize the messiahship, or even the divinity of Jesus; b) Jews do not recognize the New Testament as Scripture; c) Jewish teachers do not believe in Original Sin. For them, what happened at Creation in the Garden of Eden was not Adam's Fall, but Adam and Eve's realization that they were human; d) In Judaism, contrary to Christianity, faith alone is not enough; the practice of Mitzvot is required; e) There are no sacraments in Judaism, only Mitzvot. Similarly, Judaism takes exception to some of Paul's ideas that the flesh is evil; that there is vicarious salvation; that the authority of the Hebrew Bible is abrogated; that Jesus will return; and that only those who believe will be saved and others will be lost to perdition.

## Jewish–Christian Dialogue

Constructive religious dialogue between Jews and Christians is relatively new. In the past, most formal contacts between these two groups were set up as disputations trying to prove the correctness of a particular point of view. For example, the medieval Jewish commentator Nahmanides of Gerona was forced to meet with a group of Catholic clergy in 1263, Barcelona, Spain, in order to argue whether or not the Messiah had arrived. In recent times many efforts have been made to further a serious and open dialogue between Christians and Jews, albeit with mixed success. Even though major Jewish organizations, such as the American Jewish Committee, The International B'nai Berith, and the Central Conference of American Rabbis (Reform) supported the effort, other Jews failed to see any value in it. Among those who opposed the dialogue was the celebrated Orthodox Rabbi Joseph Soloveitchik of Yeshiva University, who in his 1964 article titled, "Confrontations,"[4] stated that we could discuss with the Christians many social issues, such as poverty, natural resources, anti-Semitism, but on religious matters, we have nothing to tell them.

After the Second World War, the Catholic Church, horrified by the results of the Holocaust, issued in 1965 a document entitled "Declaration on the Relation of the Church to non-Christian Religions" ( *Nostra Aetate*, for short; see text at the end of this chapter) during the papacy of Paul VI. In this historic text, the Vatican confirmed the spiritual bond with Jews, "Abraham's stock," deplored anti-Semitism, stated that Jews "should not be presented or rejected as accursed by God," and admitted that "the Jews still remain most dear to God because of their fathers." However, it failed to mention the modern State of Israel. In 1975, the Vatican published further guidelines about the implementation of *Nostra Aetate*, and even made some changes: not only did the Church "deplore" anti-Semitism, but actually "condemned" it; furthermore, it stated that it is important "to understand Jews as they understand themselves." The text of *Nostra Aetate* was further clarified through "Notes for Preaching and Catechesis" of 1985, which affirm the Jewishness of Jesus, the existence of the State of Israel, and that Jews are presented as "the people of God of the Old Testament, which has never been revoked by God."

In response, a group of Jewish academics issued a document called *Dabru Emet* ("Speak the Truth"; cf. Zech. 8:16; see text at the end of this chapter) in Sept 2000, where they declared among others, that a) Jews and Christians worship the same God; b) Jews and Christians seek authority from the same book—the Bible (Tanak); c) Christians can respect the claim of the Jewish people upon the land of Israel; d) Jews and Christians accept the moral principles of Torah; e) Nazism was not a Christian phenomenon; f) The humanly irreconcilable difference between Jews and Christians will not be settled until God redeems the entire world as promised in Scripture; g) A new relationship between Jews and Christians will not weaken Jewish practice; h) Jews and Christians must work together for justice and peace.

*Dabru Emet* was well received by many Jews. In support of an authentic religious dialogue, many Jewish books appeared on various aspects of this topic. Among them is *Christianity in Jewish Terms* by Tikva Freymer-Kensky and others[5], as well as a collection of articles by D. F. Sandmel, R.M. Catalano, and C.M. Leighton called *Irreconcilable Differences?*[6]

In Sept. 2002, a prominent group of Christian theologians published a document called, "A Sacred Obligation: Rethinking Christian Faith in Relation to Judaism and the Jewish People," in which they affirmed the following: a) God's covenant with the Jewish people endures forever; b) Jesus of Nazareth lived and died as a faithful Jew; c) Ancient rivalries must not define Christian-Jewish relations today; d) Judaism is a living faith, enriched by many centuries of development; e) The Bible both connects and separates Jews and Christians; f) Affirming God's enduring covenant with the Jewish people has consequences for Christian understanding of salvation: g) Christians should not target Jews for conversion; h) Christian worship that teaches contempt for Judaism dishonors God; i) Affirming the importance of the land of Israel for the life of the Jewish people; j) Christians should work with Jews for the healing of the world. The interest in Jewish–Christian dialogue continues in earnest in our time. As part of this effort, a new Jewish commentary on the New Testament appeared with the title of *The Jewish Annotated New Testament* (2011) by Amy-Jill Levine and Marc Z. Brettler.[7]

However, in recent times, there has also been some negative reaction to this religious dialogue. In 2009, a group of Palestinian Christian clergy issued a document called "A Moment of Truth," popularly known as "Kairos [Greek for the right or opportune moment] 2009," which not only demonizes the Israelis but also renews the old teaching of Christian supersessionism long rejected today by main line churches. Although some Christians supported the statement, others strongly criticized it.

It is hoped that the efforts on the part of Jewish and Christian teachers and religious leaders to continue with an open and mutually respectful dialogue will keep getting stronger, and will even trickle down to the congregational level, thus becoming guiding posts in the personal relationship between ordinary Jews and Christians.[8]

## Jews And Muslims

Jews and Muslims have had a long history of coexistence. The so-called Golden Age of Spain (8th to 15th centuries) was one of the shiniest spots in Jewish history when significant number of Jews reached great prominence in Spain living under Muslim rulers.

Main line Judaism and Islam (Sunni or Shiite) have a great deal in common: a) Both are monotheists; b) Islam recognizes both Jews and Christians as the "People of the Book"; c) The patriarch Abraham is claimed by both as their ancestor (Jews saying they are the descendents of Abraham and Isaac, whereas Muslims asserting they are the descendents of Abraham and Ishmael, Isaac's half-brother); d) Both practice circumcision; e) Both prohibit the eating of pork; f) Neither one accepts icons or paintings of human beings in their sanctuaries; g) Like Judaism, Islam is a religion of law (Shari'a); h) Historically speaking Jews fared better living under Muslim rule than under Christian rule, even when both Jews and Christians had a restrictive life in Muslim countries, living as *dhimmis* ("protected people") and paying certain taxes.

On the other hand, Judaism and Islam differ in the following areas: a) Islam claims that it represents the ultimate fulfillment of Judaism and Christianity; b) Jews do not recognize the Qur'an as Holy Scripture; c) Jews do not accept Muhammad as a prophet; d) Many Muslims claim that modern Israel is built on what Muslims call, *dar al-Islam* ("the abode of Islam"). This delegitimizes the State of Israel, which has its roots in biblical times, long before Arabs emerged onto the historical scene. It is hoped that visionaries on both sides will eventually open the doors of true dialogue, accepting not only the similarities but also the differences that separate them. [9]

## Jews And Other Religions

Today, Jews and the members of other world monotheistic religions live, as Mark Washofsky said, in "creative tension."[10] There is a great deal of interaction between liberal

Jews, Christians, and Muslims in a variety of social, cultural, and religious issues. It is not uncommon for these groups to get together for interfaith religious services, for example. Orthodox Jews are more reluctant in this area. However, many Jewish teachers would have issues with other world religions, such as Hinduism and Native American religions, which are not purely monotheistic, and therefore would consider it inappropriate for Jews to take part in their religious rituals.

## Is Judaism The True Religion?

Rabbi Louis Jacobs, a British-Jewish theologian, maintains that there are three different attitudes among Jews today regarding the relationship between Judaism and other religions:[11]

a. Judaism is the only true religion: This is the medieval point of view that claimed that all other religions, outside of Judaism, are false. However, comparative studies on religion have made it clear that many religions share the same high ideals, including the belief in God, however conceived. So there is truth in other religions too.

b. There is more truth in Judaism than in other religions. This is the point of view of Rabbi Jacobs who maintains that the belief in One God and the centrality of the Torah have not been superseded by any other religion. This does not mean, he adds, that other religions do not have any truths or that God has not revealed some truths to other people. But there more of it in Judaism.

c. All religions are equally true or false: This relativistic concept is unacceptable because the "highest insights" of each particular religion are often incompatible with those of other religions. So if one is true, the other has to be false.

To these three options, we can add a fourth one: Judaism is true for me. Anyone who chooses a religion for him/herself must be convinced of the validity of the religion's teachings. Otherwise, why opt for it? For those who accept Judaism as a way of life as well as a religious discipline, Jewish teachings have to ring true. This does not mean that everything in Judaism is perfect, or that Jews cannot learn from others. But the basic assumptions have to be accepted as authentic, commanding loyalty and respect.

## I. Declaration On The Relation Of The Church To Non-Christian Religions *Nostra Aetate* Proclaimed By His Holiness Pope Paul Vi On October 28, 1965

1. In our time, when day by day mankind is being drawn closer together, and the ties between different peoples are becoming stronger, the Church examines more closely her relationship to non-Christian religions. In her task of promoting unity and love among men, indeed among nations, she considers above all in this declaration what men have in common and what draws them to fellowship.

One is the community of all peoples, one their origin, for God made the whole human race to live over the face of the earth.[1] One also is their final goal, God. His providence, His manifestations of goodness, His saving design extend to all men,[2] until that time when the elect will be united in the Holy City, the city ablaze with the glory of God, where the nations will walk in His light.[3]

Men expect from the various religions answers to the unsolved riddles of the human condition, which today, even as in former times, deeply stir the hearts of men: What is man? What is the meaning, the aim of our life? What is moral good, what sin? Whence suffering and what purpose does it serve? Which is the road to true happiness? What are death, judgment and retribution after death? What, finally, is that ultimate inexpressible mystery which encompasses our existence: whence do we come, and where are we going?

2. From ancient times down to the present, there is found among various peoples a certain perception of that hidden power which hovers over the course of things and over the events of human history; at times some indeed have come to the recognition of a Supreme Being, or even of a Father. This perception and recognition penetrates their lives with a profound religious sense.

Religions, however, that are bound up with an advanced culture have struggled to answer the same questions by means of more refined concepts and a more developed language. Thus in Hinduism, men contemplate the divine mystery and express it through an inexhaustible abundance of myths and through searching philosophical inquiry. They seek freedom from the anguish of our human condition either through ascetical practices or profound meditation or a flight to God with love and trust. Again, Buddhism, in its various forms, realizes the radical insufficiency of this changeable world; it teaches a way by which men, in a devout and confident spirit, may be able either to acquire the state of perfect liberation, or attain, by their own efforts or through higher help, supreme illumination. Likewise, other religions found everywhere try to counter the restlessness of the human heart, each in its own manner, by proposing "ways," comprising teachings, rules of life, and sacred rites. The Catholic Church rejects nothing that is true and holy in these religions. She regards with sincere reverence those ways of conduct and of life, those precepts and teachings which, though differing in many aspects from the ones she holds and sets forth, nonetheless often reflect a ray of that Truth which enlightens all men. Indeed, she proclaims, and ever must proclaim Christ "the way, the truth, and the life" (John 14:6), in whom men may find the fullness of religious life, in whom God has reconciled all things to Himself.[4]

The Church, therefore, exhorts her sons, that through dialogue and collaboration with the followers of other religions, carried out with prudence and love and in witness to the Christian faith and life, they recognize, preserve and promote the good things, spiritual and moral, as well as the socio-cultural values found among these men.

3. The Church regards with esteem also the Moslems. They adore the one God, living and subsisting in Himself; merciful and all- powerful, the Creator of heaven and earth,[5] who has spoken to men; they take pains to submit wholeheartedly to even His inscrutable decrees, just as Abraham, with whom the faith of Islam takes pleasure in linking itself, submitted to God. Though they do not acknowledge Jesus as God, they revere Him as a prophet. They also honor Mary, His virgin Mother; at times they even call on her with devotion. In addition, they await the day of judgment when God will render their deserts to all those who have been raised up from the dead. Finally, they value the moral life and worship God especially through prayer, almsgiving and fasting.

Since in the course of centuries not a few quarrels and hostilities have arisen between Christians and Moslems, this sacred synod urges all to forget the past and to work sincerely for mutual understanding and to preserve as well as to promote together for the benefit of all mankind social justice and moral welfare, as well as peace and freedom.

4. As the sacred synod searches into the mystery of the Church, it remembers the bond that spiritually ties the people of the New Covenant to Abraham's stock.

Thus the Church of Christ acknowledges that, according to God's saving design, the beginnings of her faith and her election are found already among the Patriarchs, Moses and the prophets. She professes that all who believe in Christ-Abraham's sons according to faith[6] are included in the same Patriarch's call, and likewise that the salvation of the Church is mysteriously foreshadowed by the chosen people's exodus from the land of bondage. The Church, therefore, cannot forget that she received the revelation of the Old Testament through the people with whom God in His inexpressible mercy concluded the Ancient Covenant. Nor can she forget that she draws sustenance from the root of that well-cultivated olive tree onto which have been grafted the wild shoots, the Gentiles.[7] Indeed, the Church believes that by His cross Christ, Our Peace, reconciled Jews and Gentiles, making both one in Himself.[8]

The Church keeps ever in mind the words of the Apostle about his kinsmen: "theirs is the sonship and the glory and the covenants and the law and the worship and the promises; theirs are the fathers and from them is the Christ according to the flesh" (Rom. 9:4-5), the Son of the Virgin Mary. She also recalls that the Apostles, the Church's mainstay and pillars, as well as most of the early disciples who proclaimed Christ's Gospel to the world, sprang from the Jewish people.

As Holy Scripture testifies, Jerusalem did not recognize the time of her visitation,[9] nor did the Jews in large number, accept the Gospel; indeed not a few opposed its spreading.[10] Nevertheless, God holds the Jews most dear for the sake of their Fathers; He does not repent of the gifts He makes or of the calls He issues-such is the witness of the Apostle.[11] In company with the Prophets and the same Apostle, the Church awaits that day, known to God alone, on which all peoples will address the Lord in a single voice and "serve him shoulder to shoulder" (Soph. 3:9).[12]

Since the spiritual patrimony common to Christians and Jews is thus so great, this sacred synod wants to foster and recommend that mutual understanding and respect which is the fruit, above all, of biblical and theological studies as well as of fraternal dialogues.

True, the Jewish authorities and those who followed their lead pressed for the death of Christ;[13] still, what happened in His passion cannot be charged against all the Jews, without distinction, then alive, nor against the Jews of today. Although the Church is the new people of God, the Jews should not be presented as rejected or accursed by God, as if this followed from the Holy Scriptures. All should see to it, then, that in catechetical work or in the preaching of the word of God they do not teach anything that does not conform to the truth of the Gospel and the spirit of Christ.

Furthermore, in her rejection of every persecution against any man, the Church, mindful of the patrimony she shares with the Jews and moved not by political reasons but by the Gospel's spiritual love, decries hatred, persecutions, displays of anti-Semitism, directed against Jews at any time and by anyone.

Besides, as the Church has always held and holds now, Christ underwent His passion and death freely, because of the sins of men and out of infinite love, in order that all may reach salvation. It is, therefore, the burden of the Church's preaching to proclaim the cross of Christ as the sign of God's all-embracing love and as the fountain from which every grace flows.

5. We cannot truly call on God, the Father of all, if we refuse to treat in a brotherly way any man, created as he is in the image of God. Man's relation to God the Father and his relation to men his brothers are so linked together that Scripture says: "He who does not love does not know God" (1 John 4:8).

No foundation therefore remains for any theory or practice that leads to discrimination between man and man or people and people, so far as their human dignity and the rights flowing from it are concerned.

The Church reproves, as foreign to the mind of Christ, any discrimination against men or harassment of them because of their race, color, condition of life, or religion. On the contrary, following in the footsteps of the holy Apostles Peter and Paul, this sacred synod ardently implores the Christian faithful to "maintain good fellowship among the nations" (1 Peter 2:12), and, if possible, to live for their part in peace with all men,[14] so that they may truly be sons of the Father who is in heaven.[15]

# Endnotes

1. Cf. *Acts* 17:26
2. Cf. *Wis.* 8:1; *Acts* 14:17; *Rom.* 2:6-7; 1 *Tim.* 2:4
3. Cf. *Apoc.* 21:23f.
4. Cf 2 *Cor.* 5:18-19
5. Cf St. Gregory VII, *letter XXI to Anzir (Nacir), King of Mauritania* (Pl. 148, col. 450f.)
6. Cf. *Gal.* 3:7
7. Cf. *Rom.* 11:17-24
8. Cf. *Eph.* 2:14-16
9. Cf. *Lk.* 19:44
10. Cf. *Rom.* 11:28
11. Cf. *Rom.* 11:28-29; cf. dogmatic Constitution, *Lumen Gentium* (Light of Nations) AAS, 57 (1965) pag. 20
12. Cf. *Is.* 66:23; *Ps.* 65:4; *Rom.* 11:11-32
13. Cf. *John.* 19:6
14. Cf. *Rom.* 12:18
15. Cf. *Matt.* 5:45

# II. Dabru Emet (You Shall Tell the Truth)

In recent years, there has been a dramatic and unprecedented shift in Jewish and Christian relations. Throughout the nearly two millennia of Jewish exile, Christians have tended to characterize Judaism as a failed religion or, at best, a religion that prepared the way for, and is completed in, Christianity. In the decades since the Holocaust, however, Christianity has changed dramatically. An increasing number of official Church bodies, both Roman Catholic and Protestant, have made public statements of their remorse about Christian mistreatment of Jews and Judaism. These statements have declared, furthermore, that Christian teaching and preaching can and must be reformed so that they acknowledge God's enduring covenant with the Jewish people and celebrate the contribution of Judaism to world civilization and to Christian faith itself. We believe these changes merit a thoughtful Jewish response. Speaking only for ourselves—an interdenominational group of Jewish scholars—we believe it is time for Jews to learn about the efforts of Christians to honor Judaism. We believe it is time for Jews to reflect on what Judaism may now say about Christianity. As a first step, we offer eight brief statements about how Jews and Christians may relate to one another.

1. Jews and Christians worship the same God.

Before the rise of Christianity, Jews were the only worshippers of the God of Israel. But Christians also worship the God of Abraham, Isaac, and Jacob; creator of heaven and earth. While Christian worship is not a viable religious choice for Jews, as Jewish theologians we rejoice that, through Christianity, hundreds of millions of people have entered into relationship with the God of Israel.

2 Jews and Christians seek authority from the same book—the Bible (what Jews call "Tanakh" and Christians call the "Old Testament").

Turning to it for religious orientation, spiritual enrichment, and communal education, we each take away similar lessons: God created and sustains the universe; God established a covenant with the people Israel, God's revealed word guides Israel to a life of righteousness; and God will ultimately redeem Israel and the whole world. Yet, Jews and Christians interpret the Bible differently on many points. Such differences must always be respected.

3 Christians can respect the claim of the Jewish people upon the land of Israel.

The most important event for Jews since the Holocaust has been the reestablishment of a Jewish state in the Promised Land. As members of a biblically based religion, Christians appreciate that Israel was promised—and given—to Jews as the physical center of the covenant between them and God. Many Christians support the State of Israel for reasons far more profound than mere politics. As Jews, we applaud this support. We also recognize that Jewish tradition mandates justice for all non-Jews who reside in a Jewish state

4. Jews and Christians accept the moral principles of Torah.

Central to the moral principles of Torah is the inalienable sanctity and dignity of every human being. All of us were created in the image of God. This shared moral emphasis can be the basis of an improved relationship between our two communities. It can also be the basis of a powerful witness to all humanity for improving the lives of our fellow human beings and for standing against the immoralities and idolatries that harm and degrade us. Such witness is especially needed after the unprecedented horrors of the past century..

5. Nazism was not a Christian phenomenon.

Without the long history of Christian anti-Judaism and Christian violence against Jews, Nazi ideology could not have taken hold nor could it have been carried out. Too many Christians participated in, or were sympathetic to, Nazi atrocities against Jews. Other Christians did not protest sufficiently against these atrocities. But Nazism itself was not an inevitable outcome of Christianity. If the Nazi extermination of the Jews had been fully successful, it would have turned its murderous rage more directly to Christians. We recognize with gratitude those Christians who risked or sacrificed their lives to save Jews during the Nazi regime. With that in mind, we encourage the continuation of recent efforts in Christian theology to repudiate unequivocally contempt of Judaism and the Jewish people. We applaud those Christians who reject this teaching of contempt, and we do not blame them for the sins committed by their ancestors.

6. The humanly irreconcilable difference between Jews and Christians will not be settled until God redeems the entire world as promised in Scripture.

Christians know and serve God through Jesus Christ and the Christian tradition. Jews know and serve God through Torah and the Jewish tradition. That difference will not be settled by one community insisting that it has interpreted Scripture more accurately than the other; nor by exercising political power over the other. Jews can respect Christians' faithfulness to their revelation just as we expect Christians to respect our faithfulness to our revelation. Neither Jew nor Christian should be pressed into affirming the teaching of the other community.

7. A new relationship between Jews and Christians will not weaken Jewish practice.

An improved relationship will not accelerate the cultural and religious assimilation that Jews rightly fear. It will not change traditional Jewish forms of worship, nor increase intermarriage between Jews and non-Jews, nor persuade more Jews to convert to Christianity, nor create a false blending of Judaism and Christianity. We respect Christianity as a faith that originated within Judaism and that still has significant contacts with it. We do not see it as an extension of Judaism. Only if we cherish our own traditions can we pursue this relationship with integrity.

8. Jews and Christians must work together for justice and peace.

Jews and Christians, each in their own way, recognize the unredeemed state of the world as reflected in the persistence of persecution, poverty, and human degradation and misery. Although justice and peace are finally God's, our joint efforts, together with those of other faith communities, will help bring the kingdom of God for which we hope and long. Separately and together, we must work to bring justice and peace to our world. In this enterprise, we are guided by the vision of the prophets of Israel: It shall come to pass in the end of days that the mountain of the Lord's house shall be established at the top of the mountains and be exalted above the hills, and the nations shall flow unto it and many peoples shall go and say, "Come ye and let us go up to the mountain of the Lord to the house of the God of Jacob and He will teach us of his ways and we will walk in his paths." (Is 2:2-3)

Tikva Frymer-Kensky, *The Divinity School, University of Chicago Chicago, IL*
David Novak, *University of Toronto Toronto, Canada*
Peter Ochs, *University of Virginia Charlottesville, VA*
Michael Signer, *University of Notre Dame South Bend, IN*

"These are the things that you must do: Speak the truth to one another. At your gates, administer fair judgment conducive to peace." (Zec 8:16)

## ENDNOTES

1. On Creation stories see Richard J. Clifford, *Creation Accounts in the Ancient Near East and in the Bible.* The Catholic Biblical Quarterly Monograph Series, 26, Washington, DC: The Catholic Biblical Association of America, 1994; ANET, 501–512; Rifat Sonsino, *Did Moses Really Have Horns?* 25–37.
2. For the Deluge story, see ANET, 93–97; Rifat Sonsino, op.cit. 60–69.
3. Walter Jacobs, *Contemporary American Reform Responsa*, #68.
4. *Tradition: A Journal of Orthodox Thought*, 1964 volume 6, #2.
5. Tikva Freymer-Kensky, David Novak, Michael Signer, Peter Ochs, and David Sandmel, Westview Press, 2000.
6. D. F. Sandmel. R.M. Catalano, C.M. Leighton, Westview Press, 2001.
7. Oxford University Press, 2011.
8. The material on Judaism and Christianity is extensive. Among others, see Hershel Shanks, *Christianity and Rabbinic Judaism* (Biblical Archaeology Society, 1993); documents listed in the Center for Christians-Jewish Learning, Boston College, (www.bc.edu/research/cjl).
9. On Islam and Judaism, see, Khalid Duran, *Children of Abraham.* Hoboken, NJ: Ktav, 2001; Reuven Firestone, *An Introduction to Islam for Jews.* Philadelphia: Jewish Publication Society, 2008.
10. Mark Washofsky, *Jewish Living.* New York: Union for Reform Judaism Press, 2001, 271.
11. Louis Jacobs, *A Jewish Theology*, 284–291.pillars, as well as most of the early disciples who proclaimed Christ's Gospel to the world, sprang from the Jewish people.

# CHAPTER TEN

# PRESENT AND FUTURE CHALLENGES

The survival of the Jewish people is like a miracle today. Over a period of close to four thousand years, Jews managed to exist in spite of all the attempts to destroy them, and, in fact, were able to create a viable and often flourishing culture that sustained them in hard times as well as in periods of relative comfort. Some Jews would attribute this to the biblical covenant that God made with the people of Israel, promising to keep them safe (e.g., Gen. 17:3-8). Others would argue that their continuous existence is because they were scattered all over the world, and, in each case, they made their best to adapt themselves to local conditions, and when conditions became unbearable, or when they were expelled from their countries (e.g., 1492 from Spain), they found refuge in other parts of the world (e.g., the Ottoman Empire) in order to establish a new life for themselves. However, they never forgot the sacred land that gave birth to their culture, and always hoped to be able to return to the Land of Israel in order to live once again freely. That event finally took place in 1948 when the State of Israel was set up as a haven of refuge for Jews all over the world. This explains why Jews, who are loyal citizens of their own respective countries today, are so concerned about the well-being of Israel, and collectively rise in support when it is threatened by its enemies.

Of the approximately thirteen and a half million Jews today, over six million live in Israel, five and a half million in the United States, and the rest are scattered about the world. Some countries are friendlier to Jews than others. Whereas most Jews live comfortably in some parts of the world, other Jews need to watch their back in order to survive.

In spite of their many achievements, Jews all over the world still face a number of challenges. Here below are some of them:

# 1. The Israeli–Palestinian Conflict

Non-Jews often confuse local citizens with Israelis, and think that all Jews agree with the policies of the Israeli government. Even though most Jews strongly support the reality and existence of the State of Israel, they are divided, just as it is within Israel, with regard to the attitude and action of a given Israeli government.

There is no doubt that the Israeli–Palestinian conflict, which dates back even before the establishment of the State of Israel in 1948, affects Jews all over the world. Most people now realize that both Jewish Israelis and Palestinian Arabs have conflicting claims to the land, and that peace will come only when each side truly recognizes the existence and legitimacy of the other, and is ready to make painful compromises. The Jewish Israelis are not going to leave Israel and the Palestinians will not give up on their hope to establish a country of their own in the West Bank and Gaza. The peace process will inevitably be long and difficult, but there is no other viable alternative.

# 2. Anti-Semitism

Anti-Semitism is usually defined as hatred toward or discrimination against Jews. The term was invented in 1879 by Wilhelm Marr, a German-Lutheran political activist, who claimed that Jews attack gentiles in order to achieve world domination. The term is misleading because it could also be directed at Arabs who are Semites. A more accurate expression would be "bigotry against Jews."

Anti-Semitism has a long and ugly history.[1] It has taken various forms: There is political and economic anti-Semitism, going back to Cicero (106 BCE–43 CE) who claimed that Jews took up arms against Rome, to, more recently, Father Charles Coughlin of Royal Oak, MI, who in the 1930's claimed that all Jews were Communists. In the early 1900's a devastating document entitled "The Protocols of the Elders of Zion" was published that claimed that there was a Jewish plot for world domination. This document was even disseminated in the United States by Henry Ford, the automaker, who paid for the publication of 500,000 copies throughout the country, but then recanted. Ultimately, the document was proven to be a forgery, a creation of the Russian Secret police. There is also religious anti-Semitism usually attributed all the way back to bishop Melito of Sardis, who preached that Jews killed Jesus and the Jewish people bear the guilt for this act. Thomas Aquinas (13th cent.) referred to Jews as infidels, and Martin Luther (16th cent.) asked that Christians avenge the death of Jesus by oppressing Jews. In our time, anti-Semitism is also conflated with anti-Zionism. In fact, in 1975, the United Nations voted that Zionism is "a form of racism and racial discrimination," but the vote was revoked in 1991.

It is not clear at all why anti-Semitism exists. Some thinkers point to economic reasons; others think that Jews are scapegoated by projection of guilt and displaced aggression. Yet others argue that anti-Semitism exists because Jews are viewed as outsiders. And some even believe that it is totally irrational. However, Jews for centuries have suffered because of these unfounded allegations.

Today anti-Semitism is condemned by many international bodies. For example, in 1994, for the first time, the United Nations' Human Rights Commission in Geneva passed a resolution requiring constant monitoring of anti-Semitism around the world. The resolution was passed without opposition by the Arab countries. Among international religious bodies, the Catholic Church, in the document *Nostra Aetate*, dated 1965 (see Chapter Nine) had stated, "The Church, mindful of the patrimony she shares with the Jews and moved not by political reasons but by the Gospel's spiritual love, decries hatred, persecutions, and displays of anti-Semitism directed against Jews at any time and by anyone." In 1975, the Church went even further. In the guidelines about the implementation of *Nostra Aetate*; it did not only "deplore" anti-Semitism, but even "condemned it."

Anti-Semitism may have diminished in some parts of the world, but is still in evidence as bigotry against the Jews in many other countries, based often on ignorance or prejudice. Even in the United States, where Jews feel most comfortable, the Anti-Defamation League's annual *Audit of Anti-Semitic Incidents* recorded 1,239 anti-Semitic incidents across the United States in 2010, which represents a 2.3% increase over 2009. [2]

# 3. Women's Rights

The function and status of women in Judaism were affected in the past by the patriarchal structure of society. Men were considered the head and protector of the family. During biblical times, however, some women attained greatness as matriarchs (e.g., Sarah, Rebekah, Rachel, and Leah), as leaders (e.g., Deborah), as prophetess (e.g., Huldah), and as successful businesswomen (e.g., Prov. 30). But, overall, women played the part of wife and mother within the family. During the rabbinic period, women were required to fulfill all the negative commandments (*mitzvot lo ta'ase*), except for trimming one's beard and viewing the dead, and were virtually exempt from all the positive commandments (*mitzvot a'se*) that are restricted by time, such as praying in the morning, residing in a Sukah, listening to the shofar, or even say the Shema', the watchword of the Jewish faith (BT Kid. 33b).

Sensitive to women's rights today, major changes are taking place within the Jewish community. Except for the Orthodox movement in Judaism, all other religious denominations have ordained women Rabbis, the first one being Sally Priesand, who received her ordination from the Hebrew Union College-Jewish Institute of Religion in 1972. (See Chapter Seven.)

Women now function as cantors in many non-Orthodox congregations. There are women presidents in various synagogues across the United States and Europe today. Under the influence of many women Jewish theologians, contemporary liturgies are becoming more and more gender sensitive. New prayerbooks are also being published to meet the new understanding of women in society. The Reform Jewish movement has even come out with a *Women's Torah Commentary* in 2008, edited by Tamara Cohn Eskenazi and Andrea L. Weiss (New York: Women of Reform Judaism).

Yet other challenges remain. The Orthodox Jewish movement refuses to ordain women Rabbis or Cantors, based on their understanding of Jewish law that places women in a different, some would say lower, category. For example, according to Jewish law today, a woman cannot serve as a witness in a religious case involving marriage, divorce, and conversion; she cannot divorce her husband (i.e., only a husband can divorce his wife), is not counted as part of a prayer quorum of ten, cannot act as worship leaders (see Chapter Seven), and, if her husband has disappeared, she cannot remarry, remaining as *a'gunah* ("chained") for the rest of her life. Non-Orthodox movements have ignored these restrictions and give women full access to Jewish life. [3]

## 4. The Tension Between Patrilineal and Matrilineal Descent

As noted in Chapter Two, in the biblical period, religious identity was derived from the father. In the rabbinic period, for reasons that are not clear, heredity of identity was switched to originating with the mother, so that if the mother is Jewish, the child is automatically considered Jewish. When the Reform Jewish movement passed its Patrilineal Descent Resolution in 1983, accepting both the biblical and rabbinic possibilities, it also created a major split in the Jewish community. (See full text in Chapter Two.) Today Orthodox Jews refuse to accept the child of a Jewish father and a non-Jewish mother as Jewish. Most of the Reform congregations outside the States accept only the matrilineal definition. So the identity of a child of a Jewish father in an interfaith marriage, though accepted as Jewish by Reform congregations in the USA, remains in limbo in the rest of the world. But there are so many Reform temples in the USA that one does not feel its impact.

The problem emerges when a patrilineally defined Jew moves to Israel or to another Jewish community outside of the States. In Israel, for example, he/she will not be able to marry another Jew, because the Orthodox establishment that controls all life-cycle events refuses to accept him/her as Jewish. Pressure was placed on the American Reform movement to eliminate the patrilineal definition in favor of the rabbinic matrilineality, but so far it has not worked, and it is unlikely that the Reform Jewish leadership, especially in view of the rise of interfaith marriages in the country, would make any changes. So, the conflict continues.

# 5. INTERFAITH MARRIAGES

The number of interfaith marriages in the Jewish world has been rising considerably, and is not likely to stop soon. The 1990 National Jewish Population Survey reported an intermarriage rate of 52 percent among American Jews. One of the main reasons for this increase is that Jews are now more accepted in society, and, therefore, non-Jews do not consider Judaism a major impediment to an interfaith marriage.

Orthodox and Conservative Judaism are opposed to interfaith marriages. The Reform movement is also on record as being against interfaith marriages. The CCAR's 1973 Resolution on Rabbinic Officiation at mixed marriages clearly states "its opposition to participation by its members in any ceremony which solemnizes a mixed marriage," even though recognizing that "historically its members have held and continue to hold divergent interpretation of Jewish tradition." Consequently, some Reform Rabbis officiate at interfaith marriages, in order to support the Jewish partner, and others do not. In fact, in 1983, one hundred Reform Rabbis who refuse to do interfaith weddings issued a statement saying that "a marriage ceremony involving a person who is not a member of the Jewish people is not a Jewish ceremony." Yet, a group of Rabbis who do officiate came up with a resolution in 1985 saying, "We will not deny the blessings of Judaism to our children."

The overwhelming majority of Reform Rabbis in congregations outside of the United States do not officiate at interfaith marriages. In the States, the debate continues between those who do and those who do not, with no clear solution in sight.

# 6. POST-DENOMINATIONALISM?

In the past, the only religious group that existed within Judaism was various shades of Orthodoxy, depending on the country in which Jews lived. Once the Reform movement was started in the early 19th century, things changed forever. Up until a few decades ago, it was much easier to distinguish a Reform Jew from other Jews. Today, the line of demarcation is not so clear. There is hardly any difference now in theology or practice between Reconstructionism and Reform. Furthermore, there are some Reform Jews who are as observant as Conservative Jews, and there are many Conservative Jews who act and think like Reform Jews. It is also not uncommon for Jews, who move around the country, to join a different congregation from their original hometown, simply because of convenience and local custom.

The palpable religious difference among Jews today is between halakhically bound Jewry and the rest of the other movements. As we noted before, Orthodox Judaism, by definition, maintains that the Torah has been divinely revealed, and, therefore, it is authoritative and binding, whereas the others assume that it is a human document, subject to free interpretation, and that it is to be followed as tradition or folkways. As Rabbi Mordecai Kaplan, the founder of Reconstructionism, put it, "Tradition has a vote, not a veto." The disagreement is so basic that it is unlikely that it will be resolved easily or that it can be resolved at all. The best that we can expect is to establish mutual respect and cooperation between all religious movements of our time.

# 7. Lower Birthrate

Recent studies have shown that the birth rate among Jews in Israel went up by 1.7%, whereas among Jews in the diaspora it is down by 0.2%. The birthrate among liberal Jews is much lower than that of Orthodox Jews all over the world. If this trend continues, it is estimated that the number of Jews in Israel will continue to increase, whereas the Jewish population in the Diaspora will progressively decrease. Liberal Jews appear to use more birth control methods, limit the number of their children, or decide not to have children at all. To counteract this trend, most rabbis encourage parents to bring more children into the world. Thus, the *Gates of Mitzvah* (a Reform publication, 1979) clearly states: "In considering family size, […] parents should be aware of the tragic decimation of our people during the Holocaust and of the threats of annihilation that have pursued the Jewish people throughout history. Thus, while Reform Judaism approves of the practice of birth control, couples are encouraged to consider the matter of family size carefully and with due regard to the problem of Jewish survival" (p. 11). In fact, a position paper on Jewish Family Planning, presented to the 1977 Central Conference of American Rabbis' Convention, states that "couples are encouraged to have at least two or three children."

# CONCLUSION

Judaism is a religion and culture that has a long and rich history. It has survived all its enemies in the past, and continues to create a remarkable culture that nourishes Jews today. In spite of the internal divisions, all Jews feel a sense of kinship, a historical bond, that goes back for centuries, all the way back to the first patriarch of the Jewish people, Abraham, to whom God said, "I will make you an great nation, and I will bless you" (Gen. 12:2), and feel responsible for one another by religious and cultural bonds and a sense of common fate. These connections are most likely to remain for a long, long time.

*a'm yisrael hai,* The Jewish people live.

# ENDNOTES

1. The literature on this subject is vast. A good start is Dennis Prager and Joseph Telushkin, *Why the Jews? The Reasons for Antisemitism* (Touchstone, 1983, 2003) and Phyllis Goldstein, *A Convenient Hatred: The History of Antisemitism.* (Facing History and Ourselves, 2012).
2. See, for more details, http://www.adl.org/main_Anti_Semitism_Domestic/2010_Audit
3. On the problem of *Agunah* read E.J. Vol. 1, 2nd Ed. 210–250.

# Excursus

## Faith Statements

### 1. MOSES MAIMONIDES' THIRTEEN PRINCIPLES OF FAITH

In the 10th century, the Jewish philosopher Sa'adia Gaon and in the 11th century, the Jewish thinker Bahya ibn Pakudah formulated certain specific beliefs derived from the Torah, but it was Moses Maimonides' Thirteen Principles of Faith, found in his Commentary on the *Mishnah* (San. Ch. 10:1), that became the main pronouncement for many traditional (Orthodox) Jews of the past as well as the present.[1]

## The text

### Principle I. To know the existence of the Creator

To believe in the existence of the Creator and that this Creator is perfect in all manner of existence. He is the cause of all existence. He causes them to exist and they exist only because of Him. And if you could contemplate a case, such that He was not to exist... then all things would cease to exist and there would remain nothing. And if you were to contemplate a case such that all things would cease to exist aside from the Creator, His existence would not cease. And He would lose nothing; and oneness and kingship is His alone. Hashem of strength is His name because He is sufficient with His own existence, and sufficient [is] just Him alone, and needs no other. And the existences of the angels, and the celestial bodies, and all that is in them and that which is below them...all need Him for their existence. And this is the first pillar and is attested to by the verse, "I am Hashem your God."

## Principle II. The unity of God

That is to say, to accept that this is the quintessential idea of Oneness. It is not like the oneness of a pair (i.e., pair of shoes—one group) and not one like a species. And not like man that has many individual (members) nor like a body that divides into many different parts until no end (every part being divisible). Rather, God is one and there is no other oneness like His. This is the second principle and is taught in what it says, "Hear Israel, Hashem is Our God, Hashem is one."

## Principle III. The denial of physicality in connection with God

This is to accept that this Oneness that we have mentioned above (Principle II) is not a body and has no strength in the body, and has no shape or image or relationship to a body or parts thereof. This is why the Sages of blessed memory said with regards to heaven there is no sitting, nor standing, no awakeness, nor tiredness. This is all to say that He does not partake of any physical actions or qualities. And if He were to be a body then He would be like any other body and would not be God. And all that is written in the holy books regarding descriptions of God, they are all anthropomorphic. Thus said our great Rabbis of blessed memory, "The Torah speaketh in man's language" (i.e., using human terms to offer some understanding). And the Rabbis have already spoken at length on this issue. This is the third pillar and is attested to by the verse, "For you saw no image" meaning that you did not see an image or any form when you stood at Sinai because as we have just said, He has no body, nor power of the body.

## Principle IV. God's Antiquity

This is that God existed prior to everything, and exists after everything. This is proved many times throughout scripture and is attested to by the verse, "Meuna Elokei kedem."

## Principle V. That God, blessed be He is worthy that we serve Him, to glorify Him, to make known His greatness, and to do His commands.

But not to do this to those that are below Him in the creation. Not to the angels or to the stars or the planets or anything else, for they are all created things in nature and in their functioning, there is no choice or judgment except by God Himself. Also it is not fitting to serve them as intermediaries to God. Only to God should you incline your thoughts and your actions. This is the fifth principle and it warns against idolatry and most of the Torah speaks out against this.

## Principle VI. Prophecy

And this is that it is known to man that these (prophets) are a type of man who are created beings of great stature and perfection of the character traits. Who have tremendous knowledge until a different intelligence attaches to them when the intelligence of the person clings to the intelligence of God and it rests upon him. And these are the prophets;

and this is prophecy; and the idea of it. The explanation of it is very long and the intention is not to bring a sign for every fundamental and to explain it all, encompassing of all knowledge (i.e., God's knowledge) but it is mentioned to us in a story form and all of the Torah attests to this.

### Principle VII. The prophetic capacity of Moses our Teacher, peace be upon him

And this is that we accept that he was the father of all prophets that were before him and that will be after him. He was on a qualitatively different level than any other, and he is chosen from all other people before and after him of any that have any knowledge of God; for his was the greatest. And he, peace be upon him, rose to the levels of the angels. He was granted all areas of knowledge and prophecy and his physical attributes did not diminish. His knowledge was different and it is through this difference that it is ascribed to him that he spoke to God without any intermediary or angel.

My intention was to explain this puzzling concept and to open up the sealed areas in the Torah regarding the verses of "face to face" and other similar references, but its length would be tremendous and it would require numerous proofs from the Torah and other sources and encompass many areas. Even to write it the briefest of briefest it would require 100 pages, so I will save it and write it in another book. I will now return to the intent of this seventh fundamental that the prophecy of Moses our teacher, peace be upon him, was different from all others in four ways:

1) Regarding all other prophets, God spoke to them through intermediaries. Regarding Moses, it was without one, as it says, "face to face I spoke to him."

2) Regarding all other prophets, prophecy came to them at night while they were asleep in a dream as it says, "in a dream of the night" and other such references; or in the day but only after a deep sleep-like state came over them, and all their senses were shut off except their thoughts. Not so by Moses. Moses would receive a prophecy any time when he would stand between the two figures [fixed] on the ark, as God attests to it, "and I will make it known to you there" and "not so my servant Moses. Face to face I speak to him."

3) When a prophet would receive prophecy he would not be able to stand the intense effect and he would shake and not be able to stand, as it relates regarding Daniel in his encounter with the angel Gabriel. Regarding Moses, he did not suffer from this. As it says, "Face to face do I speak to him as a person speaks to his friend." And even though this is the greatest connection to God, still, he did not suffer.

4) All other prophets could not receive prophecy at their will, [but] only when God desired to tell them. Some would go days or months without prophecy. Even if they wanted or needed something, sometimes it would be days or months or years or even never that they would be told [a prophecy]. Some, such as Elisha, would have people play music to put them in a good mood. But Moses, peace be upon him, received prophecy whenever he wanted, as it says, "Stand here and listen to what God will tell you what to

do" and "God said to Moses tell Aaron your brother that he can't come to the holy of holies at any time [he wants]." Our rabbis said, "Aaron was prohibited to come whenever he wanted, but not Moses.

### Principle VIII. That the Torah is from heaven [God]

And this is that you believe that all of this Torah that was given by Moses our teacher, peace be upon him, that it is all from the mouth of God. Meaning that it was received by him entirely from God. And it is not known how Moses received it except by Moses himself, peace be upon him, that it came to him. That he was like a stenographer that you speak to him and he writes all that is told to him: all the events and dates, the stories, and all the commandments. There is no difference between "And the sons of Cham were Kush, and Mitzraim, and his wife was Mehatbe'el" and "Timnah was his concubine" and "I am Hashem your God" and "Hear Israel [Hashem your God, Hashem is one]" for it was all given by God. And it is all Hashem's perfect Torah; pure, holy, and true. And he who says that these verses or stories, Moses made them up, he is a denier of our sages and prophets worse than all other types of deniers [form of heretic] for he thinks that what is in the Torah is from man's flawed heart and the questions and statements and the dates and stories are of no value for they are from Moses Rabbeinu, peace be upon him. And this area is that he believes the Torah is not from heaven. And on this our sages of blessed memory said, "he who believes that the Torah is from heaven except this verse that God did not say it but rather Moses himself did [he is a denier of all the Torah]." And this that God spoke this and that, each and every statement in the Torah, is from God and it is full of wisdom (each statement) and benefit to those who understand them. And its depth of knowledge is greater than all of the land and wider than all the seas and a person can only go in the path of David, the anointed of the God of Jacob who prayed and said "Open my eyes so that I may glance upon the wonders of Your Torah" (Psalms 119). And similarly the explanation of the Torah was also received from God and this is what we use today to know the appearance and structure of the sukka and the lulav and the shofar, tzitzis, tefillin, and their usage. And all this God said to Moses and Moses told to us. And he is trustworthy in his role as the messenger and the verse that teaches of this fundamental is what is written (Numbers 16), "And Moses said, with this shall you know that Hashem sent me to do all these actions (wonders) for they are not from my heart."

### Principle IX. The completeness of the Torah

And this is that the Torah is from God and is not lacking. That to it you can't add or take away from. Not from the written Torah or from the oral Torah, as it says, "Do not add to it and do not take away from it" (Deut 3). And we already explained what needs to be explained about this fundamental at the beginning of this essay.

**Principle X. That God knows man's actions and does not remove His eye from them**

His knowledge is not like someone who says God abandoned the land but rather like it says (Jer. 32) "Great in council and mighty in deed, Your eyes are cognizant to all the ways of mankind." "And God saw for the evil of man on the land had grown greatly." (Gen. 6) And it says, "The disgust of Sodom and Amorrah is great" and this demonstrates the 10th principle.

**Principle XI. That God gives reward to he who does the commandments of the Torah and punishes those that transgress its admonishments and warnings**

And the great reward is the life of the world to come and the punishment is the cutting off of the soul [in the world to come]. And we already said regarding this topic what these are. And the verse that attests to this principle is (Exodus 32) "And now if You would but forgive their sins—and if not erase me from this book that You have written." And God answered him, "He who sinned against Me I will erase from My book." This is a proof that God knows the fulfiller and the sinner in order to mete out reward to one and punishment to the other.

**Principle XII. The era of the Messiah**

And this is to believe that in truth that he will come and that you should be waiting for him even though he delays in coming. And you should not calculate times for him to come, or to look in the verses of Tanach to see when he should come. The sages say: The wisdom of those who calculate times [of his coming] is small and that you should believe that he will be greater and more honored than all of the kings of Israel since the beginning of time as it is prophesied by all the prophets from Moses our teacher, peace be upon him, until Malachi, peace be upon him. And he who doubts or diminishes the greatness of the Messiah is a denier in all the Torah for it testifies to the Messiah explicitly in the portion of Bilam and the portion of "You are gathered (toward the end of Deut)." And part of this principle that there is no king of Israel except from the house of David and from the seed of Solomon alone. And anyone who disputes this regarding this family is a denier of the name of God and in all the words of the prophets.

**Principle XIII. Resurrection of the dead**

And we have already explained it. And when the person will believe all these fundamentals and his faith will be clear in them he enters into the nation of Israel and it is a mitzva to love him and to have mercy on him and to act to him according to all the ways in which God commanded us regarding loving your neighbor. And even if he did all of the sins in the Torah due to desire of the emotions, and from his physical aspect's conquering him, he will be punished for his sins, but he still has a share in the world to come and is among the sinners of Israel. However if he rejects one of these fundamentals he leaves the nation and is a denier of the fundamentals and is called a heretic, a denier, etc., and it is a mitzva to hate him and to destroy him (financially—not physically to kill him. And not to steal either). And regarding him it is said (Psalms 139) "Behold will not the enemy of God be my enemy?"

I have expounded at length many things and I have left the topic of my composition but I have done it for I saw a need in the dealings of the fundamentals of faith and I have gathered together many different and spread-out areas. Therefore know them and succeed in understanding them and review them many times and know them very well [i.e., not just memorization but full understanding and ability to support them and know their proofs]. Therefore if after one or ten times you think you have understood them, God knows that you are just involved in falsehood. Therefore do not read them quickly because I have not written them as it suddenly entered into my mind. But rather, after a deep and careful study of the whole area, and after I have seen many clear and true ideas and I have seen what is proper to believe of them [as the fundamentals], I have brought proofs and logical demonstrations for each and every one of them. May it be God's will that I have been correct that He helped me through this area on the good path and now I will return to my explanation of this chapter [in the Talmud].

## 2. THE PLATFORMS OF REFORM JUDAISM

Reform Judaism has attempted to define itself through various platforms, as indicated below.

### a) The Pittsburgh Platform, 1885

Toward the end of the 19th century, large numbers of Jews began to arrive from Europe, mostly from Germany but some from Eastern Europe as well, each group with its own religious culture. It is estimated that by the 1880's there were about 300,000 Jews in the country. Most of these Jews were either Reform or Orthodox. There were very few Conservative Jews at the time. Given their background, these Jewish groups clashed over issues of Jewish theology and religious observance. The few Reform rabbis in the country then felt the necessity to clarify their position not only against the criticism of the Orthodox but also to respond to the broad humanitarian universalism of the prominent Jewish rationalist Felix Adler, who was the son of Rabbi Samuel Adler (Reform) of New

York City, and the founder of Ethical Culture. Even though a few Reform rabbis had issued a position paper in 1869 in Philadelphia, there was a need for a more comprehensive approach by the Reform rabbinate as a whole. On Nov. 1, 1885, Rabbi Kaufmann Kohler, an outstanding Reform rabbi of New York City, later to become one of the presidents of the Hebrew Union College, invited his colleagues to a conference "for the purpose of discussing the present state of American Judaism." In response to this invitation, nineteen Rabbis came to Pittsburgh, Pennsylvania. After serious deliberation, they issued the Pittsburgh Platform.

In this platform, Reform rabbis declared themselves a religious community, not a nation praying for the return to Palestine. They committed themselves to social action for the benefit of society; asserted their belief in the immortality of the soul, instead of bodily resurrection; affirmed their assumption in a progressive revelation that welcomes the teachings of science; eliminated the difference between Cohen-Levi and Israel in legal matters; and held that all laws that "regulate diet, priestly purity, and dress, originated in ages past and under the influence of ideas altogether foreign to our present mental and spiritual state," and, therefore, are not binding now, thus making all the laws of *kashrut* and synagogue attire (including head covering) irrelevant.

The Pittsburgh Platform established harmony among Reform Jewish leaders, and guided the movement for about half a century. Its teachings are reflected in the Union Prayer Book (UPB), the first official prayerbook of the Reform movement in America, which was edited by Rabbi Kaufmann Kohler and published by the CCAR in 1895. It replaced Rabbi Wise's prayerbook, Minhag America, and other prayer texts issued by individual Reform Rabbis before. Orthodox and Conservative Jews, however, attacked the Pittsburgh Platform as "a radical creed." The Conservatives, in particular, were so displeased by this platform that they set up their own rabbinic school, the Jewish Theological Seminary (JTS) in 1886.

## The Text

Convening at the call of Kaufmann Kohler of New York, Reform rabbis from around the United States met from November 16 through November 19, 1885 with Isaac Mayer Wise presiding. The meeting was declared the continuation of the Philadelphia Conference of 1869, which was the continuation of the German Conference of 1841 to 1846. The rabbis adopted the following seminal text:

1. We recognize in every religion an attempt to grasp the Infinite, and in every mode, source or book of revelation held sacred in any religious system the consciousness of the indwelling of God in man. We hold that Judaism presents the highest conception of the God-idea as taught in our Holy Scriptures and developed and spiritualized by the Jewish

teachers, in accordance with the moral and philosophical progress of their respective ages. We maintain that Judaism preserved and defended midst continual struggles and trials and under enforced isolation, this God-idea as the central religious truth for the human race.

2. We recognize in the Bible the record of the consecration of the Jewish people to its mission as the priest of the one God, and value it as the most potent instrument of religious and moral instruction. We hold that the modern discoveries of scientific researches in the domain of nature and history are not antagonistic to the doctrines of Judaism, the Bible reflecting the primitive ideas of its own age, and at times clothing its conception of divine Providence and Justice dealing with men in miraculous narratives.

3. We recognize in the Mosaic legislation a system of training the Jewish people for its mission during its national life in Palestine, and today we accept as binding only its moral laws, and maintain only such ceremonies as elevate and sanctify our lives, but reject all such as are not adapted to the views and habits of modern civilization.

4. We hold that all such Mosaic and rabbinical laws as regulate diet, priestly purity, and dress originated in ages and under the influence of ideas entirely foreign to our present mental and spiritual state. They fail to impress the modern Jew with a spirit of priestly holiness; their observance in our days is apt rather to obstruct than to further modern spiritual elevation.

5. We recognize, in the modern era of universal culture of heart and intellect, the approaching of the realization of Israel's great Messianic hope for the establishment of the kingdom of truth, justice, and peace among all men. We consider ourselves no longer a nation, but a religious community, and therefore expect neither a return to Palestine, nor a sacrificial worship under the sons of Aaron, nor the restoration of any of the laws concerning the Jewish state.

6. We recognize in Judaism a progressive religion, ever striving to be in accord with the postulates of reason. We are convinced of the utmost necessity of preserving the historical identity with our great past. Christianity and Islam, being daughter religions of Judaism, we appreciate their providential mission, to aid in the spreading of monotheistic and moral truth. We acknowledge that the spirit of broad humanity of our age is our ally in the fulfillment of our mission, and therefore we extend the hand of fellowship to all who cooperate with us in the establishment of the reign of truth and righteousness among men.

7. We reassert the doctrine of Judaism that the soul is immortal, grounding the belief on the divine nature of human spirit, which forever finds bliss in righteousness and misery in wickedness. We reject as ideas not rooted in Judaism, the beliefs both in bodily resurrection and in Gehenna and Eden (Hell and Paradise) as abodes for everlasting punishment and reward.

8. In full accordance with the spirit of the Mosaic legislation, which strives to regulate the relations between rich and poor, we deem it our duty to participate in the great task of modern times, to solve, on the basis of justice and righteousness, the problems presented by the contrasts and evils of the present organization of society.

## 6) The Columbus Platform, 1937

In the early part of the 20th century, Jews started to arrive in America in very large numbers. This had a great impact on the make-up of the Jewish community. By 1935, there were about four and a half million Jews in the country, most of them originally from the Eastern European countries. Reform Jews, mostly from Germany, slowly became a minority. Their numbers showed a negligible increase. Thus, for example, in 1920 there were 205 congregations affiliated with the UAHC; by 1935, only 256. The newcomers were more Zionists and brought a new appreciation for traditional ceremonies, such as the use of *Shofar*, the practice of *Bar Mitzvah*, the chanting of the *Kiddush*. As these Eastern European Jews began to enter Reform congregations, they demanded changes in the liturgy and fostered a new attitude toward the peoplehood of Israel. Furthermore, with the rise of Nazism in Germany, anti-Semitism was threatening Jews, not only in Europe but also in the States. The increasing activities of the anti-black, anti-Catholic but also anti-Semitic group, Ku Klux Klan (originally set up in the South in 1865); the publication by the automobile tycoon Henry Ford of the English version of the Protocols of the Elders of Zion; and the restrictions imposed on Jews in hotels, resorts, and other vacation places began to alarm the leaders of the Jewish community, including the Reform. Some Reform Rabbis, such as Bernard Felsenthal, Stephen S. Wise, and Abba Hillel Silver became ardent Zionists, and pushed the Reform movement to change its attitude. It became clear that there was a need to revive the religious loyalties of American Reform Jews, and to come up with a new platform that would reflect the condition of American Jewry of the time. This was accomplished by the Columbus Platform of 1937. (For the full text, see below.)

Prepared by a committee led by Rabbi Samuel Cohon, a professor at the Hebrew Union College, it was presented at the CCAR convention in Columbus, Ohio, in 1937 that was attended by 110 Reform Rabbis, and was adopted with only five votes against it.

"The Guiding Principles of Reform," as it was called, did not differ significantly from the Pittsburgh Platform in its basic approach to Judaism, but introduced a few very important concepts in Reform Jewish thought: It referred to the reality of "the Jewish people"; it spoke of "our sacred literature," implying both biblical and rabbinic; it affirmed the validity of "The Torah, both written and oral"; and, in a major departure, it stated, "We affirm the obligation of all Jewry to aid in its (Palestine's) upbuilding as a Jewish homeland by endeavoring to make it not only a haven of refuge for the oppressed but also a center of Jewish culture and spiritual life." Furthermore, in response to the prospect of the Second World War, it stressed the need for "universal peace," and "physical and spiritual disarmament." The platform promoted a stronger identification and emotional attachment to Judaism through intensive religious practices. Specifically, it's noted, "Judaism as a way of life requires, in addition to its moral and spiritual demands, the preservation of the Sabbath, festivals, and holy days, the retention and development of such customs, symbols and ceremonies as possess inspirational value, the cultivation of distinctive forms of religious art and music and the use of Hebrew, together with the vernacular, in our worship and instruction."

The teachings of the Columbus Platform are reflected in the next prayerbook of the Reform movement, *The Gates of Prayer* (GOP), edited by Rabbi Chaim Stern. This book replaced the old Union Prayer Book (UPB) that had already gone through some revisions in 1922 and then in 1941. The GOP, published in 1975, includes Sabbath services with multiple theological approaches, from Theism to Religious Naturalism, contains more Hebrew than the UPB, and a service for Yom Ha-Atzmaut (Israel Independence Day) as well as one for Yom Hashoa-ah (Holocaust). (The High Holiday Prayerbook *Gates of Repentance* was published by the CCAR in 1978).

## The Text

In view of the changes that have taken place in the modern world and the consequent need of stating anew the teachings of Reform Judaism, the Central Conference of American Rabbis makes the following declaration of principles. It presents them not as a fixed creed but as a guide for the progressive elements of Jewry.

### A. Judaism and Its Foundations

1. *Nature of Judaism.* Judaism is the historical religious experience of the Jewish people. Though growing out of Jewish life, its message is universal, aiming at the union and perfection of mankind under the sovereignty of God. Reform Judaism recognizes the principle of progressive development in religion and consciously applies this principle to spiritual as well as to cultural and social life. Judaism welcomes all truth, whether written in the pages of scripture or deciphered from the records of nature. The new discoveries of science, while replacing the older scientific views underlying our sacred literature, do not conflict with the essential spirit of religion as manifested in the consecration of man's will, heart, and mind to the service of God and of humanity.

2. *God.* The heart of Judaism and its chief contribution to religion is the doctrine of the One, living God, who rules the world through law and love. In Him all existence has its creative source and mankind its ideal of conduct. Though transcending time and space, He is the indwelling Presence of the world. We worship Him as the Lord of the universe and as our merciful Father.

3. *Man.* Judaism affirms that man is created in the Divine image. His spirit is immortal. He is an active co-worker with God. As a child of God, he is endowed with moral freedom and is charged with the responsibility of overcoming evil and striving after ideal ends.

4. *Torah.* God reveals Himself not only in the majesty, beauty, and orderliness of nature, but also in the vision and moral striving of the human spirit. Revelation is a continuous process, confined to no one group and to no one age. Yet the people of Israel, through

its prophets and sages, achieved unique insight in the realm of religious truth. The Torah, both written and oral, enshrines Israel's ever-growing consciousness of God and of the moral law. It preserves the historical precedents, sanctions and norms of Jewish life, and seeks to mold it in the patterns of goodness and of holiness. Being products of historical processes, certain of its laws have lost their binding force with the passing of the conditions that called them forth. But as a depository of permanent spiritual ideals, the Torah remains the dynamic source of the life of Israel. Each age has the obligation to adapt the teachings of the Torah to its basic needs in consonance with the genius of Judaism.

5. *Israel.* Judaism is the soul of which Israel is the body. Living in all parts of the world, Israel has been held together by the ties of a common history, and above all, by the heritage of faith. Though we recognize in the group loyalty of Jews who have become estranged from our religious tradition a bond that still unites them with us, we maintain that it is by its religion and for its religion that the Jewish people has lived. The non-Jew who accepts our faith is welcomed as a full member of the Jewish community. In all lands where our people live, they assume and seek to share loyally the full duties and responsibilities of citizenship and to create seats of Jewish knowledge and religion. In the rehabilitation of Palestine, the land hallowed by memories and hopes, we behold the promise of renewed life for many of our brethren. We affirm the obligation of all Jewry to aid in its upbuilding as a Jewish homeland by endeavoring to make it not only a haven of refuge for the oppressed but also a center of Jewish culture and spiritual life. Throughout the ages it has been Israel's mission to witness to the Divine in the face of every form of paganism and materialism. We regard it as our historic task to cooperate with all men in the establishment of the kingdom of God, of universal brotherhood, Justice, truth, and peace on earth. This is our Messianic goal.

### B. Ethics

6. *Ethics and Religion.* In Judaism religion and morality blend into an indissoluble unity. Seeking God means to strive after holiness, righteousness, and goodness. The love of God is incomplete without the love of one's fellow men. Judaism emphasizes the kinship of the human race, the sanctity and worth of human life and personality, and the right of the individual to freedom and to the pursuit of his chosen vocation. Justice to all, irrespective of race, sect, or class, is the inalienable right and the inescapable obligation of all. The state and organized government exist in order to further these ends.

7. *Social Justice.* Judaism seeks the attainment of a just society by the application of its teachings to the economic order, to industry and commerce, and to national and international affairs. It aims at the elimination of man-made misery and suffering, of poverty and degradation, of tyranny and slavery, of social inequality and prejudice, of ill-will and strife. It advocates the promotion of harmonious relations between warring classes on the basis of equity and justice, and the creation of conditions under which human personality may flourish. It pleads for the safeguarding of childhood against exploitation. It champions the

cause of all who work and of their right to an adequate standard of living, as prior to the rights of property. Judaism emphasizes the duty of charity, and strives for a social order that will protect men against the material disabilities of old age, sickness, and unemployment.

8. *Peace.* Judaism, from the days of the prophets, has proclaimed to mankind the ideal of universal peace. The spiritual and physical disarmament of all nations has been one of its essential teachings. It abhors all violence and relies upon moral education, love, and sympathy to secure human progress. It regards justice as the foundation of the well-being of nations and the condition of enduring peace. It urges organized international action for disarmament, collective security, and world peace.

### C. Religious Practice

9. *The Religious Life.* Jewish life is marked by consecration to these ideals of Judaism. It calls for faithful participation in the life of the Jewish community as it finds expression in home, synagogue, and school and in all other agencies that enrich Jewish life and promote its welfare. The Home has been and must continue to be a stronghold of Jewish life, hallowed by the spirit of love and reverence, by moral discipline and religious observance and worship. The Synagogue is the oldest and most democratic institution in Jewish life. It is the prime communal agency by which Judaism is fostered and preserved. It links the Jews of each community and unites them with all of Israel. The perpetuation of Judaism as a living force depends upon religious knowledge and upon the education of each new generation in our rich cultural and spiritual heritage.

Prayer is the voice of religion, the language of faith and aspiration. It directs man's heart and mind Godward, voices the needs and hopes of the community, and reaches out after goals that invest life with supreme value. To deepen the spiritual life of our people, we must cultivate the traditional habit of communion with God through prayer in both home and synagogue.

Judaism as a way of life requires, in addition to its moral and spiritual demands, the preservation of the Sabbath, festivals, and Holy Days; the retention and development of such customs, symbols, and ceremonies as possess inspirational value; and the cultivation of distinctive forms of religious art and music and the use of Hebrew, together with the vernacular, in our worship and instruction.

These timeless aims and ideals of our faith we present anew to a confused and troubled world. We call upon our fellow Jews to rededicate themselves to them, and, in harmony with all men, hopefully and courageously to continue Israel's eternal quest after God and His kingdom.

## c) Reform Judaism, A Centenary Perspective: 1976

At the end of the Second World War, Germany and its allies were defeated, the former Soviet Union and the USA, first allies, then became involved in a "cold war," the West began to realize the enormity of the genocide perpetrated by the Nazis on Jews (The Holocaust) and others, and, in the shadow of this tragedy, the State of Israel was established in 1948. Reform Jews, too, reacting to all these developments, showed significant signs of change. Their numbers grew considerably. Whereas in 1873 there were only 28 Reform congregations in America, by 1980s, the number went up to 800. Reform was now the leading Jewish religious movement in the country. The challenges for Reform Jews were numerous: how to give change positive meaning and direction; how to ensure unity in diversity; how to establish co-operation with others in a pluralistic society; and how to make Reform synonymous with educated, committed, and enthusiastic Jewish living. Reform Jews were now more comfortable with rituals, with Hebrew, with Israel; it became obvious to many leaders of Reform Judaism that a new platform was needed to formulate the newest Reform position on many topics of interest, so as to unify the movement and set it ion a new path.

With the approach of the 100th anniversary of the UAHC (now URJ) in 1873, and of the Hebrew Union College in 1875, and in order to present a comprehensive view of Reform Judaism after the Holocaust and the establishment of the State of Israel, the CCAR leadership recommended that a new platform be issued. The draft of the new platform was prepared by a CCAR committee, led by Rabbi Eugene Borowitz, a professor at the Hebrew Union College-Jewish Institute of Religion, New York campus. Entitled "A Centenary Perspective," it was adopted overwhelmingly at its 1976 convention in San Francisco.

Recognizing that Reform Jews operate with the principle of "personal autonomy," Perspective states, "We stand open to any position thoughtfully and conscientiously advocated in the spirit of Reform Jewish beliefs." It also admits that Reform Judaism not only tolerates diversity, "but actually engenders it." Within this diversity, Perspective acknowledges that "we have experienced and conceived of God in many ways." However, it adds, "we ground our lives, personally and communally, on God's reality and remain open to new experiences and conceptions of the Divine." Using a Buberian dialogical approach, it also asserts that "Torah results from the relationship between God and the Jewish people," whose study becomes a religious obligation. Perspective sidesteps the Orthodox belief in the concept of resurrection, personal Messiah, or the hope for the rebuilding of the Third Temple, but, for the first time, it uses the terms of "duty and obligation" regarding Jewish observance as a way to holiness, and adds that religious practice must be accepted "on the basis of commitment and knowledge." Perspective takes a strong position regarding Israel: "We are bound to that land and to the newly reborn State of Israel by innumerable religious and ethnic ties," and even mentions the possibility of Aliyah ("going up" in

Hebrew), and refers to immigration to Israel: "We encourage *aliyah* for those who wish to find maximum personal fulfillment in the cause of Zion."

## The Text

The Central Conference of American Rabbis has on special occasions described the spiritual state of Reform Judaism. The centenaries of the founding of the Union of American Hebrew Congregations and the Hebrew Union College-Jewish Institute of Religion seem an appropriate time for another such effort. We therefore record our sense of the unity of our movement today.

## One Hundred Years: What We Have Taught

We celebrate the role of Reform Judaism in North America, the growth of our movement on this free ground, the great contributions of our membership to the dreams, and achievements of this society. We also feel great satisfaction at how much of our pioneering conception of Judaism has been accepted by the Household of Israel. It now seems self-evident to most Jews: that our tradition should interact with modern culture; that its forms ought to reflect a contemporary esthetic; that its scholarship needs to be conducted by modern, critical methods; and that change has been and must continue to be a fundamental reality in Jewish life. Moreover, though some still disagree, substantial numbers have also accepted our teachings: that the ethics of universalism implicit in traditional Judaism must be an explicit part of our Jewish duty; that women have full rights to practice Judaism; and that Jewish obligation begins with the informed will of every individual. Most modern Jews, within their various religious movements, are embracing Reform Jewish perspectives. We see this past century as having confirmed the essential wisdom of our movement.

## One Hundred Years: What We Have Learned

Obviously, much else has changed in the past century. We continue to probe the extraordinary events of the past generation, seeking to understand their meaning and to incorporate their significance in our lives. The Holocaust shattered our easy optimism about humanity and its inevitable progress. The State of Israel, through its many accomplishments, raised our sense of the Jews as a people to new heights of aspiration and devotion. The widespread threats to freedom, the problems inherent in the explosion of new knowledge and of ever-more-powerful technologies, and the spiritual emptiness of much of Western culture have taught us to be less dependent on the values of our society and to reassert what remains perenially valid in Judaism's teaching. We have learned that the survival of the Jewish people is of highest priority and that in carrying out our Jewish responsibilities we help move humanity toward its messianic fulfillment.

## Diversity Within Unity, the Hallmark of Reform

Reform Jews respond to change in various ways according to the Reform principle of the autonomy of the individual. However, Reform Judaism does more than tolerate diversity; it engenders it. In our uncertain historical situation we must expect to have far greater diversity than previous generations knew. How we shall live with diversity without stifling dissent and without paralyzing our ability to take positive action will test our character and our principles. We stand open to any position thoughtfully and conscientiously advocated in the spirit of Reform Jewish belief. While we may differ in our interpretation and application of the ideas enunciated here, we accept such differences as precious and see in them Judaism's best hope for confronting whatever the future holds for us. Yet in all our diversity, we perceive a certain unity and we shall not allow our differences in some particulars to obscure what binds us together.

1. *God*—The affirmation of God has always been essential to our people's will to survive. In our struggle through the centuries to preserve our faith, we have experienced and conceived of God in many ways. The trials of our own time and the challenges of modern culture have made steady belief and clear understanding difficult for some. Nevertheless, we ground our lives, personally and communally, on God's reality and remain open to new experiences and conceptions of the Divine. Amid the mystery we call life, we affirm that human beings, created in God's image, share in God's eternality despite the mystery we call death.

2. *The People Israel*—The Jewish people and Judaism defy precise definition because both are in the process of becoming. Jews, by birth or conversion, constitute an uncommon union of faith and peoplehood. Born as Hebrews in the ancient Near East, we are bound together like all ethnic groups by language, land, history, culture, and institutions. But the people of Israel is unique because of its involvement with God and its resulting perception of the human condition. Throughout our long history our people has been inseparable from its religion with its messianic hope that humanity will be redeemed.

3. *Torah*—Torah results from the relationship between God and the Jewish people. The records of our earliest confrontations are uniquely important to us. Lawgivers and prophets, historians and poets gave us a heritage whose study is a religious imperative and whose practice is our chief means to holiness. Rabbis and teachers, philosophers and

mystics, gifted Jews in every age amplified the Torah tradition. For millennia, the creation of Torah has not ceased and Jewish creativity in our time is adding to the chain of tradition.

4. *Our Religious Obligations:* Religious Practice—Judaism emphasizes action rather than creed as the primary expression of a religious life, the means by which we strive to achieve universal justice and peace. Reform Judaism shares this emphasis on duty and obligation. Our founders stressed that the Jew's ethical responsibilities, personal and social, are enjoined by God. The past century has taught us that the claims made upon us may begin with our ethical obligations but they extend to many other aspects of Jewish living, including creating a Jewish home centered on family devotion; lifelong study; private prayer and public worship; daily religious observance; keeping the Sabbath and the holy days; celebrating the major events of life; involvement with the synagogues and community; and other activities that promote the survival of the Jewish people and enhance its existence. Within each area of Jewish observance Reform Jews are called upon to confront the claims of Jewish tradition, however differently perceived, and to exercise their individual autonomy, choosing and creating on the basis of commitment and knowledge.

5. *Our Obligations:* The State of Israel and the Diaspora—We are privileged to live in an extraordinary time, one in which a third Jewish commonwealth has been established in our people's ancient homeland. We are bound to that land and to the newly reborn State of Israel by innumerable religious and ethnic ties. We have been enriched by its culture and ennobled by its indomitable spirit. We see it providing unique opportunities for Jewish self-expression. We have both a stake and a responsibility in building the State of Israel, assuring its security, and defining its Jewish character. We encourage aliyah for those who wish to find maximum personal fulfillment in the cause of Zion. We demand that Reform Judaism be unconditionally legitimized in the State of Israel.

At the same time that we consider the State of Israel vital to the welfare of Judaism everywhere, we reaffirm the mandate of our tradition to create strong Jewish communities wherever we live. A genuine Jewish life is possible in any land, each community developing its own particular character and determining its Jewish responsibilities. The foundation of Jewish community life is the synagogue. It leads us beyond itself to cooperate with other Jews, to share their concerns, and to assume leadership in communal affairs. We are therefore committed to the full democratization of the Jewish community and to its hallowing in terms of Jewish values.

The State of Israel and the Diaspora, in fruitful dialogue, can show how a people transcends nationalism even as it affirms it, thereby setting an example for humanity which remains largely concerned with dangerously parochial goals.

6. *Our Obligations:* Survival and Service—Early Reform Jews, newly admitted to general society and seeing in this the evidence of a growing universalism, regularly spoke of Jewish purpose in terms of Jewry's service to humanity. In recent years we have become freshly conscious of the virtues of pluralism and the values of particularism. The Jewish

people in its unique way of life validates its own worth, while working toward the fulfill-ment of its messianic expectations.

Until the recent past our obligations to the Jewish people and to all humanity seemed congruent. At times now these two imperatives appear to conflict. We know of no simple way to resolve such tensions. We must, however, confront them without abandoning ei-ther of our commitments. A universal concern for humanity unaccompanied by a devotion to our particular people is self-destructive; a passion for our people without involvement in humankind contradicts what the prophets have meant to us. Judaism calls us simultane-ously to universal and particular obligations.

## Hope: Our Jewish Obligation

Previous generations of Reform Jews had unbound confidence in humanity's potential for good. We have lived through terrible tragedy and been compelled to reappropriate our tradition's realism about the human capacity for evil. Yet our people has always refused to despair. The survivors of the Holocaust, being granted life, seized it, nurtured it, and, rising above catastrophe, showed humankind that the human spirit is indomitable. The State of Israel, established and maintained by the Jewish will to live, demonstrates what a united people can accomplish in history. The existence of the Jew is an argument against despair; Jewish survival is warrant for human hope.

We remain God's witness that history is not meaningless. We affirm that with God's help people are not powerless to affect their destiny. We dedicate ourselves, as did the generations of Jews who went before us, to work and wait for that day when "They shall not hurt or destroy in all My holy mountain for the earth shall be full of the knowledge of the Lord as the waters cover the sea" [Isa. 11:8].

## d) A Statement of Principles for Reform Judaism, 1999

During the latter part of the 20th century, new issues and concerns began to surface in the Jewish world: people were more concerned about the environment and the preservation of individual rights, including those of gay, lesbian, and transgendered individuals. Reform Jews were more comfortable with traditional Jewish religious practices. Many people felt that in the past, the task was how to find the way to reform Judaism so as to make it more relevant; today, however, the concern was to reform Jews, and make them more proud of their tradition.

In response to these issues, Rabbi Richard N. Levy, the President of the CCAR, sug-gested and, in fact, produced the first draft of a new position paper on Reform Judaism, and urged that, after further discussion by all the members, it should be put to vote at the

CCAR Convention in Pittsburgh. This was done in May, 1999, and with a vote of 324-68, the CCAR members approved "A Statement of Principles for Reform Judaism."

The document, drafted using the three traditional Jewish rubrics, God, Torah, and Israel, affirms a number of mainline Reform Jewish beliefs and practices, but opens the door wider to traditional practices for those who wish. Regarding God, this Statement (Note: It is not "The Statement" but "A Statement") acknowledges the diversity of opinions among Reform Jews in this area, and still maintains the standing Jewish belief in "the reality and oneness of God" (thus denying the legitimacy of the Jewish Humanists that God is an "idea" and not a "reality"); it reaffirms the covenant with God and the sacredness of every human being as well as all creation (thus, echoing the warnings of the environmentalists); it also repeats the standing Reform Jewish commitment to social action as well as the ultimate expectation for the realization of the messianic age (not the arrival of the personal Messiah).

Concerning Israel, both the land and the people, this Statement contains strong support for the State of Israel, and "encourages aliyah," but denies the centrality of Israel in the Jewish world; instead, it speaks of the "interdependence" between Israel and the Diaspora. It affirms the value of *kelal Yisrael* ("the totality of the Jewish people"), it also stresses the movement's historical commitment to "complete equality of women and men in Jewish life"; the primacy of the synagogue over other Jewish community organizations; it opens the door to Judaism, to anyone, including converts and interfaith-married, "regardless of their sexual orientation."

In clarifying the Reform's present position on religious practices, and contrary to past approaches that defined Reform by what we do not do, this Statement chooses to speak of what we must do, by placing Torah at the center of Jewish life, by stressing the importance of studying Hebrew, and by opening the study of "the whole array of Mitzvot," and "the fulfillment of those that address us an individuals and as community," thus accepting the present reality that many Reform Jews today follow the laws of *Kashrut*, use *tallit* and *tefillin*, go to the Mikveh, and pay more attention to the observance of *Shabbat* and festivals.

Though the text represents a compromise between the traditionalists and the classicists within Reform Judaism in the USA today, it brings the Reform movement much closer to the mainstream of Jewish life, and in line with other Reform congregations around the world. As Rabbi Levy put it, "The Pittsburgh Platform [of 1885] explicitly rejected all but the ethical Mitzvot; no Reform statement of principles [except this one] has explicitly given us the freedom to confront the totality of Mitzvot."

The teachings of this Statement are reflected in the Reform movement's newest prayerbook, *Mishkan T'filah: A Reform Siddur for Shabbat, Weekdays, and Festivals*, which was edited by Rabbi Elyse D. Frishman and published by the CCAR in 2007. This prayerbook came out with in two versions, one with transliteration and the other without it. The English translation is gender-sensitive and God is often addressed as

Adonai. In light of theological diversity of the Reform Movement, the prayers are written in the broadest terms, and at times providing alternative texts for the same theme. In one case, this is clearly done even in the Hebrew: realizing some Reform Jews subscribe to the idea of immortality of the soul whereas others accept resurrection of the body after death, the prayerbook offers both versions of the closing blessing after the Gevurot in the T'filah, "*Blessed are You, Adonai, who gives life to all [m'chayeih hakol] (who revives the dead [m'chayeih hameitim])*." For the first time the prayerbook also comes with some commentaries at the bottom of each page.

## The Text

## Preamble

On three occasions during the last century and a half, the Reform rabbinate has adopted comprehensive statements to help guide the thought and practice of our movement. In 1885, fifteen rabbis issued the Pittsburgh Platform, a set of guidelines that defined Reform Judaism for the next fifty years. A revised statement of principles, the Columbus Platform, was adopted by the Central Conference of American Rabbis in 1937. A third set of rabbinic guidelines, the Centenary Perspective, appeared in 1976 on the occasion of the centenary of the Union of American Hebrew Congregations and the Hebrew Union College-Jewish Institute of Religion. Today, when so many individuals are striving for religious meaning, moral purpose, and a sense of community, we believe it is our obligation as rabbis once again to state a set of principles that define Reform Judaism in our own time.

Throughout our history, we Jews have remained firmly rooted in Jewish tradition, even as we have learned much from our encounters with other cultures. The great contribution of Reform Judaism is that it has enabled the Jewish people to introduce innovation while preserving tradition, to embrace diversity while asserting commonality, to affirm beliefs without rejecting those who doubt, and to bring faith to sacred texts without sacrificing critical scholarship.

This "Statement of Principles" affirms the central tenets of Judaism—God, Torah, and Israel—even as it acknowledges the diversity of Reform Jewish beliefs and practices. It also invites all Reform Jews to engage in a dialogue with the sources of our tradition, responding out of our knowledge, our experience, and our faith. Thus we hope to transform our lives through *kedushah*, holiness.

# God

We affirm the reality and oneness of God, even as we may differ in our understanding of the Divine presence.

We affirm that the Jewish people is bound to God by an eternal *berit* covenant, as reflected in our varied understandings of Creation, Revelation, and Redemption.

We affirm that every human being is created *b'tzelem Elohim* in the image of God, and that therefore every human life is sacred.

We regard with reverence all of God's creation and recognize our human responsibility for its preservation and protection.

We encounter God's presence in moments of awe and wonder, in acts of justice and compassion, in loving relationships, and in the experiences of everyday life.

We respond to God daily: through public and private prayer, through study and through the performance of other *mitzvot* sacred obligations *bein adam la Makom* to God, and *bein adam la-chaveiro* to other human beings.

We strive for a faith that fortifies us through the vicissitudes of our lives—illness and healing, transgression and repentance, bereavement and consolation, despair and hope.

We continue to have faith that, in spite of the unspeakable evils committed against our people and the sufferings endured by others, the partnership of God and humanity will ultimately prevail.

We trust in our tradition's promise that, although God created us as finite beings, the spirit within us is eternal.

## In all these ways and more, God gives meaning and purpose to our lives.

# Torah

We affirm that Torah is the foundation of Jewish life.

We cherish the truths revealed in Torah, God's ongoing revelation to our people, and the record of our people's ongoing relationship with God.

We affirm that Torah is a manifestation of *ahavat olam*, God's eternal love for the Jewish people and for all humanity.

We affirm the importance of studying Hebrew, the language of Torah and Jewish liturgy, that we may draw closer to our people's sacred texts.

We are called by Torah to lifelong study in the home, in the synagogue, and in every place where Jews gather to learn and teach. Through Torah study we are called to *mitzvot*, the means by which we make our lives holy.

We are committed to the ongoing study of the whole array of *mitzvot* and to the fulfillment of those that address us as individuals and as a community. Some of these *mitzvot*, sacred obligations, have long been observed by Reform Jews; others, both ancient and modern, demand renewed attention as the result of the unique context of our own times.

We bring Torah into the world when we seek to sanctify the times and places of our lives through regular home and congregational observance. *Shabbat* calls us to bring the highest moral values to our daily labor and to culminate the workweek with *kedushah*, holiness; *menuchah*, rest; and *oneg*, joy. The High Holy Days call us to account for our deeds. The Festivals enable us to celebrate with joy our people's religious journey in the context of the changing seasons. The days of remembrance remind us of the tragedies and the triumphs that have shaped our people's historical experience both in ancient and modern times. And we mark the milestones of our personal journeys with traditional and creative rites that reveal the holiness in each stage of life.

We bring Torah into the world when we strive to fulfill the highest ethical mandates in our relationships with others and with all of God's creation. Partners with God in *tikkun o'lam*, repairing the world, we are called to help bring nearer the messianic age. We seek dialogue and joint action with people of other faiths in the hope that together we can bring peace, freedom, and justice to our world. We are obligated to pursue *tzedek*, justice and righteousness, and to narrow the gap between the affluent and the poor, to act against discrimination and oppression, to pursue peace, to welcome the stranger, to protect the earth's biodiversity and natural resources, and to redeem those in physical, economic, and spiritual bondage. In so doing, we reaffirm social action and social justice as a central prophetic focus of traditional Reform Jewish belief and practice. We affirm the *mitzvah* of *tzedakah*, setting aside portions of our earnings and our time to provide for those in need. These acts bring us closer to fulfilling the prophetic call to translate the words of Torah into the works of our hands.

# In all these ways and more, Torah gives meaning and purpose to our lives.

## Israel

We are Israel, a people aspiring to holiness, singled out through our ancient covenant and our unique history among the nations to be witnesses to God's presence. We are linked by that covenant and that history to all Jews in every age and place.

We are committed to the *mitzvah* of *ahavat Yisrael*, love for the Jewish people, and to *k'lal Yisrael*, the entirety of the community of Israel. Recognizing that *kol Yisrael arevim zeh ba-zeh*, all Jews are responsible for one another, we reach out to all Jews across ideological and geographical boundaries.

We embrace religious and cultural pluralism as an expression of the vitality of Jewish communal life in Israel and the Diaspora.

We pledge to fulfill Reform Judaism's historic commitment to the complete equality of women and men in Jewish life.

We are an inclusive community, opening doors to Jewish life to people of all ages, to varied kinds of families, to all regardless of their sexual orientation, to *gerim*, those who have converted to Judaism, and to all individuals and families, including the intermarried, who strive to create a Jewish home.

We believe that we must not only open doors for those ready to enter our faith, but also to actively encourage those who are seeking a spiritual home to find it in Judaism.

We are committed to strengthening the people Israel by supporting individuals and families in the creation of homes rich in Jewish learning and observance.

We are committed to strengthening the people Israel by making the synagogue central to Jewish communal life, so that it may elevate the spiritual, intellectual, and cultural quality of our lives.

We are committed to *Medinat Yisrael*, the State of Israel, and rejoice in its accomplishments. We affirm the unique qualities of living in *Eretz Yisrael*, the land of Israel, and encourage *aliyah*, immigration to Israel.

We are committed to a vision of the State of Israel that promotes full civil, human and religious rights for all its inhabitants and that strives for a lasting peace between Israel and its neighbors.

We are committed to promoting and strengthening Progressive Judaism in Israel, which will enrich the spiritual life of the Jewish state and its people.

We affirm that both Israeli and Diaspora Jewry should remain vibrant and interdependent communities. As we urge Jews who reside outside Israel to learn Hebrew as a living language and to make periodic visits to Israel in order to study and to deepen their relationship to the Land and its people, so do we affirm that Israeli Jews have much to learn from the religious life of Diaspora Jewish communities.

We are committed to furthering Progressive Judaism throughout the world as a meaningful religious way of life for the Jewish people.

## In all these ways and more, Israel gives meaning and purpose to our lives.

*Baruch she-amar ve-haya ha-olam.* Praised be the One through whose word all things came to be. May our words find expression in holy actions. May they raise us up to a life of meaning devoted to God's service And to the redemption of our world.

## 3. WHAT IS CONSERVATIVE JUDAISM?

In 1988, Robert Gordis authored a long pamphlet called "Emet ve-Emunah: Statement of Principles of Conservative Judaism" (New York: The Jewish Theological Seminary). In it we read:

### The Text

"In the beginning God ..." Though we differ in our perceptions and experiences of reality, we affirm our faith in God as the Creator and Governor of the universe. His power called the world into being; His wisdom and goodness guide its destiny. Of all the living creatures we know, humanity alone, created in His image and endowed with free will, has been singled out to be the recipient and bearer of Revelation. The product of this human–divine encounter is the Torah, the embodiment of God's will revealed pre-eminently to the Jewish people through Moses, the Prophets, and the Sages, as well as to the righteous and wise of all nations. Hence, by descent and destiny, each Jew stands under the divine command to obey God's will.

Second, we recognize the authority of the *Halakhah*, which has never been monolithic or immovable. On the contrary, as modern scholarship has abundantly demonstrated, the *Halakhah* has grown and developed through changing times and diverse circumstances. This life-giving attribute is doubly needed today in a world of dizzying change.

Third, though the term was unknown, pluralism has characterized Jewish life and thought through the ages. This is reflected in the variety of views and attitudes of the biblical legislators, priests, prophets, historians, psalmists, and Wisdom teachers, the hundreds of controversies among the rabbis of the Talmud and in the codes and responsa of their successors. The latter-day attempt to suppress freedom of inquiry and the right to dissent is basically a foreign importation into Jewish life.

Fourth, the rich body of *Halakhah* and *Aggadah* and the later philosophic and mystical literature, all seeking to come closer to God's presence, are a precious resource for deepening the spiritual life of Israel and humankind.

Fifth, all the aspects of Jewish law and practice are designed to underscore the centrality of ethics in the life of the Jews.

Sixth, Israel is not only the Holy Land where our faith was born and developed, but it also plays an essential role in our present and future. Israel is a symbol of the unity of the Jewish people the world over, the homeland for millions of Jews, and a unique arena for Jewish creativity. Together with our responsibility to Israel is our obligation to strengthen and enrich the life of Jewish communities throughout the world—including, it need hardly be said, our own.

Seventh, Jewish law and tradition, properly understood and interpreted, will enrich Jewish life and help mold the world closer to the prophetic vision of the Kingdom of God.


# 4. WHAT IS HUMANISTIC JUDAISM?

The Society for Humanistic Judaism mobilizes people to celebrate Jewish identity and culture consistent with a humanistic philosophy of life, independent of supernatural authority. As the central body for the Humanistic Jewish Movement in North America, the Society assists in organizing new communities, supporting its member communities, and in providing a voice for Humanistic Jews.

### Humanistic Jews Affirm That...

...A Jew is someone who identifies with the history, culture, and future of the Jewish people.

...Jewish identity is best preserved in a free, pluralistic environment.

...Jewish history is a human saga, a testament to the significance of human power and human responsibility.

..Judaism is the historic culture of the Jewish people.

...We possess the power and responsibility to shape our own lives independent of supernatural authority.

...Ethics and morality should serve human needs.

...The freedom and dignity of the Jewish people must go hand in hand with the freedom and dignity of every human being.

Source: http://www.shj.org/mission.htm

## 5. WHAT IS JEWISH RECONSTRUCTIONISM?

Rabbi Lester Bronstein, of Bet Am Shalom Synagogue in White Plains, NY, writes:

### A Crash Course on Reconstructionist Judaism

If you advertise yourself as a Reconstructionist rabbi, people will inevitably corner you with "the" question: "Can you tell me—*in a few words*—what Reconstructionist Judaism is all about?"

In formulating a response that I could quickly pull out of my back pocket, I long ago decided not to lead people into the abyss of "two civilizations," "vote-not-a-veto," and other cul-de-sacs of Reconstructionist jargon. Instead, I like to approach the question by mentioning three arms which are vitally central to *every* form of Judaism, and I try to show people how Reconstructionist Jews (and, truth be told, a myriad of Jews around the world) view these matters in a way that is different from traditional Judaism, but surprisingly close to the *spirit* of that tradition.

My three litmus topics are Torah, prayer and ritual, and *mitzvot*. Here are my few words on each.

**Torah:** Tradition tells us that the Torah was dictated by God to Moses, and then transmitted through the generations. Reconstructionist Jews see the Torah as the Jewish people's response to God's presence in the world (and not God's gift to us). That is to say, the Jews wrote the Torah. But that is *not* to say that the Torah is merely a human creation. It is a *response* to the sacred. It is an attempt to convince an entire people to view everyday life in a sacred way.

Yes, it is intriguing to apply the tools of history, science and chronology to the Torah. These vehicles give us the historical and natural *context* of the Torah. But they don't give us the *essence* of the Torah. The essential Torah is neither the tidal explanation for the parting of the sea, nor the geological definition of the primordial flood nor the cosmological identification of "let there be light." The essential Torah consists in the truth deep within these stories, a truth that radiates a picture of a society based on courts of justice and on social empathy. God didn't *write* that Torah, since God does not write per se. But God is everywhere in the details of it.

**Prayer and Ritual:** On the face of it, the text of the *siddur* suggests that our prayers are direct recitations and petitions to a God who is "other" and who, we hope, is listening and contemplating a favorable response. Reconstructionist Jews retain the traditional language of Jewish prayer, but not the obvious understanding of its meaning and function.

Rather, we understand prayer to help us perform the task of awakening. We need to awaken ourselves to the miracle that is life and to the obligations that inhere in that life. We believe that we are the primary respondents to our own prayers, and that we need prayer to remind us of the Godly values behind our benevolent actions in the world. We also understand prayer as a way of calling out to others in the world, in the hope that they, too, would sign on to the Godly enterprise of healing, caring, and righting injustice.

**In sum, prayer and ritual are the Jewish people's way of heightening our awareness of the sacredness of life, of clarifying and reiterating our moral values and of marking time and space in a sacred way.**

*Mitzvot*: The word *mitzvah* means "commandment," and tradition literally understands mitzvot to be direct commandments from God, via the Torah. As such, we might utilize a *mitzvah* as an opportunity for meaningful relationship with God or our own souls, but we are obligated to perform the deed in any case, regardless of any spiritual uplift it may or may not provide.

As you would expect, Reconstructionist Judaism teaches that the *mitzvot* are our own invention. *Mitzvot* **are our particularly Jewish ways of responding to the universal God.** We perceive God as demanding sacredness in general, and the Jewish *mitzvot* are our people's way of bringing that universal sacredness to the minutiae of daily life in our own specifically Jewish context.

In this system, God does not choose the Jews to be performers of the commandments. Rather, the Jews choose to be called by God by means of a vast network of sacred acts (*mitzvot*) ranging from balancing work and rest (*Shabbat*), to establishing courts and laws, to sexual fidelity, filial respect, medical ethics, and the rhythms of the seasons. (Hence, *asher ker'vanu la'avodato*, "who has called us to your service.") Paradoxically, it is the *mitzvot* that keep us Jewish, but which simultaneously attune us to the greater universe of which we are a tiny part.

How do people respond to these sorts of answers? Clearly, most have never heard them before. They are not the answers they were expecting. Some love the responses, some are skeptical and some know that they simply have to let the information seep in. My hope is that this crash course in Reconstructionist Judaism leads people to see this movement not as a loosely defined "anything goes" religion, but as a serious modern attempt to understand Judaism as a discipline, as a life path and as a *response* to the holiness that fills our world.

## ENDNOTES

1. For a discussion of this text, see Menachem Kellner, *Must a Jew Believe Anything?* London: The Littman Library of Jewish Civilization, 1999, and the literature listed in it.

# INDEX

**A**

A'gunah  139, 198
Alef  xvi, 175
A'liyah  75, 77, 89
A'm yisrael  37, 153, 201
A'ravah  116
Aron ha-Kodesh  160
A'tid lavo  149
Avel  141

**B**

Bar/bat mitzvah  65, 70, 132, 133, 134
Berit  31, 72, 222
Berit milah  31, 128, 129, 130
Bet keneset  158
Bet midrash  158
Bet tefilah  158
Bikkur holim  139
Bimah  56, 87, 160

**D**

Devekut  18
Dibbuk  152

**E**

En sof  18, 31, 40, 55
Erusin  137
Etrog  115, 116
E'zrat nashim  161

**G**

Gan e'den  150
Gaon  9, 24, 58, 163, 203
Ge-hinnom  150
Genizah  160
Ger  179
Ger/ giyoret/gerim  71, 72, 179, 224
Get  88, 138, 139
Geulah  34

Gilgul 152
Goel 36

# H

Hadar 115
Haggadah 103, 111, 175
Hag ha-Asif 115
Hag ha-Katzir 112
Hag ha-Matzot 103
Hag Shavuo't 112
Hai 153, 175, 201
Ha-i'vri xvi
Haknasat orehim 170
Halakhah xviii, 51, 53, 56, 64, 67, 69, 105,
    107, 109, 225, 226
Hametz 104, 111
Ha-motzi 97
Hanukah 7, 85, 119, 120, 121, 125, 161,
    172
Hanukiyah 119, 172
Hatafat dam 72
Hatan 135
Hatimah tovah 100
Havdalah 97, 100, 171
Hazzan 165
He-hag 115
Hesed 38
Het ix, 32, 175
Hoshanah rabba 115
Hoshen 55, 160
Huppah 135

# I

I'bbur 152

# K

Kabbalah 18, 40, 54, 152

Kaddish 59, 141, 142, 144, 163
Kadosh xviii, xix
Kallah 135
Kashrut/kasher 55, 90, 92, 105, 107, 176,
    177, 178, 209, 220
Kedushah 170, 221, 223
Keria'h 143
Keter 160
Ketubah 135, 136, 137, 138
Kibbud av va-em 170
Kiddush 97, 171, 211
Kiddushin xviii, 68, 134, 137
Kippah 136, 174
Kitniyot 104, 105
Kol Nidre 100, 102

# L

Lag Ba-O'mer 124
Lehitpallel 34
Le-Shanah Tovah 100
Lulav 115, 116, 206

# M

Magen david 174
Mamzer 70, 139
Maror 103
Mashiah 36
Mazal tov 137
Medinat yisrael 36, 77, 224
Mehayye ha-kol 151, 221
Mehitzah 88, 161
Menorah 119, 161, 172
Mezuzah 170, 171
Midrash 53, 57, 62, 158
Minyan 59, 142, 163
Mishnah xii, 8, 9, 12, 49, 50, 51, 57, 62, 68,
    97, 104, 111, 112, 118, 132, 165, 203
Mitzvah xvii, xix, 60, 61, 65, 70, 71, 75, 89,

91, 105, 107, 108, 109, 127, 128,
130, 131, 132, 133, 134, 139, 140,
141, 142, 146, 171, 173, 177, 200,
211, 223, 224, 228
Mitzvot xviii, 170, 173, 177
Mohel/mohelet/mohalim 72, 129, 130
Moshia' 34

**N**

Ner tamid 161
Nissuin 137

**O**

O'lam ha-ba 149
O'mer 135
O'neg Shabbat 97

**P**

Parokhet 160
Pesah 95, 103, 112
Pidyon Haben 130
Pikuah nefesh 144
Purim 95, 121, 122, 123, 125

**R**

Rimonim 160
Rosh ha-shanah 99, 101
Rosh hodesh 96, 124, 133

**S**

Sandek 129
Seder peredah 138
Sefer ha-Hinukh 148
Sefer hasidim 18
Sefer torah 159

Sefirot 18
Selihot 99
Seudat havraah 142
Sevivon 121
Shabbat xii, xix, 11, 56, 59, 90, 96, 97, 98,
108, 125, 133, 134, 142, 170, 171,
220, 223, 228
Shabbat shalom xix, 97
Shaddai 31, 170
Shalom xix, 36, 92, 97, 163, 170, 181, 227
Shavuo't 95, 103, 111, 112, 124, 134, 135
Sheelot uteshuvot 59
Shekhinah 31, 39, 150
Shelom bayit xix
Sheloshim 142
Shema' 29, 140, 163, 197
Shemini A'tzeret 115
Shemirah 143
Sheol 148, 149
Shevirat ha-kelim 18, 40
Shiva'h 142
Shoftim 4
Simhat bat 130
Sofer 159
Sufganiot 121
Sukkah/sukkot 95, 103, 114, 115, 116, 118,
119, 121, 125, 135, 142, 171

**T**

Takhrikhim 142
Tallit 135, 136, 137, 143, 172, 173, 220
Talmud xi, 1, 7, 9, 12, 17, 18, 50, 51, 55,
57, 68, 104, 105, 106, 108, 127, 128,
131, 151, 182, 208, 226
Talmud torah 131
Tashlih 99
Tefillin 133, 173, 206, 220
Tehiyyat ha-metim 149, 151
Tevah 87, 160

Tevilah 72

Tikkun o'lam 18, 40, 89, 93, 223

Tisha Be-Av 125, 135, 173

Torah xiii, xvii, xviii, 3, 7, 8, 11, 24, 29, 31,
33, 45, 46, 49, 51, 52, 54, 55, 56, 57,
58, 59, 65, 70, 71, 75, 88, 89, 92, 93,
106, 107, 108, 109, 111, 112, 113,
114, 115, 116, 123, 128, 130, 131,
132, 133, 134, 136, 149, 150, 158,
159, 160, 161, 165, 170, 174, 181,
185, 187, 192, 193, 198, 200, 203,
204, 205, 206, 207, 211, 212, 213,
215, 217, 218, 220, 221, 222, 223,
224, 225, 227, 228

Torah she-bea'l pe 49

Torah she-bikhtav 49

Tosafot 18

Tu Bi-Shvat 125

Tzaddik 23

Tzedakah 123, 172, 223

Tzimtzum 18, 40

**V**

Viddui 140

**Y**

Yad 55, 65, 66, 67, 68, 129, 160

Yahrzeit 142

Yehudi xiv, xv

Yemot ha-mashiah 149

Yetzer ha-ra' 33

Yetzer ha-tov 33

YHVH 3, 29, 30, 31, 46, 48, 180

Yihud 137

Yom ha-Atzmaut 124

Yom ha-Bikkurim 112

Yom ha-Shoah 124

Yom Kippur 95, 99, 100

**Z**

Zeman matan toratenu 112

Zeved ha-bat 130

Zohar 18, 43, 54, 55, 62, 152

CPSIA information can be obtained
at www.ICGtesting.com
Printed in the USA
LVHW010302020120
642244LV00005B/13/P

9 781621 314370